Shari'ah on Trial

Shari'ah on Trial

Northern Nigeria's Islamic Revolution

Sarah Eltantawi

UNIVERSITY OF CALIFORNIA PRESS

University of California Press, one of the most distinguished university presses in the United States, enriches lives around the world by advancing scholarship in the humanities, social sciences, and natural sciences. Its activities are supported by the UC Press Foundation and by philanthropic contributions from individuals and institutions. For more information, visit www.ucpress.edu.

University of California Press
Oakland, California

Library of Congress Cataloging-in-Publication Data

Names: Eltantawi, Sarah, 1976– author.
Title: Shari'ah on trial : Northern Nigeria's Islamic revolution / Sarah Eltantawi.
Description: Oakland, California : University of California Press, [2017] | Includes bibliographical references and index.
Identifiers: LCCN 2016042864 (print) | LCCN 2016044226 (ebook) | ISBN 9780520293779 (cloth : alk. paper) | ISBN 9780520293786 (pbk. : alk. paper) | ISBN 9780520967144 (ebook)
Subjects: LCSH: Islamic law—Nigeria, Northern. | Islamic courts—Nigeria, Northern. | Islam and politics—Nigeria, Northern. | Islam and state—Nigeria, Northern.
Classification: LCC KTA469.5 .E45 2017 (print) | LCC KTA469.5 (ebook) | DDC 349.669/8—dc23
LC record available at https://lccn.loc.gov/2016042864

Manufactured in the United States of America

26 25 24 23 22 21 20 19 18 17
10 9 8 7 6 5 4 3 2 1

CONTENTS

ACKNOWLEDGMENTS

This book and the story it tells are the result of a collective effort, made possible by the generosity and courage of too many people to name. These thanks can only be abridged, but I will start with my greatest debt, to my friends and interlocutors in Nigeria. Salisu Balarabe, Hamidu Bobboyi, Ahmed Garba, Saudatu Mahdi, Aliyu Yerima, Mustapha Guadebe, Aliyu Ibrahim, Ibraheem Sulaiman, Khadija Asaiko, and the late Bilkisu Yusuf opened their homes, offices, minds, and hearts to me in ways I will never forget, instilling in me a love and unending support for Hausaland and Nigeria. I also thank the staff of the Arewa House Centre for Historical Documentation and Research in Kaduna and the Waziru Junaidu archives in Sokoto for their invaluable support and guidance. I am deeply grateful to my wonderful and skilled editors at the University of California Press, Eric Schmidt and Maeve Cornell-Taylor, who have been a joy to work with. I also thank Production Editor Jessica Moll for her able stewardship of the final manuscript, and Richard Earles for his tremendous copyediting skill and patience. I also owe an incredible debt of gratitude to Ramzi Ben Amara, Maren Milligan, and Philip Ostien, three scholars whose work on Nigeria has inspired my own and whose friendship and kindness opened many doors for me in Nigeria. At Harvard University, where I began this work as a doctoral student, my advisor and dear mentor Leila Ahmed showed me a priceless example of scholarly elegance and precision, as well as personal kindness and integrity. I must also thank Jacob Olupona, who in his warm and deeply dedicated way taught me the history and politics of Nigeria, as well as making it possible for me to go there. Michael D. Jackson was an incredible intellectual inspiration, giving me dozens of profound insights, in addition to consistent generosity. I also had many deeply important, trenchant conversations about this work and beyond with the late Shahab Ahmed, who made everything I did better and who has left us far too soon. I also thank Kecia Ali, Khaled El-Rouayheb, Baber Johansen, Maria Pia Di Bella, and Nur Yalman for extremely useful resources and feedback on this work; as well as William Granara for his general, kind support and Arabic language precision; the late Wolfhart Henrichs for the same; and Lori De Lucia Connolly for teaching me Hausa. Juliane Hammer gave me helpful and brilliant comments on the manuscript in her review, for which I am very grateful. My deep appreciation as well to Ahmad Mahdavi-Damghani for the honor of a yearlong private study with him in Shiite law in the best possible company. I thank Ronald Heifetz for giving me the opportunity to workshop key parts of this work as a predoctoral Fellow in Public Leadership at Harvard's John F. Kennedy School of Government, and I am grateful for the Center for Public Leadership's fellowship support. I also thank Harvard's Department of African and African American Studies, Harvard Divinity School, and the Harvard Center for International Studies for providing grants that supported this work. In Berlin, I am greatly indebted to Gudrun Krämer for her many essential insights, and for offering me a wonderful opportunity to complete the manuscript as a predoctoral fellow at the Berlin Graduate School of Muslim Cultures and Societies at Freie Universität Berlin—and also for her later stewardship, along with that of Georges Khalil, when I was an EUME (Europe in the Middle East, Middle East in Europe) postdoctoral fellow at the Forum Transregionale at the Wissenschaftskolleg zu Berlin, where I completed the manuscript. I also wish to express my appreciation to Lisa Fishbayn Joffe at the Hadassah-Brandeis Center at Brandeis University, where I was a postdoctoral scholar-in-residence, for giving me invaluable insights and mentorship on questions of gender and religious law. I am incredibly grateful to my dear friend and colleague at the Evergreen State College, Therese Saliba, who carefully read the manuscript and gave me endless substantive and editorial insights, to my friend and colleague Sean Williams, for guiding me through loose ends at exactly the right time, and to Amjad Faur for his support, and whose photography inspired this book's cover art. At Evergreen, I would also like to thank John McClain, who patiently steered me in the direction of fellowships that would allow me to complete the production stage of this work. My most precious gift from John's guidance was a very fine research fellow, Joshua Pollock. Josh provided an initial copyedit of the manuscript with exemplary skill and speed. A very partial list of friends I would like to thank for their generous intellectual and moral support of this project are Manan Ahmed, Ahmad Al-Jallad, Yasmin Amin, Diana Allan, Fares Al-Suwaidi, Sa'ed Atshan, Ayesha Chaudhry, Karimah Judy Cheley, Matthew Ellis, Nader Elmakawi, David Freidenreich, Nuri Friedlander, Ellis Goldberg, Genevieve Negrón-Gonzales, Jason Negrón-Gonzales, Bilal Ibrahim, Aaron Isaksen, James D. Hastings, Ahmed Kanna, Hun Kim, Dominic Longo, Clara Masnatta, Michael Moyer, Wendy Pearlman, Kristian Petersen, Junaid Quadri, Omid Safi, Nahed Samour, Sadia Shirazi, Daniel Silver, Fiona Smith, Stephanie Thomas, Saadia Yacoob, and Maged Zaher. A special thank-you to Moustafa Soliman for his years of support for me and this project. To my late sister-friend Jenna Hansen, I love you and miss you every day. My deepest gratitude goes to my parents, Salaheddin and Hoda Eltantawi, for always supporting me, and for listening to me talk about stoning for over a decade, any time, day or night. My brother Kareem Eltantawi has also provided priceless comic relief. I am also deeply grateful to my sister-in-law Erin Vites and the memory of her wonderful father, Harold. I also thank my family in Egypt, especially Nabil Taha, Adaala Hasanain, and their children and grandchildren; my late aunt, Noor Eltantawi; and my late grandmother, Bahaia Moawad Amin, for their endless support, depth, and joyfulness.

NOTE ON TRANSLITERATION

Arabic and Hausa words are italicized throughout the book, with the exception of words that have made their way into the English lexicon (e.g., Sufi and Qur'an); the latter also appear without diacritical marks, as ease of pronunciation is assumed. Some words that are in the English lexicon and easily pronounced (e.g., *jihad*) appear without diacritics but are italicized to highlight their divergent meanings in Arabic. All other Arabic words are rendered with diacritics, following the standards set by the *International Journal of Middle East Studies.*

CHRONOLOGY

610	Islam is founded by the Prophet Muḥammad in the Arabian Peninsula.
644	ʻUmar b. al-Khaṭṭāb, Islam's second caliph and protagonist of key *aḥadīth* concerning the stoning punishment, dies.
ca. 700s	Islam first comes to West Africa through trade with North Africans.
795	Mālik b. Anas, who founded the Mālikī school of Islamic law in Medina, dies.
990	King of Songhay (now Central Mali to Niger and Nigeria) converts to Islam.
1365	Sīdī Khalīl dies, author of *al-Mukhtasar,* the most important compendium of the Mālikī legal school (still used widely in northern Nigeria).
1380–1893	Borno Empire, a continuation of the Kanem Empire, rules what is now northeastern Nigeria.
1804	Sokoto Caliphate is founded by Uthmān Dan Fodio, who brought the Qādariyya Sufi order and the Mālikī school of *fiqh* to Hausaland.

1808	Fulani warriors associated with Uthmān Dan Fodio's *jihad* conquer Ngazargamu, capital of the Bornu Empire.
1809	Dan Fodio's son, Muhammad Bello, founds the city of Sokoto, which will become the capital of the Sokoto Caliphate.
1817	Uthmān Dan Fodio dies.
1828–30	Tijāniyya Sufi order is established in West Africa.
1900	The British vice-regent to Hausaland, Lord Frederick Lugard, outlaws the stoning punishment, declaring it "antithetical to natural justice."
1903	Sokoto Caliphate falls to British cannons in Kano.
1960	On October 1, Nigeria gains independence from the British and declares itself a federal republic.
1978	Izālat al-Bid'ah wa Iqāmat al-Sunnah (Izālā) is established in Jos, Nigeria, to fight what they characterized as the *bid'ah* (unlawful innovation) of the Sufis.
1986	Northern Nigerian historian Ibraheem Sulaiman writes a hagiographic history of Uthmān Dan Fodio, *A Revolution in History: The Jihād of Uthman Dan Fodio.*
1999	Shari'ah is declared the law of the land in Zamfara State by Governor Ahmed Sani Yerima.
1999–2007	Ahmed Sani Yerima is governor of Zamfara State. Olusegun Obasanjo is the first Pentecostal Christian president of Nigeria and the first military ruler in Africa to hand over power to a civilian government.
2002	Boko Haram, self described as "al-Wilāyat al-Islāmiyya Gharb Afrīqiyyah" and "Jamā'at Ahl al-Sunna l-Da'wah w-al-Jihād," is established in Nigeria by Muhammad Yusuf in Maiduguri.
	On January 15, Amina Lawal and Yahayya Muhammad Kurami are arraigned for committing the crime of *zinā* (illegal sexual activity).

	On March 22, Lawal is sentenced to death by stoning. On March 28, Lawal appeals the ruling, having been visited by her newly retained attorney, Aliyu Musa Yauri.
2003	On September 25, Amina Lawal is acquitted of all charges in an Islamic court.
2007–10	Umaru Musa Yar'adua is president of Nigeria.
2010	Fieldwork is conducted for this book.
2015	Boko Haram, a symbol of the shari'ah experiment's failure, swears its allegiance to ISIS. They declare the Izālā heretics for their willingness to work with the Nigerian government.

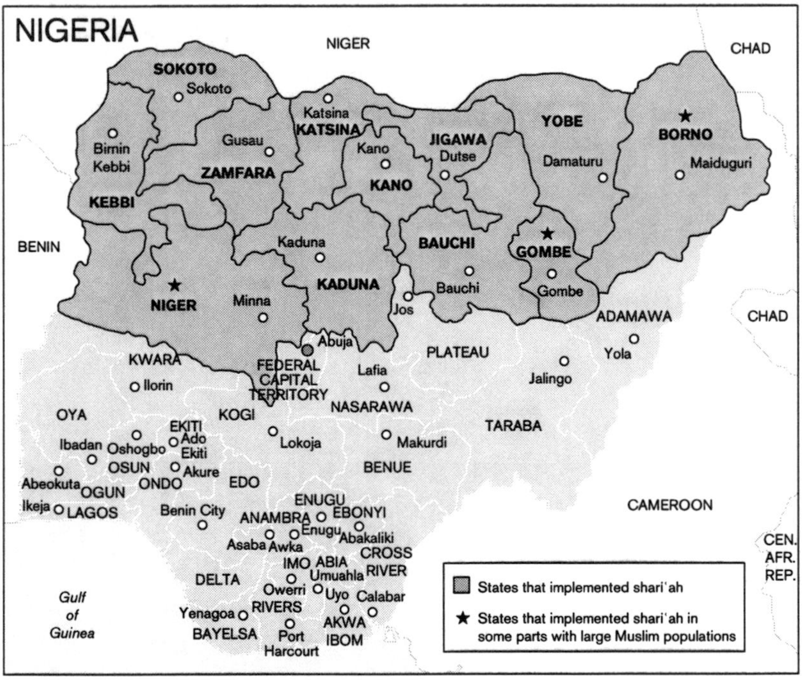

Northern Nigerian states that have implemented shari'ah since 1999.

Introduction

Why did the people of Hausaland—the twelve states of the northern region of Nigeria—clamor into the streets in November 1999 to demand reimplementation of the strictest possible iteration of full Islamic shari'ah law? And why would many of them, two years later, support the death sentence by stoning of a peasant woman, Amina Lawal, for committing the crime of *zinā,* or illegal sexual activity? This book delves deeply into the 1999 shari'ah revolution in Nigeria, a moment crucial to understanding subsequent Nigerian history.

I was in a meeting of civil rights leaders in Washington, D.C., one afternoon in the spring of 2002, when I could no longer ignore the incessant ringing of my phone. Something unusual had obviously happened, and it was time to duck out of the room to find out what it was. I was the national communications director of a major American Muslim organization, with the responsibility for drafting policies and talking points to be disseminated in the media regarding whatever issue concerned the community that day. Around 2002, a year after 9/11 and as the war on Iraq was being prepared, this work was without end. On that particular afternoon, Amina Lawal had just been sentenced to death by stoning. Could I offer the "Muslim" opinion on stoning, violent punishment, women's rights, and Islamic notions of justice? I posed the journalists' questions to my colleagues present at the meeting. A group of mostly affluent professionals of varied ideological persuasions, they nonetheless expressed a common sentiment: stoning is not called for in Islam; this sort of thing "only happens in Africa"; and the concern over what is happening in Nigeria is all simply Western sensationalism.

My colleagues' first assertion is simply untrue. Lawal was in fact being sentenced according to classical Islamic law, specifically a reduced version of Sīdī Khalīl's (d. 766 A.H./1365 C.E.) *Mukhtasar,* a legal compendium used for centuries not only in Hausaland, but also throughout the Muslim-majority world. The Mālikī school of Sunni law, out of which this particular set of laws has grown, is not unique; the three other major Sunni schools, as well as the Shiite school of law, all legalize stoning for convicted married adulterers. My colleagues' second assertion, that "these things only happen in Africa," is therefore equally untrue. And although "Western sensationalism" almost certainly played some role in our understanding of what was happening in Nigeria, the widespread textual basis for stoning in Islamic law makes it clear that Western attitudes cannot explain the whole story.

As I mulled over my colleagues' reactions, I supposed they had something to do with the fact that we constituted one of the most privileged Muslim populations in the world, both economically and socially. They focused on staving off criticism of "Islamic law" in the United States, a legal code to which they were not subject, rather than asking tough questions about stoning and its place in the Islamic tradition. Our discussions that day—and my sense that these issues desperately needed the careful treatment that I felt Western Muslims avoided—led me to this project. During several years of research and writing, however, my assumptions about the causes of Lawal's trial and release changed quite dramatically. While I continue to believe that American Muslim organizations and Muslim intellectuals must seriously and systematically address questions of penal law, gender, and patriarchal norms in the contemporary Islamic world, my analysis has led me to understand that this particular expression of Islamic law cannot, at any level, be separated from its context in contemporary northern Nigeria. In other words, I'm convinced that "Nigeria" is more essential than "Islam" to understanding what is happening in Nigeria, and that there is little or no ahistorical "Islam" that can be separated from a particular cultural manifestation. However, I do not argue that Islamic law exerts no causal influence whatsoever on a society that implements it, which is why I chose the phrase "little or no" in the previous sentence. I consider that the Islamic legal tradition transmits some transhistorical ethics across time, just as long as that tradition is considered divine by the Muslim *umma* (community of believers). This, I believe, is what distinguishes religious phenomena from secular topics that are subjected to the method of historical materialism, and I think my respondents and friends in Nigeria who support the shari'ah would agree with my proposition that religion is "different." Hence, one of the main concerns of this book is to understand how social and cultural manifestations of religion interact with a canon of overdetermined divine religious texts.

In order to understand the influence and power of both texts and culture, we must also study the power of tradition, and how tradition works to motivate a contemporary Muslim society to change its present through a revolution. In the Nigerian case, the interaction of three layers of history must be understood to see how this cultural power works: first, the present tense and its concerns; second, the nineteenth-century Sokoto Caliphate, which serves as a model of strength and self-determination for today's northern Nigerians; and finally the classical, Prophetic period of Islam—a particularly idealized version of which animates and inspires the previous two layers. I call this dialectic triad the "sunnaic paradigm" (from the concept of the sunnah, a Muslim's desire to emulate the example of the Prophet Muḥammad). I contend that this is a particularly Islamic paradigm that thinks about and interprets history in a different mode. I see this paradigm used most often by Muslims who favor the modalities of political Islam, or Islamism.

To deepen our understanding of the sunnaic paradigm's power in the case of Nigeria, we must begin with the paradigm's first layer:

discussions by northern Nigerians concerning the social conditions that gave rise to the 1999 shari'ah revolution, which I transmit here in their own words. This support for Islamic penal law extended to support of stoning, which is contained within that penal law. It must be noted, however, that "support" for the legality of the stoning punishment is quite different from support for meting out the punishment. Stated support for stoning is overwhelming, whereas support for actually stoning someone is not. The deeper, second layer of the sunnaic paradigm is the nineteenth-century Sokoto Caliphate (r. 1809–1903 C.E.), a successful caliphate founded by native sons, whose rule contemporary Nigerians often look to as a social and political ideal. The polemical literature of the Sokoto Caliphate (and the Sokoto *jihad* leaders' subsequent historiography) places itself in a linear history tracing back directly to the classical, Prophetic period of Islam, which makes up the third and deepest layer of the sunnaic paradigm.

This powerful sunnaic paradigm gave a sense of power to Nigerians as they embarked on the 1999 shari'ah experiment to overcome their nation and society's significant challenges. The quick rise of stoning after the first of twelve northern states began to (re)implement full Islamic shari'ah codes reflects the general state of decline of Islamic law and jurisprudence that has occurred in this and many other contemporary Muslim-majority societies in the age of postcoloniality. This reductionist version of Islamic law *(fiqh)*, colloquially referred to in Nigeria as shari'ah,[1] is literally illustrated in Amina Lawal's trial—a careful analysis of which reveals the amalgam of cultural priorities that are authoritative today. I also look at aspects of Lawal's background: her country, her region, her ethnic group, and their traditions; as well as the Islamic legal traditions that have been operative in one form or another in the area since the eighth century, declining only when the encroachment of European colonial powers began in the nineteenth century. We also encounter Islamic legal history, both in Hausaland during the era of the Sokoto Caliphate, when textual Islamic law became dominant in the region, and in the classical period when the Islamic legal tradition developed.

Finally, we must consider the sustained ambivalence toward stoning in Islamic thought, from the classical tradition that reluctantly legalized it to contemporary concerns in northern Nigeria. On a rhetorical level, a vocal minority of Muslim populations around the world demands the strictest possible iteration of Islamic law as a means of ordering a chaotic social situation. But digging deeper into the social, historical, and theological reality, one finds ambivalence toward Islamic law, stoning, political shari'ah, and the course of Amina Lawal's case. Zoom the lens out even further and we find evidence of this ambivalence in the Islamic intellectual tradition at large, in which exegetists and jurists expressed their trepidation over the severity of the punishment in Islam's earliest discussions. All these layers of history and historiography played themselves out in the light-blue courtroom that housed Amina Lawal's trial. This book will explore that moment and its outcomes.

Given that the current rise of Boko Haram in Nigeria can be directly attributed to the failure of the 1999 Islamic revolution, the book will offer broader insights into the question of political Islam in the contemporary world. Since the "Arab Spring" began in Tunisia in late 2010, several states in the Muslim-majority world have found themselves contending for political power with often long-suppressed Islamist movements. While a rich literature on this phenomenon has arisen, few analysts of the Arab Spring have looked to the example of northern Nigeria—or explored links with the West African experience in general—to gain broad insights from what happened when an Islamist movement took power and earnestly began to activate its politico-theological agenda.

The instinct to "look back" into Islamic history to legitimate a new shari'ah order in the present (the sunnaic paradigm) may lead to the conclusion that political Islam in Nigeria—and perhaps more generally—works best as a resistance narrative rather than a positive governing platform and agenda. The reason for this is that looking back to a utopian past is an idealization, most pointed as a form of protest against a distressing present. Dismantling actual structures of colonial rule, global politics, and poverty has proved more difficult across the Muslim-majority world. Nigeria is very much included in this problem, and these difficulties are no less profound once Islamists take power.

Chapter 1, "A Revolution for Shari'ah," takes us to northern Nigeria's present—a society plagued by poverty and corruption, and one in which the legitimacy and efficacy of the federal government is in a state of steady weakening. This state of affairs has only worsened as of 2016, when the Nigerian military is engaged in a protracted battle with Boko Haram that seems, at this point, ineffective. In 2015, President Goodluck Jonathan postponed the presidential elections scheduled for February 14 by more than a month, citing that the military was too busy fighting Boko Haram to provide security. Boko Haram, for its part, has now declared its allegiance to Abu Bakr al-Baghdadi, the caliph of the "Islamic State" (ISIS).

Tracing how this distressing state of affairs came to be, I draw on ethnographic material gathered during fieldwork in northern Nigeria in 2010, in addition to books, conference procedures, popular poetry, and oral artifacts (all largely unpublished or unpublished outside Nigeria) to explain the symbolic value of post-1999 shari'ah for contemporary northern Nigerian citizens. In order to explain this symbolic capital across class and social strata, I introduce a distinction between "idealized shari'ah" and "political shari'ah." Idealized shari'ah is a yearning on the part of the common man for an end to corruption—particularly of their governors—and for the creation of a welfare state to aid the poor by instilling a divinely inspired fear in their leaders as well as through the facilitation of practical and fair disbursement of *zakāt* (almsgiving). Stories of the Prophet and his Companions, especially ones that emphasize fair play, moral exactitude, and the leveling of all people before the power of a just and judging God, are regularly evoked. Idealized shari'ah—the ideal of God's justice in the classical theological understanding—is, in this schema, used nearly interchangeably with "Islamic law," which, in turn, is used nearly interchangeably with "natural order," or the elevation of man above the animal level. It becomes clear as chapter 1 unfolds that "idealized shari'ah" does not relate in a straightforward way to "Islam" proper. It is a signifier upon which a set of beliefs about the good and the just life are placed. Law is the means for this signifier to manifest itself politically.

By contrast, I use "political shari'ah" to explain manifestations of post-1999 shari'ah that do not meet the standards of the ideal. Many Nigerians concluded, with varying degrees of grief, that by 2010 the entire project had fallen under the category of "political shari'ah." I argue that this bifurcation between the ideal of shari'ah and its inevitable political dispensation—which subjected the ideal to the same social and political dynamics that caused the shari'ah revolution to begin with—is necessitated by a cultural desire to uphold a shari'ah ideal against a distressing, corrupt material reality. The reasons for the desire to uphold the shari'ah ideal are in part doctrinal and theological, but I argue that at a more fundamental level they are a function of survival under difficult circumstances. The first chapter also introduces the theme, which began in the late eighteenth century, of Hausaland looking eastward to affiliate itself with a larger Arab–Islamic epistemological and political heritage, even as it insisted on its independent identity and culture.

Chapter 2, "Hausaland's Islamic Modernity," takes us deeper into the dialectical sunnaic triad to the Sokoto *jihad* period. I argue that the concept of stoning and other violent punishments *(ḥudūd)* prescribed in the Qur'an function as a "legitimizing horror" in the eighteenth- and nineteenth-century polemical literature of the Sokoto Caliphate. What this means is that the severity of the stoning punishment is held up as demonstrating the ultimate seriousness of Islamic law and, by extension, Islam.

I begin with an overview of the arrival of Islam to West Africa beginning in the eighth century C.E., showing how houses of power from Songhay to Borno and beyond mandated Islamic law to consolidate new forms of rule. I argue that the *jihad* launched by Uthmān Dan Fodio (d. 1817) in the late eighteenth and early nineteenth centuries can be read as the culminating moment in a long movement away from the synchronistic religious practices that had dominated West Africa and toward the full application of a textual, legally oriented "shari'ah society." This new order was facilitated in Hausaland through the explicit adoption of the Mālikī school of law. Confirmed texts, in this context, were the bearer of legal authority. The instantiation of a shari'ah society in the Sokoto *jihad* and the later Sokoto Caliphate period also reflects broader trends throughout the Arab and Islamic world in the early modern period. Evidence for a growing relationship with the wider Islamic world is found in Uthmān Dan Fodio's teacher's reported interaction with Muḥammad ibn 'Abd al-Waḥḥab (d. 1792) in the Arabian Peninsula during his *hajj* (pilgrimage). I also note some of the Arabic/Islamic legal, theological, and literary texts that were in circulation in Hausaland during this period and studied by *jihad* leaders. The chapter ends with the arrival of the Europeans to Hausaland, bringing an end to the Sokoto Caliphate in 1903, when the city of Kano fell to British cannons and Sultan/Emir al-Mu'minīn was exiled to the city of Sokoto.

Chapter 3, "Origins of the Stoning Punishment," takes us to the deepest level of the sunnaic triad, which exposes several fissures that are at work both in the present (manifested in "political shari'ah") and in the Islamic legal tradition to which contemporary actors refer. I examine how the seventh-century Islamic legal legacy interacts with twenty-first-century northern Nigerian social and political realities. Two general observations can be made that challenge the "seriousness" and "stability" that contemporary northern Nigerians claim about stoning. First, the punishment was certainly borrowed from another, or several other, legal systems; whether this or these are Judaic, Roman, Mesopotamian, or Ancient Arabian Custom is the subject of scholarly debate. Second, stoning did not take legal force in Islamic law smoothly; while stoning for *zinā* is forbidden in authoritative Sayings of the Prophet *(ḥadīth)*, the Qur'an's prescription of flogging punishment for what can plausibly be construed as the same crime necessitated subtle hermeneutic devices to harmonize the sometimes opposed pronouncements within the legal tradition.

I attempt to "proof text" the Nigerian notion that a strict-constructionist application of Islamic law offers "stability." The result—that stoning entered the Islamic tradition by way of a fraught, contested, "contradictory," and, in a sense, anthropomorphic process (in considering the role played in stoning's legalization by Islam's second caliph, 'Umar b. Al-Khaṭṭāb (d. 23 A.H./644 C.E.)—suggests that the same Islamic law that is sought after to offer stability is itself, in some instances, on shaky epistemological ground.

Chapter 4, "Colonialism: Then and Now," examines the legal and social changes that occurred during Hausaland's encounter with European businessmen, explorers, and military colonizers. Were it not for northern Nigeria's colonial encounter with the British, the contemporary desire to aggressively reach back into history to cleanse and preserve their society would have been far less acute. I examine in detail the most important event of the early British colonial era—the promulgation of the Native Courts Proclamation in 1900. Issued by British High Commissioner for the Northern Region Lord Frederick Lugard, the proclamation holds that "no punishment, involving mutilation, torture or grievous bodily harm, or repugnant to natural justice and humanity, may be inflicted."[2] This clause outlawed stoning and amputations—a fact that is often recalled in contemporary, post-1999 shari'ah discourse in northern Nigeria—even though the punishment was never enacted by Sokoto Caliphate leaders, which even the Islamic legal scholar Joseph Schacht, sent to the region by the British crown, admitted. What is striking (as the chapter examines in detail) is that even though the British claim positions itself against a universalized conception of self-evident "repugnan[ce] to natural justice and humanity," the contemporaneous British penal code that replaced the Islamic one sanctified flogging, whipping, imprisonment in stocks or irons, field imprisonment, and other punishments, many of which (in the case of treason against the colonial authorities) could be carried out until death.

Chapter 5, "The Trial of Amina Lawal," digs deeply into the instincts and events that drove the stoning trial and surprisingly reveals that two elements fade into the background: Amina Lawal herself and stoning. Lawal's trial was the theater within which the parameters, purpose, and authoritative legal arguments and methods for postmodern Nigerian shari'ah were enacted—while Lawal's person, testimony, and indeed the facts of the case largely left the stage after her first trial. This prioritization, whereby primary source material, namely Qur'an and *ḥadīth,* were debated in trial in lieu of a discussion of the facts of the case, veers considerably from court records from Hausaland's colonial period. This shift reflects contemporary priorities that, I argue, are characteristic of "postmodern Islamic law" in northern Nigeria. I analyze the form of argumentation used by the prosecution and defense, both of which emphasized interpretations of Qur'an and *ḥadīth* over jurisprudence, the latter playing a more symbolic role in the proceedings. Western legal forms, including the form of the proceedings and the deployment of the 1999 Nigerian constitution, were also present in the trial, despite one of the stated purposes of reintroducing shari'ah presented in chapter 1—to distance the north from the federal structure.

Chapter 6, "Gender and the Western Reaction to the Case," examines in detail how the massive international reaction to Lawal's case influenced its final outcome. It also excavates the roles of women and gender in the shari'ah revolution. Although Lawal's fate was the stated cause of the massive international reaction to her trial—with everyone from human rights organizations to governments to famous public figures advocating her freedom—Lawal as an individuated subject virtually disappeared from view. Instead, the particular interests of European and North American reactors and respondents took center stage in a post-9/11 context in which the war on Iraq was being prepared, and "fuel" to attack the region was a valuable currency. As for how many stoning cases are awaiting trial in Nigeria, it is very difficult to say—the number is somewhere between twelve and several hundred, according to my sources there. We do know that governors are reluctant to mete out the punishment after Lawal's case, and therefore many sentenced to death by stoning are languishing in prison, in legal purgatory.

This book wrestles throughout with how the past (a legal–theological discussion and legacy from the seventh century C.E. in the Arabian Peninsula) affects the present (twenty-first-century northern Nigeria). An idealized shari'ah perspective would understand the practice of Islam and Islamic law as a means to create an unbroken chain between these two moments. Political shari'ah, however—that is, the version of shari'ah that expresses itself through politicized society, which includes all expressions of shari'ah in the lived world—places Islam and Islamic law within history. As post-1999 shari'ah in northern Nigeria seeks to re-enliven an "authentic" Islam to counter societal ills that are seen as imposed and illegitimate, gender most powerfully exposes the "political" in the political shari'ah that is ultimately manifested. Concerns about women and gender betray the limitations of a static understanding of shari'ah: women are more invested in seeking the "universal message" of Islam over the specifics of shari'ah when those specifics tend to affect their lives negatively and disproportionately. I also examine which kinds of voices and ideas for reform on the question of gender are considered valid and acceptable in Nigerian society, and which are not. On the topic of that which is "unthinkable," the book ends by considering how welcome critical thinking is in a society that perceives itself as under threat. The sunnaic paradigm is an example of critical thinking under such circumstances of feeling threatened—a masculinist and reductionist one—while societal desires to change gender norms express themselves within the historicized field of political shari'ah.

CHAPTER ONE

A Revolution for Shari'ah

Corruption

O Lord of the worlds help our nation
To get rid of the scourge of debilitating corruption
By day and night from top to bottom
People are aware of this rotten disease
That the rich and poor suffer without
Cure and solution like AIDS epidemic....
Looking at the police man as of now
Standing as wretched as a hungry cow
With uniforms so dirty and tattered like crow
From top to bottom unwieldy lined in a row
Never smart never alert or battle ready with a bow...
A man in the street in Nigeria
Is like a man on death roll
As a common man everything is like hell fire
For there is nowhere for him to get cool
Everywhere is suffering he has to suffer
Its corruption left and right in every pool
Its corruption up and down and everywhere...
This is our home we have nowhere to go
And our poverty is never alleviated not even near
And yet we are kept in a hell of suffering
Now we resort to looking for the MESSIAH to come...

M.M. Abdulkarim, "The Poems for the New Generation" (found in a bookshop in Kaduna, Nigeria, 2010)

On any day, *tashar motaci* (transport stations) across northern Nigeria are bustling with commerce: hawkers sell pirated Hausa videos, sliced papaya and watermelon, the day's newspaper, or hard-boiled eggs as travelers wait with impressive patience—often in extreme heat—for bush taxis to fill to maximum capacity before setting out on potholed roads that the drivers have a special knack for maneuvering. But in November 1999, northern Nigeria's *tashar motaci* saw something remarkable: tens of thousands of Nigerians crowding in to make their way, mostly westward, to Zamfara State to witness Governor Ahmed Sani Yerima's special "launching" of shari'ah.[1] Some sold their belongings to afford the journey, and in a widely remarked-upon development, taxi drivers reduced their fares in celebration. Governor Yerima—known for his sharp political instincts, if not for his special Islamic piety—had struck a geyser of popular support with his announcement that Zamfara State was to restore full shari'ah penal law for the first time since British High Commissioner for the Protectorate of Northern Nigeria Lord Frederick Lugard issued a native courts ordinance in 1900 declaring some aspects of Islamic penal law—including stoning and hand amputations—antithetical to "natural justice, equality, and good conscience."[2] Lugard's announcement came just a few years before Kano's clay city walls crumbled under British cannons in 1903, signaling the death-knell of the Sokoto Caliphate and marking the beginning of direct colonial rule.

In the same year that Yerima launched shari'ah in Zamfara, 1999, the Transparency International Corruption Perceptions Index ranked Nigeria the second-most-corrupt country in the world.[3] Ordinary Nigerians had suffered under the weight of corrupt military rule and then, starting in 1999, corrupt civilian rule. Conditions had never been worse since Nigeria won its independence in 1960, and in recent decades Nigerians had seen their standard of living fall to heretofore unseen depths, particularly after the adoption of an International Monetary Fund (IMF) structural adjustment program that significantly withdrew the government from the public sector, affecting, among other things, food and education subsidies.[4] Many therefore remarked with some irony that the trouble began when the military-backed government yielded to democracy, which had done nothing to quell the government's ritual dipping into the public coffers. Against this backdrop, Nigerians greeted Yerima's news of the restoration of God's law with exuberance, calling him a *mujadid* and declaring Zamfara State "holy."[5] By 2002, twelve reluctant governors of northern states, chastened and pressured by massive grassroots support for shari'ah, introduced Islamic penal codes under their jurisdiction. Among these was Katsina State, whose then governor, Umaru Musa Yar'adua, would later become president of Nigeria (2007–10) following controversial elections in 2007.

On January 15, 2002, Corporal Idris Adamu of Nigeria Police Bakori, on behalf of the Katsina State commissioner of police, arraigned a peasant woman, Amina Lawal, and her lover Yahayya Muhammad Kurami before the shari'ah court in Bakori for committing the crime of *zinā,* or illegal sexual activity.[6] The day before, on January 14, one Police Corporal Rabiu Dauda and another officer of Nigeria Police Bakori had arrested Lawal and Kurami and charged them with the offense.[7] Kurami was shortly thereafter released upon swearing his innocence before the court, while Lawal, who had given birth nine days earlier, was held, in accordance with Mālikī law, on the basis of her confession to the crime and because of her pregnancy. Almost two years later, on September 25, 2003, Lawal, whose case had since attracted unprecedented international attention, was acquitted before attentive eyes worldwide.

This chapter is an ethnography of what I call idealized versus political shari'ah, based on my own research in northern Nigeria in 2010. "Idealized shari'ah" is what was demanded on the streets of northern Nigeria in 1999; it is a constructed shari'ah imbued with what Nigerians most urgently want to see in their societies—an end to poverty and corruption. An end to poverty and corruption thus became synonymous with idealized shari'ah. "Political shari'ah" is a phrase developed by Nigerians on the ground to describe what happened when shari'ah took hold in the same corrupt political process that had prompted the revolution to begin with. While the ideal persists, the political manifestation of the ideal brings with it great grief—and, in the age of Boko Haram, grave dangers for ordinary Nigerians. The following section describing idealized shari'ah makes up the first and outermost layer of the sunnaic paradigm described in the Introduction.

IDEALIZED SHARI'AH

> In 2000, shari'ah spread—and the impossible happened.
> Dr. Haruna Wakili

"Islam"

On a very hot day in February 2010, I sat in the office of Aliyu Musa Yauri, in Nigeria's capital Abuja, awaiting my appointment to discuss his work as the lead attorney in Amina Lawal's trial.[8] His staff were not only good enough to offer me an ice-cold malt soda—a precious commodity when electricity shortages often hamper refrigeration—but also provided me great amusement as I eavesdropped on a young Hausa boy's valiant attempts to explain the virtues of conversion to Islam to his pretty, female Igbo colleague, no doubt so he could have a chance to marry her. The girl's witty, unmoved retorts to the boy's ever-more-tenacious flirting were interrupted by Mr. Yauri's emergence from his office. A kind-looking man, stout and wearing brilliant royal blue and white traditional Hausa clothing, he breathlessly asked me if we could hold the interview in his car, as he had to mediate a 15 million naira land deal immediately. A few minutes later, I leaned with relief into the air conditioning of his car and the soft murmur of BBC Hausa.

"I would even say that we are willing to see our sons die before we are willing to see the name of Islam touched," he said while maneuvering Abuja's sophisticated highways in the midst of our easy conversation. "When our sons die, we know God has a plan—but Islam ... you can do what you like to do in the north, but if you touch Islam, you are in trouble."[9] Yauri would know. Some who repeatedly threatened him, accusing him of being a non-Muslim, viewed his representation of Lawal with extreme suspicion. They were convinced that his representation of her and her subsequent release were the direct result of Western intervention in the form of money and unwelcome, imposed values. Yauri defended against these accusations by arguing that his defense of Lawal was in fact an expression of his love of Islam. As an attorney and a proud Muslim, he considers it his duty to expand the outward limits of what legal precedents for harsh punishments such as stoning and flogging should be. His words recalled a point that Hauwa Ibrahim, another of Lawal's prominent attorneys, had made to me in Cambridge, Massachusetts, some months before: "The trouble is, once stoning starts, it doesn't stop."[10]

Yauri's predicament indicates how important it is for political actors in contemporary northern Nigeria to foreground "Islam" and Islamic identity in their activism. Any agitation for change that does not cloak itself in the rhetoric of "Islam" stands almost no chance of gaining any popular support—and now, given the northern governors' widespread adoption of shari'ah in their states, no chance of elite support either. It was not always this way in northern Nigeria, where the Northern Elements Progressive Union, formed in 1950, championed socialist ideas against a backdrop of general Islamic ethical values. But today, a specific conception of Islam that includes an uncompromising fierceness of Islamic penal law (called colloquially "shari'ah") is the currency of social change. In classical Islamic accounts, shari'ah is the ideal of God's law, the perfect law. In classical Arabic, the word encompasses meanings including "the way to the watering hole [for camels]" and the ultimate mercy and redemption. This notion stands in contrast to *fiqh*, which are man-made manifestations of the shari'ah ideal, incorporated into jurisprudential schools of law that are subject to debate and refinement over time.

While the substance of some of Nigeria's shari'ah laws may have been hard to defend constitutionally, the populist power that brought them to the north is unquestionable. In the face of dwindling hope in the federal state structure, Hausaland dug deep into its history and collective memory to find an identity that would ground its passion for change. This identity was "Islam." The power of *Islam* as a proper noun is powerfully buttressed in Hausaland by the memory, now legendary for many, of the Sokoto Caliphate (r. 1809–1903 C.E.), which marked one of the most important periods of rule in African modernity. "Islam" in this construction carries the symbolic value of strength and perseverance, and a sense that all—rich or poor—are equal before God.

An eminent historian of the Sokoto Caliphate, Ibraheem Sulaiman, writes in one of his essays that "In Islam, you are born today and tomorrow you start fighting."[11] But is it all Muslims who fight against the fundamental injustices of our human predicament? Or is it Muslims who find themselves under direct attack, who are therefore commanded to defend their theological and physical borders? I believe that, for Sulaiman's part, "Islam" is a proper noun that connotes self-determination for northerners who want independence on their "own terms."[12] His essay makes it clear that the enemies to be fought are corruption, poverty, and helplessness.

But "Islam" is not simply the fight against the social problems that plague the region; Islam, here, is fundamentally oppositional. "Islam" resists powers that interfere with the subjective sense of self-determination and confidence a people need to confront their problems. According to Sulaiman, "Islam will always have to fight to survive.... Americans will always look for an excuse to fight Islam."[13] Adamu Adamu, a weekly columnist for the *Daily Star* in Nigeria, added, "There is not [a] time in Islamic history that Islam has been practiced 100%. It is always a struggle."[14]

This notion that "Islam" is always a struggle stands in for the qualities of self-determination and dignity expressed in a distinctly masculinist flavor. Dr. Usmanu Bugage, a well-known Nigerian public intellectual, said this to me of the Sokoto Caliphate: "The Hausa kingdoms were all about strong men before—but Islam says, they [the powerful] are men—and we are men."[15] "Islam" levels the playing field among "men." This contemporary iteration of Sokoto Caliphate "Islam" is understood to confer dignity to men because their allegiance is to God rather than any worldly, political force; and God—the unseeable, that which is so powerful that it cannot be apprehended by the sensory limitation of human beings—is always a greater force to direct one's allegiance to than one's mortal enemies. This God is bigger and more powerful than any Hausa ruler, modern federal republic, or geopolitical force. This masculinist account of dignity levels the playing field of power to one that is *mano a mano*—the common man at last on a par with his rulers.

Law as Natural Order

Dr. Aliyu Tilde's well-kept farm, one of the most pleasant places I visited in northern Nigeria, was a relatively unusual sight: bushes replete with violet flowers dotted the perimeter of sprawling green grasses where Dr. Tilde can often be found sitting with his laptop, writing his weekly column about Nigerian political, religious, and social affairs.[16] He interrupts his thoughts to move the table against the direction of the sun to sit in constant shade. Dr. Tilde, who has a PhD in botany from the University of Sokoto, described the Sokoto of his student days as quiet and peaceful; he used to read the Qur'an outdoors until sunset, after which he would begin reading *fiqh*[17] until late into the night. His favorite author is Abū aṭ-Ṭayyib 'Aḥmad ibn al-Ḥusayn al-Mutanabbī (d. 353 A.H./965 C.E.), who is known as one of the greatest Arab poets, and who was called a heretic in his time for his religious skepticism.[18] But Tilde, who has flirted with such unorthodox ideas himself, emerges unconvinced of their wisdom. The reason can be found in his studied observation of the dozens of cows he keeps on his property, whose delicious, sweetened milk we enjoyed while chatting as the afternoon sun slowly turned to dusk. "Unless you have law," Tilde reflected,

> Man is an animal. The law is supplied by religion, which raised man from the animal level to the human level. We must continue to refine God's law to keep man in check. Law keeps man at a high level with its potential energy. Once that energy is law, [the status of man] will drop down. As society changes, that law is modified. Our primary lawgiver comes in the form of a prophet, like Muhammad. Shari'ah is an obligation on Muslims. Shari'ah is there to regulate virtually everyone. The government [of Nigeria] is not founded on shari'ah but on the secular governance of the West. People look back to the pre-British period and they wish they could go back to the times in which they were deprived. Having said that, a Muslim society that is living in the twenty-first century has to give an interpretation of shari'ah that is better. Shari'ah is unchangeable, while *fiqh* is a changeable concept. If there is an argument that can be used to save someone's life, the jurist should use that argument.[19]

That religious law is necessary to regulate man's passions is a trope I heard often in northern Nigeria, and I believe it is one of the chief instincts motivating the clamor for shari'ah. The power of shari'ah to order and cleanse society lies in its "authenticity," as both Sulaiman and Tilde indicated—an authenticity expressed as opposition to Western forms of government, economic policies, and colonial histories that are considered to be at the root of many of Nigeria's contemporary problems.

Dr. Abdulkareem Sadiq, who directs an Islamic institute in Zaria, explicated idealized shari'ah in more detail. On the surface, the ideal is simple, and part of what makes it ideal is its simplicity—the model for northern Nigerian society is the Prophet and the four rightly guided caliphs, what is known in the Islamic tradition as the sunnah, or following the example of the Prophet Muhammad. The following stories relayed to me about the Prophet particularly illustrate the ideal. During the Prophet's time, a lady from a wealthy background was caught stealing and was brought to the Prophet. "This woman was from a noble background ... and no one had never seen the Prophet so angry when the people wanted her set free because she was of noble birth. The

Prophet swore by Allah that if his own daughter Fatima was to be caught stealing he would cut off her hand."[20] Here is an example of a great leader of Muslims, who presumably enjoyed privileges over laymen, subjecting his close family to the same rules and laws as anyone else. This moral stance is extremely attractive to northern Nigerians. A similar situation happened under the reign of the second caliph,'Umar ibn al-Khaṭṭāb (d. 23 A.H./644 C.E.), who reportedly said to his flock: "If I do anything wrong, please set me right: we'll set it right, even if it means *this*" (and he shook his sword). Another story is of Alī ibn Abī Ṭālib (d. 40 A.H./661 C.E.), the third caliph, from whom something was stolen. When Alī took the case to court, he was found guilty. The acquitted Jew accused of stealing embraced Islam, declaring it a just system.[21] Dr. Sadiq's next statement, which jolts us into the particularities of Nigeria's present, was a bit startling: "Hence if we follow the shari'ah, there will be no more immunity in the Senate.[22] In the Prophet's time, when you followed the Imam and he did something wrong, he would have immediately been told he was wrong. You only follow someone when he does something right."[23] Dr. Sadiq continued:

> In Islam, the leader has to comply with the rights of Muslims because he can be immediately removed. That's what makes shari'ah so ahead. Historically the people have heard about shari'ah and how it is all about justice. The world over, the leader is worshipped. In Islam, the leader has to comply with the rights of Muslims. People saw 'Umar crying when he was recalling that the Islamic empire has expanded and some of the unkept roads might cause a camel to stumble and fall—but look at our roads, they are stumbling blocks, and no one cares. But 'Umar was afraid of the Day of Judgment.[24]

People in northern Nigeria are afraid of the shari'ah in a manner more trenchant than their fear of other legal systems. This fear of God and the Day of Judgment is seen as fundamental to shari'ah's efficacy as a legal system. The stoning punishment is the most gruesome and powerful expression of this desire for radical order in a chaotic situation, and provides a "legitimizing horror" for the shari'ah system as a whole.

"Idealized shari'ah" interpolates an unruly order into a narrative of an *always already* perfect society. This society is made manifest through instantiations of a conception of shari'ah that is constructed as the only solution to Nigerian problems. In the face of economic decline, social disintegration, and a loss of political power in the north—and in keeping with trends in the wider Islamic world—the reimplementation of shari'ah has been a way to set boundaries around an unruly situation; for "Islam" as a symbolic category is the most powerful legitimizer of political change, moral discipline, conformity, and spiritual reflection. Dr. Muzzammil Sani Hanga, chairman of the Kano shari'ah commission, makes this point of "shari'ah as structure" by arguing that "The increased level of tolerance and the value of man and the purpose of religion is upheld by the shari'ah. It doesn't matter what he believes."[25] Dr. Hanga's statement reflects the fact that Islamic law has, by this point in history, developed as public law, one that regulates public morality and is less concerned with individual belief or hidden behavior.

Whether the above stories of the Prophet are historically "true" is beside the point. Northern Nigerian society had reached a stage by 1999 that the people desired shari'ah to mean justice. Hence, stories, *aḥadīth* (plural of *ḥadīth*), Qur'anic verses, and modes of interpreting the shari'ah that would bring swift punishments to an unruly social and political environment were sought out and promoted as shari'ah's "true" meaning. The human hand in this and many other cases is thus indelibly linked to *which* shari'ah comes to the surface in a given society, whereupon that version is accorded the status of ahistorical divinity by clergy and laypeople who accept that vision. This process of emphasizing one aspect of the shari'ah and calling it the whole was then socially canonized in northern Nigeria through naturalizing rhetoric that conflates shari'ah, Islam, and Hausaland. Dr. Aliyu Ibrahim, a professor of Islamic law at the Ahmadu Bello University, Zaria, described this conflation by saying that "Islam as a legal/political system was doing well under the Sokoto Caliphate—shari'ah is a reintroduction. Shari'ah has been here for a long time—since the British came,"[26] whereas

Dr. Asmau of the Kaduna Polytechnic University moves the argument toward further naturalization by describing shari'ah as ahistorical: "You can't 'reintroduce' shari'ah. It is simply the way you practice Islam."[27] This conflation illustrates the sunnaic paradigm.

"Democracy"

What idealized shari'ah is *not,* significantly, is a democracy. While it is tempting to explain this oft-repeated sentiment in contemporary northern Nigeria by reference to shari'ah's "naturally" undemocratic character, I believe there is no doubt that shari'ah is deemed precisely "not a democracy" in northern Nigeria because of Nigeria's failed transition to democracy after thirty years of military rule came to an end in 1999. Commenting on democracy, Dr. Guando of the University of Sokoto says, "What is this [democracy]? Islam says, whoever you are, no matter what your position, the law must take its course. Democracy gives immunity.[28] What is this?"[29] "Democracy," far from being seen as the contemporary world's most just system of government, is instead blamed for Nigeria's corruption. This corruption is today practiced under the banner of "democracy."

Aliyu Ibrahim puts the matter more starkly, claiming that the problem with democracy is that it is a Western concept that fundamentally contradicts the "Islamic": "Democracy is the sovereignty of the people and [implies] secularism—both of these are a rejection of Islam. Democracy [functions on] the basis of this popular sovereignty myth. Even if the world is paradise, we feel we are going back to God [in the end]."[30] Many northerners connect democracy, which is considered a failure in Nigeria, with secularism, and hence this religious and antireligious rhetoric is superimposed onto the political problems of Nigeria. The rhetoric of Islamic law further extends this analogy—a return to Islam is a return to general law and order. I believe that the instincts and desires described above do not contradict, but rather illuminate, Adamu Adamu's blunt summation that "The primary reason Nigerians wanted shari'ah was because of the will of God."[31]

POLITICAL SHARI'AH

> If shari'ah was from God, it will survive. But if it was politically motivated, it will fizzle out.
>
> Olusegun Obasanjo, President of Nigeria (1999–2007)

The visitor to Hausaland cannot fail to notice the near unanimity of the embodied practice of Islam.[32] Small, colorful plastic pots filled with water to make the ablutions for prayer line the dusty streets where merchants hawk their wares, and when the *iẓān*[33] sounds, all stop their business to pray, often right outside their shops on plastic or handwoven mats, or at the many corner mosques, which are often simple storefronts. Nigerians are practical about religion, starting with traditional worship, where Gods could be borrowed. I relayed my amazement to many of my new friends in Nigeria at the seemingly total rate of prayer among the population—one that I had never seen, for instance, in extensive travels through the Arab world. They replied that this order could be ascribed to the leaders of the Sokoto Caliphate, who brought textual uniformity to the region. I could not help but be impressed by these quiet scenes of people from all walks of life stopping what they were doing to wash themselves and pray, side by side, without attention to social status.

Dr. Mustapha Muhammadu Guadebe,[34] however, had a different, less romantic take: "The high rates of prayer reflect the challenge and deprivation in Nigerian society." Dr. Awalu Yadudu[35] added, when I told him my observations: "Yes. Outwardly, Allah willed them as model Muslims. But in other ways, they're the worst. They may pray, but cut corners in all other acts of worship. For example, business transactions are not fair and kept truthful."[36]

By 2010, many had declared the shari'ah experiment a failure. It made sense in cultural terms, therefore, for northern Nigerian analysts to decouple the embodied expression of Islam (e.g., prayer) from the body of evidence that would indicate moral uprightness. This cleavage is an unintended consequence of shari'ah—one that has increased public pressure to "look" Muslim, and that is also a psychosocial insistence on preserving a conception of "idealized shari'ah." There must still be something perfect and ahistorical to look to as a defense against a growingly worrisome state of affairs in the external world.

Even northern Nigeria's most enthusiastic proponents of shari'ah had to add the caveat that its process of implementation had been tragically politicized: Dr. Hanga, himself the chief of the Kano shari'ah commission, said frankly: "Those who brought about the reintroduction of shari'ah were not sincere. Shari'ah is just a legal system, not a political machine."[37] Dr. Hanga's statement reflects the fact that it was not long before the shari'ah ideals and hopes for social change, which had driven thousands to Zaria in 1999, became bitterly disappointing as shari'ah became subject to the same mechanics and personnel that were deemed corrupt to begin with. But because Hausa Islamic society cannot allow critiques of shari'ah qua shari'ah, the term "political shari'ah" was developed in northern Nigerian society to describe—and distance—the crushing disparity between the ideal of shari'ah and the far less-than-ideal reality of its implementation that was unfolding in a corrupt and inherently corrupting political space.

"ZEAL"—SHARI'AH'S EARLY DAYS

Many spoke of the "zeal" that accompanied the reintroduction of shari'ah in 1999. This first took shape in the prosecution of Buba Bello Jangebe, known in Hausa as "Kare Garke" (the ranch raider), a poor man from Zamfara State who had his hand amputated at the wrist in 2000 for stealing a cow. The zeal was so prominent that Jangebe himself hailed the decision and said to the BBC, "When I was a thief, there were lots of problems, there was no money, I had no peace. At the time, my relatives deserted me ... I now visit my relatives and they visit me ... I thank God for the amputation."[38] Today regarded somewhat like a celebrity in northern Nigeria; Jangebe was given a job after his amputation as a messenger at a secondary school in his hometown.[39]

It was only later, when it became clear that corruption had not been alleviated by shari'ah, that people began to admit that Jangebe looked malnourished when his arm was amputated. Dr. Hanga offered the following example to explain the zeal that fueled Jangebe's—and indeed Amina Lawal's—sentencing. They were in the wrong place at the wrong time and were unfortunately caught up in the zeal:

> During the Nuremberg trials in Germany, if the Nazis had been tried five years later, there would likely have been a different punishment. People were in the throes of shari'ah. In the Amina Lawal case, you can see the effects of time. At first there was intense heat: then the heat subsided and arguments were purely legal.[40]

Human nature's curtailed capacity to respect and fear the shari'ah if it is deemed too harsh or unjust was also considered by *'uṣūl al-fiqh*[41] scholars and by the contemporary thinkers who reconceptualize shari'ah for today. Shaykh Malam Sanusi Khalil, of the Izālat al-Bid'ah wa Iqāmat al-Sunnah (Izālā) movement, emphasized that the poverty level of people must be taken into account before accusing them of crimes. "In the Prophet's time, there was only one wrist cut off in twenty-three years. This is because peoples' needs were being taken care of."[42]

Idealized shari'ah entails meeting people's basic material necessities to an extent not close to being reached by contemporary Nigerian authorities. This slippage between a reality that is not conducive to shari'ah and ideal shari'ah is a well-worn theme in modernist political Islamic thought, typified by thinkers such as Syed Abul al'la Maudidi in the Indian subcontinent and Yusuf al-Qaradawi of Egypt and Qatar, both of whom were frequently cited in Nigeria as political inspirations.[43] Personnel are supposed to be properly trained to administer a new shari'ah society. There is supposed to be a reorientation of society itself, I was frequently told, a kind of renaissance—people are to be enlightened and well educated before shari'ah can be implemented. In modernist thought such as Qaradawi's, it is frequently repeated that this ideal is so far from being reached that discussions of shari'ah's actual applicability should be suspended for the foreseeable future.

KEY PLAYERS AND MOVEMENTS IN POST-1999 SHARI'AH

Shari'ah's failure to meet northern Nigerians' ideals is personified by its current political actors and movements. The following are short accounts of the main players on this scene.[44]

Ahmed Sani Yerima, Governor of Zamfara State (1999–2007)

Ahmed Sani Yerima is the former governor of Zamfara State and a member of the All Nigeria People's Party. He was the first to reintroduce shari'ah penal codes to the north, in Zamfara State in 1999. Though shari'ah rendered his reputation sterling, by the late summer of 2010 Yerima was embroiled in scandal. Khadija Asaiko described him pithily as "at the top of the list of governors who steal money. Southerners make a mockery of the north for this reason. Shari'ah was merely a cover for him. If anyone critiques him, he can now respond, 'they attack me because I am the shari'ah man.'"[45] Dr. Sadiq, who was very supportive of the shari'ah initiative and continues to be, though perhaps to a slightly lesser degree, also expressed dissatisfaction with Yerima's leadership, saying that the government has squandered a golden opportunity: they had the resources to impose a just shari'ah order of which the people were in full support. But the problem of offering immunity to corrupt government officials has persisted under the new order, and this is certainly contrary to the shari'ah. The *'ulema* (Islamic scholarly authorities), according to Dr. Sadiq, cannot prosecute the government because of immunity. Or perhaps the reason they can't prosecute the government is that the *'ulema* are being paid off.

Malam Sanusi Khalil of the Izālā sees things a bit differently, arguing that shari'ah is not new for Muslims and, therefore, that the 1999 movement back to shari'ah is not extraordinary. "Unfortunately, Muslims have criticized Yerima, but I believe Yerima, because a Muslim is only to judge actions, not one's heart."[46] In the summer of 2010, Yerima became embroiled in another scandal that severely challenged his credibility when news that he had married a child bride—a thirteen- or fourteen-year-old Egyptian girl who was reportedly the daughter of his driver in Egypt—became the talk of Nigeria. Yerima had to bring her back to Nigeria, as it is illegal in Egypt to marry a girl under eighteen.[47]

The Hisba Police

The *hisba* are a largely ad hoc police force charged with upholding the moral order as set out by the 1999 shari'ah experiment. The *hisba* are employed under an initiative called *daidatu sahu* (literally "ordering steps"), a program charged with maintaining a social order that comports with the shari'ah that was set up in the Kano, Sokoto, and Zaria shari'ah commissions. The *hisba* do not enjoy a good reputation among northern Nigerians; many citizens, including those who supported the shari'ah revolution, consider them a vigilante group composed of zealous young men.

Today the influence of the *hisba* has waned, and the civil police have regained popularity as the only constitutional body allowed to parse legal codes (it is said that only the mistakes of the *hisba* could have rehabilitated the civil police force so dramatically). Saudatu Mahdi[48] describes the hisba as "an exuberant group of young men on the verge of fanaticism. They want a moral platform to say, 'They are wrong, and we are right.'" Dr. Sadiq, on the other hand, says that while he "wouldn't be surprised if [the *hisba*] were corrupt, the police, however, are far more corrupt, for they have to show they are working."[49] Accordingly, the police's reputation for targeting the poor and the innocent was worsened by the rise of the *hisba*.

Izālat al-Bid'ah wa Iqāmat al-Sunnah

Izālat al-Bid'ah wa Iqāmat al-Sunnah[50] (Izālā) was established in Jos in 1978 by Shaykh Ismaila Idris. However, Shaykh Abubakr Gumi (1922–92), one of the most influential Islamic scholars of the 1960s, who served as the grand *qādī* of the Northern Region (1962–67), is more closely associated with the movement.[51] The Izālā are understood by many in northern Nigeria to attack traditions in Hausaland that they consider innovations in Islamic practice, such as naming ceremonies or the practice of saying *"amīn"*[52] during the five daily prayers. Traditional Sufi orders in Nigeria, especially the Tijāniyya, are particular targets, often accused of *bid'ah* for their practices of *dhikr*,[53] which offend the Izālā's belief in only the Qur'an and *ḥadīth*. The Jos faction of the Izālā is considered the most militant, known for proselytizing with loudspeakers in Christian areas. Unlike the Tijāniyya, who have been historically resistant to the British colonial masters since the nineteenth century, going so far as preventing their children from attending colonial schools, the Izālā encourage people to get a Western education in a move often understood as characteristic of an "alternative modernity." Their political focus and practical attitude toward education make them more amenable to politicians, who often sympathize with them.

Gumi, considered the spiritual founder of the Izālā, wrote his own *tafsīr*[54] of the Qur'an in Hausa and translated the Qur'an to Hausa. Gumi was critical of the cultural practices of the Hausa rulers, recalling the trope of criticizing perceived problems in society by "tightening" Islamic arguments that reach back to the *jihad* era. Uthmān Dan Fodio was a Qādarī[55], but not a Sufi, says Gumi, splitting Sufi orders in the region. This is an odd statement considering that Fodio, Hausaland's most revered figure, was an avid *murid* (follower) of the Qādariyya. In Sokoto, a man I met said, "If Gumi were alive, he would not have gone for the method used in Zamfara, i.e., translating books into English and make them into the legal code." We can see here that, by 2010, there was an attempt to distance the Izālā movement from post-1999 shari'ah.

Tijāniyya and Qādariyya (Sufi Orders)

In an implicit response to their Izālā critics, perhaps, the Qādariyya tend to emphasize that Sufis know the shari'ah by citing Imam Mālik, the eponymous founder of the Mālikī school (which dominates northern Nigeria), who wrote: *"man tasawaffa wa lam yatafaqa fa-qad tazandaqa"* (one who becomes a Sufi and doesn't become learned in Islamic law becomes a heretic).[56] The emirs of the Sokoto Caliphate, who continue to enjoy ceremonial and moral authority in Hausaland, are still part of the Qādariyya legacy, unified under one Sultan. Today, however, these movements have their fierce critics. According to Aliyu Ibrahim, "Imam Ghazālī combined beauty and law. Ibn al-Kayyām wrote about how to cure the illnesses of the heart: *Islām, Imān* and *Ihsān*.[57] Too much *Ihsān* [beauty] without shari'ah is the *Zindiq* [heresy]. They [the Sufis] are heretics."[58]

Northern Elements Progressive Union

Mustapha Guadebe credits Nigeria's independence with the political clarity offered by the Northern Elements Progressive Union, which was started by Tanko Yakasai (b. 1926), a simple tailor who became a government minister. Maalam Aminu Kano is one of the movement's most celebrated luminaries. In the 1950s, his heyday, Maalam Kano was a presidential candidate of the People's Redemption Party. Maalam Kano is still revered in Nigeria today for the perception that he was a just leader, and for his multifaceted approach to social change: known to combine Qur'an, *ḥadīth,* communist principles, and *fiqh* in his speeches and writings, his polyglot approach was condemned by the *'ulema* of his time; this historical construction places the *'ulema* on the opposing side of progress. Ironically, in today's climate, it is unlikely that Maalam Kano would garner such wide support—despite his persistent popularity as an inspirational historical figure, even among supporters of the 1999 shari'ah revolution.

Kano and Sokoto Shari'ah Commissions

Dr. A.N. Umar is the permanent secretary of the Ministry of Religious Affairs in Sokoto; his job is to coordinate among the different departments of Sokoto's shari'ah commission: shari'ah education, *zakāt*[59] collection, community service, *du'ah,*[60] and finance. Dr. Umar describes the shari'ah before 2000, when it was reintroduced in Sokoto, as "dormant and not in practice"—even though, significantly, it was always somehow there in the hearts and practices of Sokoto's residents, albeit in passive form. Sokoto replaced its magistrate courts with shari'ah courts after shari'ah was revived in 2000.

The shari'ah commissions operate on two assumptions: that shari'ah is the vehicle through which Islam becomes animated, and that morality is grounded in Islam. Many of the problems in Nigeria are diagnosed as moral problems, and shari'ah institutions are thus vested with a mandate to sanitize sin and corruption from the hearts and minds of the people. But how does an institution set upon a task as lofty as "sanitizing" hearts and minds? On the more trenchant side of this spectrum, shari'ah commissions like Sokoto's set upon improving Islamic education. They have appointed three preachers in each local government and sponsor workshops on the ethics of preaching. Politics is never far from the commission's activities: to keep the peace, and to form committees, they draw from the Tijāniyya Sufi order Jamat Nasr al-Islami, an umbrella organization bringing together the north's Islamic organization (founded by Izālā leader Abubakr Gumi) and the Izālā itself. Whereas before shari'ah there was much political rivalry between these groups, today the differences are slight; a relative political peace credited to post-1999 shari'ah has rendered the groups' differences relatively unimportant. In addition to these activities aimed at restoring morality, they have provided sixty-nine motorcycles (as of 2010) to out-of-work young men so that they can transport people around town. "Shari'ah is a way of life," Dr. Umar said. "Muslims are expected to apply shari'ah in all aspects of their life. *Ma'lims* [Hausa: Islamic scholars] could not afford Islamic books—so the government has now purchased them and distributed them according to districts in the local government."[61]

Sokoto's shari'ah commission, whose well-appointed building can be found on one of Kano's leafy side streets, was established one year after Kano's, in 2000. Kano is northern Nigeria's largest and most active shari'ah commission, serving one of West Africa's most important cities of commerce and culture. The commission is divided into four departments with specific mandates: the shari'ah commission, the *hisba* commission (which trains and appoints the *hisba* police), the *hubsi* commission (oversees issues of trade and commerce), and the *zakāt* commission (almsgiving). The primary means of contact between the shari'ah commission and everyday people is through the *daidatu sahu* initiative. Like many of the Islamic scholars I had spoken to who reflected on the deeper purpose of shari'ah, Dr. Hanga described the commission's aim as chiefly to prevent people from feeling drawn to immorality to begin with. Dr. Hanga took pains to emphasize that "the shari'ah does not go after people who hide,"[62] echoing a leitmotif of Islamic jurisprudence, whereby Islamic law is the arbiter of public morality. As such, the point is not to invade privacy or attempt to uncover sins that are hidden.[63]

It is ironic, then, that a chief concern of the commission is *zinā* (adultery, including premarital sex), one of the most private of activities. Dr. Hanga asserted that in Kano, for example, there is no longer any prostitution, and he described an incident in which the shari'ah commission brought a prostitute back to her family, saying, "Take your daughter back." But this only raises the more important questions of whether her parents could afford to resume caring for her financially; whether her sex work was unrelated to her family's poverty; and whether her parents would want her back after her moral transgressions.

Boko Haram

The terrorist group Boko Haram arose as a direct result of the the failure(s) of the post-1999 shari'ah revolution. Started in 2002 by

Muhammad Yusuf in Maiduguri, Boko Haram is today composed mainly of poor, uneducated boys who originate from Borno State. They believe that any book that is not the Qur'an is *harām* (a sin), and they do not subscribe to a particular *mathab* (school of law). Boko Haram are responsible for several instances of terrible violence in Nigeria, including a deadly clash with Nigerian security forces in 2009 that killed over seven hundred[64] and a fresh spate of killings in January 2012 that targeted schools. Aminu Gamawa, a northern Nigerian political commentator and graduate of Harvard Law School, assesses Boko Haram this way: "A failed revolution always gives way to terrorism and radicalism. The politicians promised them that when they implemented shari'ah everything would change, now they [Boko Haram] are out for total political and social revolution."[65]

SHARI'AH IS "WORKING"—A CONCENTRATION ON WOMEN'S DRESS

Over the course of my fieldwork, it has become clear to me that it is difficult to remain at the lofty level of "changing hearts," slow as the pace of this kind of change inevitably is—because, for social and political reasons, the shari'ah commission feels pressure to demonstrate that shari'ah is "working." Dress code becomes an easy means to publicly demonstrate shari'ah's efficacy, and women's dress is almost always singled out for special attention, both because of the greater emphasis on women's dress in Islamic law and because women themselves are generally less politically and socially equipped to challenge the *hisba* shari'ah police.

Other aspects of social life are also disciplined by *daidatu sahu*. Many told me that Kano was highly social before shari'ah, characterized by the Hausa word *escanche* ("loose living"). One regular man I spoke to one evening in Kano, "Umaru," recalled the promiscuity, drinking, smoking, sex, clubs, and joints that were readily on offer in Kano before shari'ah with an unmistakable whiff of nostalgia. I asked Umaru if he himself considered these activities a problem, and if he was glad shari'ah had drastically reduced them. After a long pause, he answered, "They are a problem in terms of religion," suggesting that his problem with these activities did not extend beyond abstract moral considerations—I sense that he considered his subjective opinion on this matter irrelevant. Umaru went on to add that it is a common misconception that shari'ah was deemed necessary because of a high crime rate; the reality, he added, is that the problem is actually corruption and insecurity. Before shari'ah, he reflected, there was not a lot of criminal activity.

Disrupting everyday life and infringing on personal boundaries is not what people had bargained for, yet it seems that, de facto, this is what shari'ah amounted to. Indeed, it was when the shari'ah authorities tried to crack down on social life that problems started. Policing morality began to wear on the regular citizens of Kano. More and more people began to take advantage of the fact that *daidatu sahu* regulations were almost comically easy to circumvent, as one only had to take a fifteen-minute trip from most places in Kano to the *sabon gari* (literally, the "strangers' quarters"), where the Christians in the region had traditionally lived and done business, to break the rules. In the *sabon gari* one can pass languid evenings at one of dozens of outdoor restaurants and bars and have beer, hard liquor, and wide varieties of food; the dress code is more relaxed, and at the end of the evening one could easily return home to more conservative neighborhoods.

It is important to note that this state of affairs reflects the fact that *daidatu sahu* regulations do not apply, at least directly, to non-Muslims. The free-for-all space of the Government Reserve Area in Kano, known as an exclusive area for the ultra-elite, is even more provocative to everyday Kano residents. Regular citizens often hear that unimaginable excesses take place there that go totally unpunished, including what one man I spoke to called "man-on-man acts that were overlooked because they were of a higher class."

POVERTY

A lot of Islam is the regulation between two people.
Dr. Guando, Sokoto, May 2010

The plight of the poor epitomizes what many call the fundamental root of northern Nigeria's problems: a moral decadence for which shari'ah is seen as the only real solution. Northern Nigerians are convinced that Islam is supposed to provide a check against economic imbalance; it is supposed to be "welfarist" at its core. The terrible gap between the rich and poor exists, therefore, because these very core Islamic principles have not been kept.

Many spoke of the breakdown of Nigerian society as happening in stages that led to shari'ah implementation. The first was the 1999–2000 furor, when shari'ah was a campaign issue. During that period, shari'ah was described as the antidote to a serious breakdown of social services and an IMF-sponsored structural adjustment program that marked the beginning of the end of governmental involvement in people's lives. The children of the poor could not cope with this new regime, because money was suddenly withdrawn from the public realm. This trouble all began when the military-backed government yielded to a democratically elected government. Jamila Nasr added that she believes this imbalance became exacerbated when religious scholars exploited these circumstances by "making religion more visible" in order to gain politically.[66]

According to Aliyu Ibrahim, currency devaluation and debt in Nigeria have made the current situation "ten times worse than slavery." To emphasize the point, Dr. Ibrahim recommended a book to me, *Confessions of an Economic Hit Man* by John Perkins. He told me that "Africa is dying because of debt, the plundering of riches, arms and armament—and the U.S. is the largest supporter of these arms."[67] Several other men in the room who were sipping tea with condensed milk and sugar—a drink that seems to be uniquely delicious in Nigeria—nodded and murmured approvingly.

For northerners, the shari'ah they advocated in their 1999 revolution was about advancing a welfare state, which is to say, a solution to poverty and an end to stultifying corruption. "No one should go to bed on an empty stomach. Men know their rights, and live their lives in accordance with the Prophet's last sermon. Shari'ah stands for justice and fair play."[68] According to Mustapha Guadebe, the Qur'an provides a template for the treatment of the poor and the regulation of the rich. The deprivation that Guadebe believes leads to the high rate of prayer among northerners also explains the common man's enthusiasm for shari'ah:

> The common man wants anything that can improve his own life; he believes that the Qur'an tells us how the rich and poor should live. Islam disciplines the rich; the rich should pay *zakāt*. If the poor can get *zakāt* on their own, they wouldn't have to beg. *Zakāt* is not taxed, the rich just evade it. In the shari'ah people will be obedient to God, which means: they will respect the laws brought down through religion and they will assist their neighbors. For example, if one is rich, but your neighbor is poor, Islam says there is no way you should cook what your neighbor cannot cook for themselves. Islamic society is supposed to be fair. In Nigeria the rich exploit the poor. The rich have obligations to the poor, but instead they hoard food and commodities and oversell to the poor. The rich don't pay *zakāt* because it's corrupt money and cannot be used in Allah's way. The Kano governor, who is very rich, with houses in London, is surrounded by people who cannot find a meal. Rich people are from the military or civil service. The country is declining, it's not growing.

"How do people sleep at night?" I asked, deflated by Guadebe's sadness as he spoke.

"I don't know. Maybe drugs."[69]

• • •

As Salisu Bala, the director of the Arabic Manuscript Program at Kaduna's Awera House, and I approached a vendor—of deliciously spiced baked fish wrapped in aluminum foil and stuffed with tomatoes and onions—off a side street in Kaduna, we were regaled by one of the most pathetic images I saw in northern Nigeria: dozens of young adolescent boys rushing Bala's car to beg for money in the most entreating and relentless manner. These were the *magajari,* young boys who left their hometowns to come to the city to learn Qur'an, who were supposed to be supported by the state and through *zakāt.* The pilgrimage of the *magajari* to the cities is a very old Hausaland practice, and so regular citizens come to their aid by feeding and clothing them; yet these boys had been neglected by the state for a long time and their conditions have worsened in recent years. The Kano shari'ah commission set up a task force to look into their fate.

The plight of the *magajari* is perhaps the most visible example of the failure of adequate *zakāt* collection, and is thus a source of palpable sadness for many northerners I spoke with, as the *magajari* symbolize Hausaland's rich heritage of Arabic and Qur'anic studies. Traditionally these children have survived by *zakāt* and handouts from locals, but the rich's failure to pay their *zakāt* has reduced many of these boys—frequently seen huddled in doorways writing Qur'an on wooden sheaths with ink pots—into beggars.

CORRUPTION

> The idea of full shari'ah implementation became a mirage.
> A shopkeeper in Kaduna

Anticorruption panels were set up in Kano and Zamfara's shari'ah commissions, which are well funded by those state governments. Kano's includes a public complaint commission, and Zamfara's has a separate panel to address corruption issues, but many have lamented that these are not working—to date there has been no sustained research or investigations over whether these commissions have lessened corruption. A story involving Ibrahim Shekaru, Kano's former governor, is the one most frequently used to illustrate discontent with the panels' efficacy. In 2005, then governor Shekaru was embroiled in a corruption scandal involving fertilizer distribution. He was never arraigned or tried in a shari'ah court, and now it is unclear whether Kano will ever get its money back. Dr. Sadiq had remarked that if Nigeria were to "really" implement shari'ah, the governors would be dead set against it. It is because of their lack of support for "real" shari'ah that the shari'ah experiment has died out.

The perspectives that I gathered on Nigeria's infamous problem with corruption spanned the spectrum from secular to moral and religious. Dr. Asmau is partial to a geopolitical explanation of the problem, emphasizing the United States–Nigeria relationship. The Nigerian federal government is supported by the United States, which is only interested, according to Dr. Asmau, in Nigeria's oil. Dr. Asmau then said something I found surprising: rather than advocating the United States removing itself from Nigerian affairs, she said that "The U.S. should come assist us and make our leaders listen to us." It would not be the only time I heard a plea for more U.S. involvement while at the same time hearing that the United States was responsible for aiding and abetting Nigeria's problems in the first place. Dr. Asmau believes that Nigerian leaders will listen to the United States in a way that they will not listen to their own people. Her posture toward European powers is slightly different: "These European countries should stop taking the [Nigerian oil] money, but they do, because of their own economies."[70] Nigeria's oil, which is mainly in the south of the country, is redistributed at the federal level, but that revenue rarely benefits the everyday northerner.

Dr. Hamidu Bobboyi (a prominent, American-educated northern Nigerian independent scholar and leader of an NGO promoting good governance) offers a diagnosis of Nigeria's problems focused more domestically, emphasizing that political reform is essential to weeding out corruption.[71] Nigerian politicians are expected to fund their own political campaigns, which can run into the millions of Naira. In Kano, one would need up to 250 million naira to run for governor. Thus, Nigeria's ultra-wealthy are transformed into venture capitalists who treat campaigns as a business. A rich man will take a gamble and invest in a campaign, and if the candidate happens to win, they can expect ample payback to make the investment worthwhile. If the candidate loses, the rich man will write it off as a bad investment, inevitable sometimes in the life of the marketplace. As far as the voters are concerned, an acquaintance I met in Abuja put it this way: "Before the elections, people are human. Once they get elected, you're not a human anymore."

Salisu Bala's reading of political corruption returns to the theme of "moral disease" that is quite popular with northern Nigerians. Echoing Justice Mohammed Bashir Sambo of Zamfara State, Bala believes that people are corrupt because they "do not fear God." I believe that in this context, the statement that people "do not fear God" is structurally the same as saying they "do not fear the law." As Justice Bashir Sambo says in his book *Shari'ah and Justice:* "The Prophet was asked what goodness is. The answer is: *'in ta'abudu Allah kinnaka tarāhu fa-lam takun tarāhu fa-innaka yarāk.'"* [72] (to worship Allah as if you can see Him, and if you cannot see Him, as if He can see you). Allah as the lawgiver, the judge.

With respect to authoritative Islamic legal texts—the ones that many contemporary northern Nigerians assume contain perfect answers—actually investigating them can be disappointing for Nigerians looking for a moral and legal way out of endemic corruption. Saudatu Mahdi, the secretary general of the Women's Rights Protection and Advancement Alternative, said with some disgust, "Corruption doesn't carry the same weight in the shari'ah as *zinā* (illegal sexual activity); it's merely a breach of trust." [73] Perhaps it is a result of the paucity of expected "progressive" Islamic legal readings that many of my interviewees preferred to leave the duty of mining the tradition to "the scholars." While it is de rigueur for a religious society to publicly state that everything found in the Islamic tradition must be ultimately just, I believe there is a prior instinct in northern Nigeria: a collective agreement over a set of desired values for their society—such as ending corruption and poverty—and then constructing a notion of "shari'ah" to address those concerns. When epistemological authority holders such as the *'ulema* introduce Islamic concepts that do not appeal to the collective, those concepts are challenged and called "political"—not really Islamic.

Despite doubts about this particular instantiation of shari'ah, increasingly called "political," the Kano shari'ah commission presses on with plans to try civil servant cases in corruption trials. The first order of business would be to recover stolen money, and if the money in question is mixed with personal funds, the accused will keep his own money—and then be caned one hundred lashes. In addition, his wrist will be amputated, and he will serve a life sentence.

As for the question Nigerians most want answered, Dr. Hanga, anticipating that I would ask it, said solemnly: "We are praying to God to give us a governor to try."[74]

CHAPTER TWO

Hausaland's Islamic Modernity

> We can't give one one-hundredth of the honor the jihad leaders did. Uthmān Dan Fodio is the model.
>
> Dr. Muzzammil Sani Hanga

It became clear to me, through long conversation with northern Nigerians from all walks of life, that it is important for students of contemporary Hausaland to understand what the Sokoto Caliphate—and the *jihad* of Uthmān Dan Fodio that brought it to life—has meant for the inhabitants of this region since the caliphate's founding in 1809.[1] In what follows, I distill the themes from the caliphate's history that I believe are most resonant in contemporary Hausa (roughly, northern Nigerian) society. The history of the Sokoto Caliphate and how that history is remembered makes up the second layer of the sunnaic paradigm, which explains the enthusiasm for Islamic law and shari'ah in today's northern Nigeria. The first layer, as presented in chapter 1, consists of the desires and concerns of the present. This second layer, the establishment of the Sokoto Caliphate by Uthmān Dan Fodio in 1809, helps us understand more deeply what is signified by "idealized shari'ah."

Uthmān Dan Fodio's intellectual makeup was textured and multi-textual, while the rhetoric of his political movement was rather more rigid. Dan Fodio's Islamic training reflected the lack of sharp distinction between the spiritual tradition of Sufism and the legal training that characterized premodern Islamic pedagogy. He was a *murīd* (follower) of the Qādariyya Sufi order, which had been present in Hausaland since its arrival from Baghdad in the fifth/twelfth century (A.H./C.E.), and he was trained by his father in Qur'an and *ḥadīth* sciences. However, there was a twist to his intellectual background: Dan Fadio was also a student of one Jibrīl ibn Umar, whose travels to Arabia for *hajj* on two occasions put him into contact with Muḥammad ibn 'Abd al-Waḥḥāb, the founder of the Waḥḥābī school.[2]

Dan Fodio's pastiche of intellectual influences is evident in his most important work, *Ihya' al-Sunnah wa Ikhmād al-Bid'ah* (The Enlivening of the Sunnah and the Destruction of Religious Innovation). He opens his discussion by admonishing Muslims for their failure to mete out *ḥadd* punishments (violent punishments prescribed in the Qur'an) with the regularity that they should. Dan Fodio's emphasis on *ḥadd* (plural *ḥudūd*) punishments, I think, is a way of establishing the seriousness of the Islamic legal tradition; this seriousness would then be able to penetrate human psychology at its deepest core. This seriousness, in turn, helps offer no-nonsense solutions to Hausaland's deep social and moral problems. In present-day Nigeria, I call this theme—which I believe is discernible in the *jihad* leaders' nineteenth-century literature—stoning's "legitimizing severity."

Since the eighth century C.E., a strain of intellectual production in Hausaland has understood strict adherence to Islamic law as a synecdoche for commitment to Islam in general. Islam's emphasis on literacy and its political ensconcement in the palaces of power laid the important groundwork for cultural and political fealty to Islamic law. Hausaland was also exposed to other genres of Islamic learning in the Arabic language, including Sufi theology, rhetoric *(balāgha),* and Arabic poetry. *Ḥadd* punishments in much of this literature—especially stoning—demonstrate the seriousness and, thus, the legitimacy, of Islamic law. When the British invaded the Sokoto Caliphate (which finally fell in 1903), they changed this conception of *ḥudūd* in crucial ways. Punishments that were once held at a practical distance, while supported rhetorically as symbols of the seriousness of Islamic law, were transformed into live issues after British colonial authorities singled out and banned certain *ḥadd* punishments. This history helps us further understand the symbolic power that Islamic law holds in contemporary northern Nigeria. Punishments like stoning and hand amputation are intimately tied to a sense of sovereignty and of self-determination.

EARLY HISTORY OF ISLAM IN HAUSALAND

Islam came to West Africa through nonmilitary means in the eighth century, when traders from the north, south, and west brought various iterations of the religion to the region. These included the strict Ibādīyya branch—descended from the Khawārij, who first appeared in the seventh century C.E. when they rejected Alī b Abī Tālib's rule—and two major Sufi orders, the Qādariyya and the Tijāniyya. This rich confluence of traditions produced a syncretism that ruled the history of West African Islam until its most forceful challenge, beginning in the eighteenth century with Uthmān Dan Fodio, his brother Abdullahi Dan Fodio, and his son Muḥammad Bello's *jihads* against the traditional Hausa rulers who had, previously, coexisted fruitfully with this religious syncretism. Dan Fodio aimed to establish firm adherence to orthodox Islamic law in a region under attack, not only by military means, but also through the enforcement of strict adherence to the Mālikī school of jurisprudence. Though the Mālikī school had already established deep roots in West Africa, following it to the exclusion of other faith modalities—such as belonging to Sufi orders or incorporating elements of traditional African religion—had never been mandated.

ISLAM COMES TO WEST AFRICA

In the eighth century C.E., traders traveled north across the West African savanna and the Saharan Desert to the arid plains of Hausaland—where peanut oil was gainfully produced—bringing Islam to what is now the Federal Republic of Nigeria. In the late fourteenth and early fifteenth centuries, Wangarawa-Dyula traders from the West also traveled to the kingdom of Hausaland. The eleventh century brought the most intense period of Islamization to West Africa; from the northeast, Berber and Arab traders—probably of the Ibādīyya, a branch of the Khārijite movement that opposed the Sunni succession to the Prophet Muḥammad after his death—traveled from their corner of the Sahara to Hausaland, first reaching the kingdom of Kanem-Borno. By 1810, emirates like Kano, Zaria, and Katsina were established, followed by what are known as Ilorin and Nupe in today's Nigeria.

At the start of Islamic history, Arabs set their sights on two regions south of the Sahara. In 668 C.E., under the military command of Umayyad General Uqba b. Nāfī (d. 683 C.E.), an expedition was sent to Fezza, today an administrative division of Libya. In 739 C.E., Nāfī continued southward in the direction of Lake Chad to the Bilma oasis; historian C.N. Ubah argues that this was undertaken in search of slaves and gold, and that it took the Arabs as far south as the Western Sahara. Although there are recorded attempts at military conquest, Ubah maintains that, as a general rule, it was not Arab armies from the north that brought Islam to West Africa; rather, Islam penetrated the region by various means at various times. Initially, at least, nonmilitary factors were responsible for its diffusion, and when the army was introduced as a factor in the propagation of the faith, it was not the work of the Arabs.[3]

Sufi orders began their first *jihads* into Sub-Saharan Africa around 800 C.E. by attacking the Ghana Empire at Kumbeh. Pade Badru argues that Sufi orders played the most significant role in both the initial spread and the later revival of Islam in the region; and that prior to this sustained effort, Muslim contact with black Africa was limited to long-distance trade that cut through the Saharan Desert to the Arabian Peninsula.[4] The eighteenth- and nineteenth-century *jihads* led by Uthmān Dan Fodio were pieces of a larger current of Islamic reform taking shape in the form of the nascent Waḥḥābī movement in the eastern part of the Islamic world; it was perhaps partially in the service of consolidating this transregional reform movement that the *jihad* leaders endeavored to place Hausaland within a wider Islamic legalistic, textual episteme whose epicenter was in the east.

The eleventh century, moreover, brought a great diffusion of Islamic learning in West Africa through Islam's patronage in African houses of power. Arabic and Sudanese sources agree that the first West African house to convert to Islam was in Songhay, but the exact time of this conversion is a subject of scholarly debate. In a 985 C.E. manuscript attributed to Arab geographer Abu 'l-Husayn al-Hasan b. Ahmad (d. 380 A.H./990 C.E.), we learn that the king of Songhay converted to Islam, and that some of his subjects followed suit. Later in that century War Dyabe (d. 1040 C.E.), one of the first rulers of Takrur, a kingdom founded on the banks of the Senegal, also converted to Islam. After him, the kings of Silla, and then those of Malel, converted as well. By 1086 the king of Kanem, in the region of Lake Chad, was the next important West African ruler to convert to Islam. Scholars contend that the conversions ranged from the nominal to the sincere; most put the King of Songhay's conversion in the former category, whereas the ruler of Takrur's was more authentic in that he "observed the fundamentals of the faith and introduced Islamic law into his administration."[5]

The great cities of the Mali Empire, including Niani, Jenne, Timbuktu, and Gawo (Kawkaw), and cities in modern Nigeria including Kano, Katsina, Kanem Borno, and Sokoto, were famous in the eleventh century for their Arabic and Islamic learning.[6] Scholars from these cities did not confine themselves to one geographic location; itinerant preachers moved from towns to hamlets and from cities to villages to spread learning. Some traveled as far as Cairo, as attested by one of the halls of the famed Al-Azhar University bearing the name "Borno" in recognition of its many West African students.[7] Eleventh-century scholars including ʿAbd-al-Karīm al-Maghīlī al-Tilimsānī (d. 1505 C.E.) in Algeria; Aidah Aḥmad al-Tazākti, al-Maghīlī's student; Aḥmad ʻAqiī, the grandfather of Ahmad Baba of Timbuktu; al-Suyūtī of Egypt; and Muhammad b. Masāni of Katsina all traveled with their knowledge in one context or another. Some were on their way to pilgrimage; others were invited to stay and serve as teachers, judges, and counselors at different places such as Timbuktu, Katsina, and Kano.[8]

Prescribing shari'ah was used as a cultural tool to streamline the political shift as kings and rulers of West African centralized states adopted Islam, though it would be too large a claim to argue that adherence of the populace to Islamic law indexes their "Islamic character"—it is not until the modern period that fidelity to Islamic law takes on this symbolic value. However, irrespective of whether these rulers accepted Islam for purely utilitarian reasons, their conversions and compulsion of Islamic law on their subjects allowed them to consolidate royal power. The kings of Takrur, for example, who were among the earliest to accept Islam, introduced shari'ah into their administrative system and forced their subjects to comply with the law, lending a measure of continuity and authority to their kingdoms. Islam and Islamic law also spread under royal patronage in Mali, particularly during the reigns of Mansa Musa (1312–32 C.E.) and Mansa Sulayman (1341–60 C.E.). In Kano, Muhammad Rumfa (1463–99 C.E.) was seen as a defender of the faith, as was the case with Askia Mohammad Ture of Songhay (1493–1528 C.E.) and Idris Alooma of Borno (1571–1603).[9]

Scholars agree that Islam's championship of literacy was another major cause of its spread. Ubah argues that most Islamic communities of ancient West Africa included a class of people who could read and write Arabic. These scholars were not only prized for their erudition; they were also valued because they could help merchants issue written orders or keep business records. The same skills would be useful to West African rulers for the purposes of diplomacy.

I find it fruitful to read the history of West African Islam as a gradual process of integration into a legal, textual, and pan-Islamic heritage. Nehemia Levtzion argues that the Islamization of West Africa in the first instance "preceded political domination, as traders and clerics propagated Islam under the patronage of non-Muslim rulers." Islam adapted to local environments by emphasizing its ritual and magical elements rather than its legal elements:

> There was little articulation of political content. Muslim clerics became integrated into the African sociopolitical systems because they played similar roles to those of the traditional priests; mosques, like traditional shrines, became sanctuaries. Muslim clerics, like other transcendental mediators and ritual experts, were outsiders.[10]

Levtzion argues that this era of synchronism was brought to a decisive end in the eighteenth and nineteenth centuries with Uthmān Dan Fodio's *jihad.* The distinctive feature of these *jihads* was the political ascendancy of Islam in parts of West Africa, not through conquest from the outside, but by Muslims who had lived in that area. Levtzion describes this as the "culmination of a long evolutionary process."[11] Hence, affiliating with Islam's legal heritage is both realized through a political process and is itself a political expression.

ISLAM IN HAUSALAND

When Islam first arrived in the Central Sudan region in the second half of the fourteenth century, the states of Hausaland (in today's northern Nigeria) had not yet been formed. The first Hausa state to convert to Islam was Kano. According to the *Kano Chronicle* archive, the Wangarawa under Abdurahman Zaite came to Kano from Mali, bringing Islam with him, during the reign of Sarkin (King of) Kano Yaji (r. 1349–85).[12] In another account, Muḥammad al-Hajj draws our attention to a seventeenth-century document on the basis of which it has been argued that Islam was introduced in the fifteenth century. During this latter period Mali was in decline, causing large-scale migration to the north, when Islam "took a firm grip on Hausaland."[13] It is not precisely known when Islam arrived in Katsina, Amina Lawal's home state, though it is believed that a group of Mande immigrants arrived there at about the same time they reached Kano in the fourteenth century. Muḥammad Korau was the first Muslim king of Katsina State, founding his new empire in the second half of the fifteenth century.[14] From the sixteenth century onward, the Tijāniyya and Qādariyya Sufi brotherhoods undertook the "systematic propagation and revival of Islam," as they were reportedly "appalled by the resurgence of paganic practices in many Muslim communities in West Africa particularly in Segu."[15] The Sokoto Caliphate completed the evolutionary cycle toward full adoption of Mālikī Islamic law throughout Hausaland.

UTHMĀN DAN FODIO AND HIS *JAMĀ'A*

Uthmān Dan Fodio, his brother, and a small band of followers—known in the Nigerian literature as the *jamā'a,* paralleling the name given to the Prophet Muḥammad's original followers—declared war on the Hausa Bakwai (seven Hausa kingdoms) in the late eighteenth century and provided a list of reasons they had decided to take up arms. The *jihad*'s polemical literatures portray men whose primary goal was to return to the example of the Prophet Muḥammad (sunnah). Their books read as manuals for their followers on how to conform to the Islamic sunnah in all major matters from prayer to how to conduct *jihad* to the proper administration and respect for *ḥadd* punishments.

Several of Dan Fodio's Arab contemporaries are considered among his intellectual influences. 'Abd-al-Karīm al-Maghīlī al-Tilimsānī (d. 1503/4 or 1505/6), mentioned above, was of North African origin and his works were known to have been in circulation in North and West Africa since the sixteenth century. Al-Maghīlī was militant to the degree that he was expelled from North Africa. For whatever reason, he demanded that the Jews of Morocco, who had fled there after the Roman sack of Jerusalem, should be forcibly expelled from the region—an idea that gained almost no reception among his contemporaries in al-Maghrib. With time, however, al-Maghīlī's ideas prevailed among some of his followers, who then massacred a community of Jews. Al-Maghīlī was subsequently expelled from al-Maghrib and traveled southward, first visiting Air and then successively Takida, Kano, Katsina, and Gao. In Air he was said to have built a mosque where he proselytized to the inhabitants of the region. He was held in high esteem there, and was solicited for legal and political advice—including his thoughts on how a ruler should best administer a state. Many of al-Maghīlī's theories of administration of an Islamic state are echoed in the writings of Muhammad Bello, Dan Fodio's son and champion of the emirate system; this provides a further demonstration of how the Sokoto Caliphate drew Hausaland into a wider, Arab-dominated Islamic civilizational complex.[16]

Bello is among the most important authors and *'ulema* of the Western Sahara, possessed of wide learning in the Islamic tradition. Bello was deeply versed in Arabic language, semantics, poetry, and Sufi theology. We know he studied important thirteenth- and fourteenth-century Islamic works, including Baghdādī theologian 'Abd al-Karīm al-Jīlī's (d. 1365 C.E.) *Al-Insān al-Kāmil fī Ma'rifit al-Awākhir wal-Awā'il,* a meditation on the great Sufi theological ibn 'Arabī. On the semantics of Arabic poetry, he is noted to have studied Muhammad b. 'Abd al-Rahmān al-Qizwīnī's *Talkhīs al-Miftah,* which, among other topics, comments on rhetoric and plagiarism.

Dan Fodio's brother, Abdullahī Dan Fodio, is considered the true jurist of the Sokoto Caliphate. He was trained in Mālikī *fiqh* after finishing Qur'an school (Hausa: *makarantu 'ilm*), studying the *Qawā'id* of 'Allāmah al-Shaykh 'Abd Allāh al-'Ashmāwī (d. 16th century) and the *al-Risāla* of Qaywarānī (d. 386 A.H./996 C.E.), which was used in Amina Lawal's trial. He also studied major Mālikī *fiqh* compendiums like the *Muwatta* of Mālik (d. 179 A.H./795 C.E.); the *Mukhtasar* of Sīdī Khalīl (d. 766 A.H./1365 C.E.), which was introduced to Kano in the fifteenth century; and the *Mudawwanah* of Abī Sa'īd Saḥnūn (d. 240 A.H./854–5 C.E.).

Fifteenth-century Egyptian polymath Jalāl al-Din 'Abd al-Rahmān al-Suyūtī (d. 910 A.H./1505 C.E.), who is thought to have had a special relationship with rulers of Bilād al-Takrur, is another of Dan Fodio's intellectual influences. Songhay's Askia al-Hajj Muhammad is reported to have consulted al-Suyūtī for social and political advice, and Askia Muhammad is thought to have implemented reforms in his kingdom based on those discussions. Ahmad Baba al-Timbukti (d. 1627), one of the learned men of the Mālikī *mathhab,* was also one of Dan Fodio's influences. Al-Timbukti wrote several books, the most famous of which was his biographical dictionary of the learned men of the Mālikī school of law. The work was printed on the margins of ibn Farḥūn's *al-Dibāj al-madhāhib.*[17]

Finally, special attention must be paid to 'Abd al-Qādīr al-Jaylāni (d. 561 A.H./1165 C.E.), the founder of the Al-Qādīriyya Sufi order to which Dan Fodio was a committed adherent. One of his disciples, Sidi al-Mukhtār al-Kabīr (Aḥmad al-Bakki) al-Kunti (d. 1865), was responsible for the consolidation of the Qādariyya brotherhood and the shaping of its organization in West Africa. In his book *al-Wird,* Dan Fodio describes a mystical experience he had at age forty (the same age that the Prophet Muḥammad began to receive revelations), a year before he waged his first *jihad:*

> When I reached the age of forty years, five months and [a] few nights, God drew me near to him and I found there the Master of human beings and the Jinn, our Master Muḥammad, peace and prayer of Allah be upon him, together with his companions, prophets and the saints, they welcomed me and seated me among themselves. Then the savior of the human beings and Jinn, my master 'Abd al-Qādīr al-Jaylāni came with a green cloth decorated with "there is no God but Allah and that Muḥammad is the Messenger of Allah."[18]

Having surveyed Dan Fodio's main intellectual influences, two major observations emerge. The first is that Dan Fodio was interpolated into the literary and textual heritage of the wider Islamic—and, specifically, Mālikī—legal textual heritage of the eighteenth century. Dan Fodio's immersion into traditional forms of learning is further demonstrated by the fact that he holds an *ijāza* (permission to transmit knowledge) of *Sahīh al-Bukhāri,* the most authoritative compilation of Prophetic *ḥadīth.* Muḥammad Bello's exposure to this tradition was even more varied and deep, while 'Abdullahī Dan Fodio attained mastery as a Mālikī jurist.

The second observation is that the focal point of this heritage was the Arabian Peninsula. It can therefore be argued that one of the outcomes of Dan Fodio's *jihad* was to situate Hausaland within a larger Arab–Islamic civilizational heritage, while doing so on independent terms that were suited to the needs of the *jihad* leaders' local environment in West Africa.

THE SUNNAIC PARADIGM

A deeper layer of the sunnaic paradigm, which we will explore in depth in the next chapter, is clearly on display in the polemical writings of the Sokoto Caliphate leaders. Uthmān Dan Fodio's many manuscripts are written in straightforward Arabic prose, conveying a sense of urgency as he wrote to the Hausaland elite to prepare his society for "self-determination" following his military expeditions.[19] An example of this genre of writing is found in Dan Fodio's *Kitāb 'uṣūl al-dīn wa kitāb 'ulūm al-mu'āmala.*[20] He begins a lecture on the importance of sunnah by quoting this *ḥadīth* from Mālik: "The most important matters of religion are those that are sunnah, and the most evil of matters of religion are innovations."[21] Almost two hundred years later, Nigerian Islamic scholar and politician Usmanu Bugage, whom I interviewed in Nigeria, wrote of Uthmān Dan Fodio completing the sunnah dialectic, or *silsila* of learning, "Many a *sunnah* you have brought to life, and many an error quenched while it was a live coal blazing fiercely. And you rose up in a land whose customs had become excessive and which conflicted with the joyous sunnah of the Prophet."

Dan Fodio begins his most important book, *Ihya' al-Sunnah,*[22] by explaining that a Muslim must always look back and strive to emulate the example of the Prophet to attain worldly success. For many contemporary northern Nigerians, emulating the *jihad* leaders is itself a sunnah that delivers them to the ultimate sunnah of the Prophet. The *jihad* leaders provide a local, authoritative sunnah once removed.

Ihya' al-Sunnah's understanding of "Islam" is a legalistic one. An instruction manual for Muslims on the eve of military battle, the work opens by quoting a *ḥadīth* commanding believers to kill in the name of God until the enemy says, *"la illāha il-Allah wa Muḥammad Rasūl Allah"* (There is no God but God and Muhammad is his Prophet), "until they pray, and until they give *zakāt;* if they do these things, they have mercy *['asama]* from me . . . and their judgment will be for God."[23]

Dan Fodio's style is often clipped; in a short passage describing the importance of following the sunnah *('idilat wujūb itbā' al-sunnah),* Dan Fodio proffers only one quotation from the Qur'an and the *ḥadīth* to make his case.[24] His abridged style hints at the formal influence of *tawhīd* principles from the burgeoning Waḥḥābī school, but it is probably more a literary function born of his station as an intellectual and political leader as well as a teacher intent on preaching the Prophet's sunnah to everyday people. Dan Fodio's populism is illustrated in his response to Abū Hamīd al-Ghazālī's (d. 505 A.H./1111 C.E.) statement that "it is the right of regular people to occupy themselves with worship and with their livelihoods, leaving learning to the intellectual elite": with a rare and subtle amendment to Ghazālī, Dan Fodio claims that "What [Ghazālī] means is that they might leave learning to the intellectual elite with respect to preaching, not with respect to learning."[25]

Upon reading the body of literature produced by the *jihad* leaders, one could be forgiven for thinking they were concerned mostly with idiosyncratic questions of ritual, or with imparting pointers for good governance that were inspired by religion, and that their aim was, somewhat obviously, to expedite their own power. This, however, would be too reductionist a reading. What appears to be attention to arcane matters of ritual is really a call for the people of Hausaland to take part in a set of "universal" legal performances aimed at aligning Hausaland eastward, namely within a wider Islamic civilizational complex whose center was Arabia. Framing the Sokoto Caliphate as a great civilization like other great civilizations, Sabo Bako emphasizes the degree to which the caliphate has contributed to "the development of African political thought and administration, putting it on the same and equal footing as the European, American, Asian, Arabic, and Chinese political thought and public administration."[26]

With these larger political goals in mind, it becomes easier to understand why much of the *jihad* literature is focused on the practicalities of organizing an Islamic polity. Muḥammad Bello, Dan Fodio's son, who is represented as the most learned among the *jihad* leaders in Islamic *adāb* (literature), is also, interestingly, the *jihad* leader most closely associated with the task of negotiating with imperial powers—be they German, French, or British. A practical leader, Bello deployed "occupational groups" to newly established towns of the caliphate to promote the growth of small-scale industries. His agenda was to commission craftsmen to do their work and to provide vocational and occupational opportunities for farmers, blacksmiths, dyers, tailors, grocers, physicians, carpenters, and butchers—all of whom he took to be essential to the development of urban life.[27] Even taxable earnings were divided into legal categories: compulsory *(farḍ),* commendable *(mustaḥabb),* lawful *(mubāh),* unlawful *(ḥarām),* and detested *(makrūh).* Bello also introduced the *kofa* system under his rule—*kofa* being the Hausa word for "door" and signifying an intermediary space at the court of the commander to keep himself informed of the affairs of the emirate under his jurisdiction.[28] Fear of God buttresses this system as the central ethos of the caliphate. Bello writes that a good emir is "A man whose eyes shed tears when, in his solitude, he remembers his Lord; a man who is invited *[da'atuhu]* by a beautiful, perfect woman who has filled his spirit *[mālit nafsuhu]* and says [instead], 'I fear Allah most high.'"[29] Such is the extent to which fear of God should guide a righteous man.

Before Dan Fodio's death in 1817, he replaced the Hausa kings with *umara al-'aqalīm,* or provincial governors. In his *Tanbīh al-ṣāḥib 'alā aḥkām al-makāsib* (The Dignity of Labor),[30] Bello cites al-Ghazālī's (d. 1505) *Iḥyā ulūm al-Dīn* as his source for the definition and scope of these provincial governors.[31] To source Ghazālī in one's quotidian conception of the state signals a conflation between yielding to the authority of state power and being a true Islamic believer—as if one cannot inhabit one ontological position without the other. A stark example of yielding to both authority and *belief* simultaneously can be found in the story of how Bello dealt with the main competitor for the caliphate after Uthmān Dan Fodio's death: one 'Abd al-Salām.

'Abd al-Salām was a scholar and a former student of Dan Fodio.[32] According to Shehu Yamusa's account, 'Abd al-Salām became discontented when the emirates were divided between Bello and 'Abdullahī Dan Fodio, causing 'Abd al-Salām to rebel against Bello's authority. Bello, according to Yamusa, tried to preserve order and to work through their differences peacefully, but, "when this failed, he declared 'Abd al-Salām an apostate, after learning that 'Abd al-Salām had declared himself the Commander of the Faithful and that people were declaring their oath of allegiance to him."[33] Here, the Sokoto Caliphate (and Bello) preserved their authority by claiming the unilateral power to declare apostasy—disbelief in Islam—when it was challenged. Bello justified this move by adding that 'Abd al-Salām supported infidels against Muslims—a reference to the support he gave to some Hausa kingdoms against Bello's rule. As a result of this conflation between political unruliness and loss of status as a believing Muslim, 'Abd al-Salām was killed in Bakura in 1818.[34]

A LEGALLY GROUNDED CALIPHATE: SOKOTO (1807–1903)

The Sokoto Caliphate entrenched Islamic law's deepest and most lasting roots in Hausaland, the law becoming a practical and moral reference for the social and political administration of the new empire. In a vast area of about 250,000 square miles, Dan Fodio led the Fulani ethnic group in this revolution of the practice and organization of Islam. But Dan Fodio's *jihad* did not easily take root in several parts of the erstwhile kingdom—in just one example, his followers were persecuted in Gobir. The political dynamics at play during that period are strikingly similar to Nigeria's current dynamics—which, of course, led the people to demand reintroduction of shari'ah. Historian R.A. Adeleye describes the injustices in the nineteenth century that drove regular people to embrace the *jihad*:

> The case of the persecution of the Shaikh's followers in Gobir illustrates the position of Muslims who embraced the purification of the practice of Islam in the *jamā'as* of the various states. The disabilities which the Muslim suffered by living under governments that were not based on the *sharī'ah*. This gave rise to deep-seated grievances which provided Muslims with a common cause to fight for. This factor auspiciously prepared the ground for the success of reforming preachers.[35]

This history is tilted toward the *jihad* leaders' own account of things, but Dan Fodio seized on these grievances, whether manufactured, interpreted in a particular way, or otherwise. His book *Kitāb al-Farq* is just one of many works in which Dan Fodio emphasizes the lawlessness of the local rulers: their laws were oppressive for commoners and contradicted the shari'ah, they imposed excessive taxation and forcibly took their subjects' property, they were prone to corruption and bribes, and they forced Muslims to fight in unjust wars. According to Dan Fodio, these rulers prohibited Muslims from following the sunnah by forbidding veiling for women and turbans for men. Rulers were moreover accused of "indulg[ing] in luxurious and voluptuous living; reveling in illegal music, wearing ornamented fineries and accumulating women, often as many as 1,000 in their harems."[36] Aiding the *jihad*'s success, their engagement with peasants, fishermen, and other common folk in the countryside initiated waves of religious syncretism that assured that various forms of Islam took firm root in the lands of the Sokoto Caliphate. While Dan Fodio was expansive in his efforts to convert and engage as many of the Hausa as possible, he had help proselytizing; for example, one Abubakar b. 'Uthmān (known as Buba Yero), is said to have engaged in similar conversion activities in the Old Gombe region after traveling south to learn from Dan Fodio.[37] The importance of engaging local people and customs in the *jihad*'s organizational structure was evidenced by the use of the local *ma'allams* and their *jama'āt* as instruments and transmitters of the revival. Their participation in the *jihad* lent the movement a structure that allowed the caliphate to take hold with great ease in certain areas.[38]

British historian Abdullahi Smith, who lived most of his life in northern Nigeria, categorizes the formation of the Sokoto Caliphate into five major stages. The first (1774–94) is a period of mass preaching and education of oppressed people with the aim of raising their political consciousness. The formation of the *jihad* vanguard (the *jamā'a*) is the second stage (1797–1803). The third stage, echoing the *sīra* literature (i.e., hagiographical biographies of the Prophet Muḥammad—a common echo among Nigerian historians of this *jihad* period), is described in Sokoto Caliphate historiography as the *hijra* (pilgrimage) from Dareel-Kufr *(sic)* to Dareel-Salaam *(sic)*—that is, from the kingdom of disbelief to the kingdom of Islam; or from Degel to Gudu in 1804—which is, again, an allusion to the Prophet Muḥammad and his followers' pilgrimage from Mecca to Medina in 641 C.E. The fourth stage (1810–17) is the formation of state structures and the processes of governance within the Sokoto Caliphate. Finally, the period of administration (1817–1903) is the period of governance of the state, society, and economy of the Sokoto Caliphate.[39]

Smith describes the goals of the caliphate as guided by a charge to raise the moral tone of society and to provide a social ideology in accordance with Islamic ideals. To achieve these aims, the *jihad* leaders undertook a general educational reform through training of teachers, and an economic reform through improvement of markets, for which special officials were appointed. They also developed communications by opening roads and bridges.[40] These infrastructural and moral considerations were echoed by northern Nigerians I interviewed in 2010, who believe that, at this point, the only way they will be realized is through the shari'ah. Indeed, other frameworks have not delivered results.

Contemporary northern Nigerian historiography of the *jihad* period conveys the symbolic value of the Sokoto *jihad*. Enemies of the *jihad* are depicted just as the enemies of Islam and the Prophet are portrayed in the *sīrā* . Ibraheem Sulaiman, the Nigerian historian mentioned earlier who is revered enough to have a street named after him in Kano, wrote a hagiographical account of Dan Fodio's *jihad,* titled *A Revolution in History: The Jihad of Usman Dan Fodio,* while he was on fellowship in London in 1986. As a substantive work, Sulaiman's book is a valuable history; as an object of historiographical analysis of Nigerian scholarship on the Sokoto Caliphate in the 1980s, its emphasis and tone are extremely instructive. In Sulaiman's rendering, the *'ulema* (Islamic scholarly authorities) of Dan Fodio's time possessed nearly divine authority; they occupied a role close to that of ancient Greek "philosopher kings"—seen as the best hope against times so dark that the only light capable of piercing it comes from Islam. To the best of my knowledge, Sulaiman's account of Uthmān Dan Fodio is the most widely read in modern scholarship. According to his account, Dan Fodio was consistently faced with such intractable problems, emerging from a thoroughly unjust and unequal society, that they can only be compared to the problems the Prophet faced in Arabia at the hands of the Quraysh.

THE GLORY OF THE SCHOLAR

From the eighth century to the rise of Dan Fodio's *jihad* in the seventeenth, Hausaland's popular Islamic practice was fused with traditional religions of the region and with the Qādariyya and Tijāniyya Sufi orders that had taken firm root since the twelfth century. The twelfth-century Timbuktu tradition was of essential importance for all intellectual trends in West Africa at that time, and particularly for West African Islam, in which Mālikī law was operative. Sulaiman describes the Timbuktu tradition as an intellectual edifice and a predecessor to Dan Fodio's *jihad,* painting an idealized picture of a time when scholars were never subservient to mere rulers. This hierarchy was evidenced by the fact that it was the monarch who visited the *qādī* (judge) of Timbuktu, and not the other way around. Timbuktu's decisive decline came at the hands of the Moroccan invasion of 1591 C.E., at which time all the leading scholars of the kingdom were arrested. On this point, Sulaiman argues, the deterioration of the scholars' superiority was merely quantitative—the tradition of scholarly authority was maintained in the hearts of Muslims. This is an instantiation of a common trope that posits a "natural" or "underlying" cultural affinity for traditionalist Islamic cosmology—wherein scholars rule and Islamic law serves as the foundational pillar. This naturalist theme is often repeated when northern Nigerians describe their "return" to shari'ah in 1999. Sulaiman wrote this unflagging "essence" of Islam into the *jihad* period as if to show that even when Hausaland was sinking under the weight of its "moral degradation," it took only a dedicated cadre of scholars to exhume an always nascent moral tradition and subsequent state that would commit itself entirely to Hausaland's defense and enhancement.[41]

While Sulaiman's glorification of the scholar is presented as a parallel to early Prophetic history, whereby Muslims triumphed over much more powerful adversaries on the battlefield, his narrative also evokes the specifically West African theme of *mahdism*—the notion that a great man (or men) comes along each generation to lead *tajdīd*, an enlivening (or renewal) of the Islamic tradition. In Sulaiman's rendering, Dan Fodio took inspiration from the same source that contemporary northern Nigerians do, drawing power from a Prophetic tradition that symbolizes quality, greatness, and success in fighting against oppression. Complicating this dialectic and giving it local resonance, contemporary northern Nigerians assign this same divine power to the Sokoto *jihad* leaders.

The category of "intellectual and moral tradition" is therefore that which is indestructible in the face of "quantitative" (i.e., economic and political) decline and oppression. These divine cultural resources are tools with which Hausaland can heal itself. This currency was powerful enough to sustain Dan Fodio's movement—the greatest in modern Hausaland history. The contemporary scholar/leader—like Dan Fodio—is a *mahdī* figure who has the capacity to shore up the spiritual strength of the *umma* (Islamic community), to redistribute wealth equally, and to solve other pressing social problems.

While the *mahdī*/scholar/leader drives cultural renewal by waging revolution, jurisprudence provides the grist for the mill. According to Sulaiman, scholars should be given pride of place in a developing society to form policies, lead decision making, and generally run affairs, for "such scholars are like the Prophets in former communities."[42] This is another example of the sunnaic paradigm that can serve as an organizing principle for supporters of contemporary shari'ah. This paradigm is made up of a reified understanding of the Prophet's time, the *circumstances* of which are understood to be perfect. The ideal Islamic state should guarantee the preservation of public morality, which can only be accomplished by safeguarding the sanctity of the office of the judge, who can adjudicate continuously on this question. This office, al-Maghīlī wrote to the emir of Kano, is analogous to the role played by none other than the Prophet of Allah; and therefore only men of exemplary learning and piety should be appointed judges. Rule of law should be strictly maintained and all people should be treated equally before the law, a state that is maintained through institutions of public complaint. These institutions should be strengthened continuously, and should especially defend the rights of the weak—women, children, and the poor. Criminals should be dealt with appropriately, but, warned al-Maghīlī, severity should be tempered with mercy lest the course of justice be perverted.[43]

Ibraheem Sulaiman writes of Dan Fodio's first gesture toward *jihad* in the form of a letter sent to the pre–Sokoto Caliphate emir of Gobir, "explain[ing] to him the true Islam, and order[ing] him [to observe it], and to establish justice in his lands."[44] Sending letters to rulers entreating them to accept Islam is a practice that originated with the Prophet Muhammad, who is represented in the *sīra* as sending letters to the existing rulers of surrounding empires in the early period of Islamic expansion, namely the emperors of Byzantium, Persia, and Ethiopia. In the letter, Dan Fodio reportedly asked that (1) he should be allowed a free hand to call people to Allah; (2) no hindrance should be placed before anyone who wished to respond to his call; (3) members of his *jamā'a* (following)—now identifiable by turbans for men and head-covers for women—should be treated with respect; and (4) all prisoners should be fed and people should not be burdened with heavy taxes. This representation highlights the persistent difficulty of historiography—while it is entirely possible that Dan Fodio consciously modeled his *jihad* after the Prophet, it is more plausible that Sulaiman's choice to represent the *jihad* in a direct parallel structure to the Prophetic *sīra* speaks more of the intellectual and cultural priorities of a Nigerian scholar writing in London in the 1980s than of any a priori "traveling ethic" of Prophetic history, which is divine and therefore overdetermined.

Still, there is the intriguing philosophical possibility that the Prophetic tradition has made a deterministic mark on all three periods—the classical moment that Muḥammad lived, the late-nineteenth-century moment in which the Sokoto Caliphate was formed, and the present—but the problems of historiography, which really are a reflection of our trapped-ness in time and space, make it impossible to argue for this type of traveling cultural power. It is possible, however, to note the similarity between Sulaiman's account of Dan Fodio's *jihad* and the facts on the ground in contemporary northern Nigeria. According to a certain Islamist narrative, today there is a struggle against "an enemy" that is both abstract (corruption and injustice) and local (other Nigerians who have been influenced by colonial powers and/or the contemporary West, "the Christians," or fallen Muslims). Are these historical patterns that happen to repeat, or do they arise because the narrative frame of the sunnaic paradigm presents reality in this way? Again, it is difficult to answer this question decisively.

SIGNIFICANCE OF *ḤUDŪD* PUNISHMENTS FOR *JIHAD* LEADERS

To consolidate the newly formed Sokoto Caliphate, establishing Islamic law in Hausaland was essential, so the caliphate set out to establish a legal structure as close to the classical Islamic Caliphate as possible. Islamic law would bring individual subjects under the mandate of the caliphate, legitimizing the discipline of local emirs. Alongside the shari'ah, Dan Fodio and 'Abdallahi's writings became sources on the constitution and the law. 'Abdallahi's book *Diya al-hukkām*,[45] for example, is a thorough digest of the government and its constitution; and Dan Fodio's *Bayān wijūb al-hijra*[46] covers diverse aspects of religion and state. Both of these make extensive use of direct quotations from Qur'an, *ḥadīth*, and Mālikī *fiqh*. Because Hausaland's law was now centered in Sokoto, local emirs looked there for "intellectual, religious and political leadership."[47] Thus, the emirates were supervised from Sokoto, which in 1812 divided the caliphate into two parts: the eastern provinces (east of Sokoto) were given to Dan Fodio's son Muhammad Bello, and the western provinces were given to his brother 'Abdallahi.

Uthmān Dan Fodio's *Foundations*, translated by Aisha Bewley, is today considered a good starter for the lay study of Mālikī *fiqh* in English. Jibrīl ibn 'Umar, Uthmān Dan Fodio's main teacher (mentioned earlier), taught him Sīdī Khalīl's *Mukhtasar*, a foundational work of Mālikī jurisprudence that is held in the highest esteem in Nigeria today. Dr. Hamidu Bobboyi shared a fascinating aphorism with me that has been in circulation for centuries in Nigeria: *"Nahnu Khalīliyūn—an ḍhalla, ḍhallalnā"* (We are the people of Khalīl—if he errs, we err).[48] This oral artifact attests to the deep symbolic value that Mālikī Islamic law—and Islamic law per se—has held in Nigeria since at least the Sokoto *jihad*, an inclination rooted as far back as the eleventh century. Though Uthmān Dan Fodio did not himself designate a school, preferring a policy of *istishān*, or juridical preference, Abdullahi Dan Fodio (ibn Fūdī) and Muḥammad Bello did have a preference for the Mālikī school. In the end, Dan Fodio conceded that "common people" would not be able to distinguish between the schools of law, so it would be best to champion the Mālikī school.

As I argue throughout this book, the decision to identify with shari'ah is a move to identify with the larger Islamic civilization complex that was centered eastward. This identification was epistemological—by elevating systems of knowledge transmitted through texts in Arabic—and spatial, through travel and exchange with the Arabian Peninsula. Jibrīl, Dan Fodio's teacher, made his first pilgrimage to Arabia before he started teaching Dan Fodio. Jibrīl later started the reformation campaign in Hausaland to put into practice what he had learned in Arabia concerning ridding society of *bid'ah*.

This confluence of eighteenth-century Hausaland's historical exposure to both the Mālikī school of Islamic law and a nascent Waḥḥābī sensibility raises the question of how we determine which Islamic legal works are considered particular, or even "native," to northern Nigeria. This tradition of borrowing brings up the same philosophical question raised earlier about the cultural travel life of ideas: Did northern Nigeria adopt and practice Islamic law as a direct reinscription of legal norms that were passed down through a textual canon? We have seen that at the level of society, a one-to-one relationship between shari'ah law and social behavior cannot be said to exist. Northern Nigerian society, as I have shown, acted in response to, and in accordance with, its own concerns and impulses, which were generated by the same historical factors as all in societies. But how do we account for northern Nigerians' subjective proclivities toward particular sacred texts?

In a research institute in Kaduna one evening, the electricity cut out at a different hour than usual, sending me wandering around the premises in search of the beautiful Hausa folk music that was swimming amid the warm spring air. I passed a room where a group of scholars were assembled over candlelight, laughing. They invited me to join them, and, recognizing some of my new acquaintances, I accepted and began speaking with a scholar from Libya who specialized in Mālikī law. He was in Nigeria conducting research, as he had been doing there for twenty-five years. This scholar conveyed to me the extemporaneous wisdom he had gathered about his field over the years. Through his travels, he had noticed that different aspects of the law are emphasized in different places throughout North Africa and Sub-Saharan Africa.

Certain cultures might particularly abhor *zinā* but tolerate alcohol, while in other societies alcohol consumption is unheard of and regular prayer may be a bit more lax. To his mind, prayer was extremely strict in Nigeria, while, interestingly, abhorrence of *zinā* was traditionally more lax.

ḤUDŪD AS LEGITIMACY

Dan Fodio opens his section on the sunnah of *ḥadd* punishments *(ṭarīq al-sunnah fī bāb al-ḥudūd wa al-aqīda)* with a *ḥadīth* that is still quoted today in Nigeria:

> The Prophet said of a woman who had stolen, "that which annihilated those that came before you is that they carried out the *ḥadd* punishment on the common man, setting aside the shari'ah [as a whole], and I declare by my hand [I swear] that if Fatima did the same thing that her hand would be cut."[49]

Ḥadd laws are fixed punishments for crimes outlawed by God. Dan Fodio's discussion of *ḥudūd* is embedded in an idealized legal discourse of equality before the law, irrespective of wealth or social station. It is precisely the extremity of *ḥudūd* that can guarantee this social equity. Dan Fodio goes on to admonish Muslims for failing to mete out *ḥadd* punishments as consistently as they should. The primary example of this neglect, interestingly, is a particular reticence to punish the crime of *zinā* with stoning or flogging. Dan Fodio writes, "Many have rejected (aspects of) the *ḥudūd*, such as stoning and flogging for *zinā*, desiring the matter to be satisfied with the [payment of] money,[50] and this is an innovation that has been outlawed by consensus."[51] We must question why a revolutionary religious and military leader would emphasize the *ḥadd* punishment for *zinā*—over a wealth of other topics—as the primary example of where Muslims are falling short legally.

We can make at least three significant observations based on Dan Fodio's discussion of the *ḥadd* of *zinā*. One, failing to punish the crime of *zinā,* and characterizing this failure as the primary example of *bid'ah* (innovation) in the application of *ḥadd,* suggests prior societal reluctance to apply the punishment among the "many" *(kathīr)* that came before Dan Fodio, be they judges or scholars who have written about stoning with ambivalence and severe caveats. Second, Dan Fodio specifically admonishes Muslims for failing to mete out stoning and flogging punishments, which suggests that Muslims hesitated to do just that—apply the punishments. Third, why would Dan Fodio single out the *ḥadd* of stoning for *zinā* for special emphasis among all the other *ḥadd* punishments—and indeed, among all other crimes in Islamic law—in a section aimed to educate the populace about the Prophet's sunnah, or example, when the record of the Prophet's sunnah on this matter is mixed? I suggest that these observations support my theory that the severity—and, by extension, the seriousness—of *ḥadd* punishments were used to make a case for the atemporal legitimacy of the entire corpus of Islamic law. This was a no-nonsense law.

Muhammad Bello's writings similarly give the *ḥadd* punishments pride of place in "proving" the credibility of Islamic law. As mentioned earlier, in addition to serving as one of his father's lieutenants and war commanders, Bello is remembered as a *jihad* leader of wide learning, especially as a poet. Bello's *al-Ghayth al-wabl fī sirāt al-imām al-'adl* (The Downpouring of Rain in the Biography of the Just Imām)[52] begins his section on *ḥudūd* with this *ḥadīth* narrated by Abū Hurayra: "The place taken by the *ḥadd* on God's earth is a greater blessing than forty nights of rain."[53] This *ḥadīth* is immediately followed by another: "Those who came before you—if he steals from a nobleman, exile him *(tarakahū),* but if he steals from a weak man—put the *ḥadd* upon him."[54] This ethical proclamation is emphasized with a further *ḥadīth* that points out that in the "time of God," even if Fātima herself, Muhammad's daughter, had stolen, she too would have had her hand cut off. This iteration of the *ḥadīth* tradition—one in which the law, in all its severity, is applied with razor-like precision to all human beings, regardless of station—is the iteration contemporary Nigerians reached back for through the sunnaic paradigm.[55]

ḤUDŪD TODAY

In northern Nigeria today, discussions of *ḥadd* are often preceded by the phrase "If you are Muslim and have accepted Islam. . . ." This admonition exposes a fault line in today's shari'ah debate: any hesitation or ambivalence about the stoning punishment becomes increasingly likely to result in the accusation that only "weak Muslims" (and/or those influenced by the West) would hesitate to immediately and uncritically accept "the shari'ah" in all of its facets, especially the *ḥudūd*. As shown by way of the sunnaic paradigm, *ḥadd* punishments such as stoning are valorized both in the *jihad* literature and in contemporary discussions of the punishment in northern Nigeria—as a gesture, a subtle and ironic one, to distance stoning from everyday reality by rhetorically championing the punishment's symbolic value.

For many of my respondents in Nigeria, the fact that the stoning punishment is a live issue today points more to the politicized nature of the 1999 shari'ah revolution than to its practical success. "Success" for northerners would have looked instead like a well-managed and effective welfare state, the idealized description of which makes up a large amount of the *jihad* leaders' writings.

Abba Yusuf, assistant secretary of the Kano Emirate Council, believes that shari'ah reaches far beyond *ḥudūd*—which should be a last resort. He argues that the current emphasis on *ḥudūd* can be traced, in part, to Nigeria's colonial history: "If I'm properly guided I can be more patriotic and disciplined than a PhD holder and perhaps more useful to my community. Before colonial times, people were well enlightened to their civic responsibilities: there was less corruption, more morality. Moral decadence holds back progress."[56] Yusuf added, "Most of the Western world sees shari'ah as cutting hands off. This is the wrong perception, and a misinterpretation. We have to develop human beings first, then turn to problems. If you start with structures without morally upright people, they will fail." Yusuf is arguing that Islamic law cannot work without a just society, a point made throughout Islamic history. Dr. Bashir Galadanci also believes the emphasis on *ḥudūd* amounts to a misperception: "In the West, shari'ah is stoning—but shari'ah is actually about social, economic, and political and religious life."[57]

The following statement by Dr. Abdulkareem Sadiq encapsulates perfectly, I believe, the dominant understanding of *ḥudūd*'s place in the overall shari'ah system in contemporary northern Nigeria: "When Islam came to Nigeria it was an entire way of life, not just crime and punishment. If you are Muslim and have accepted Islam, you have to abide by the shari'ah. This is beyond a personal affair."[58] On a practical level, Islam is about charity, fairness, and piety; to uphold these values, one must pronounce the totalizing quality of the entire system, within which *ḥudūd* functions as a legitimizing pillar. This does not mean that Islam is *ḥudūd*—on the contrary, punishment is de-emphasized in the tradition—but *ḥudūd* functions as an anchor for the system. Malam Sanusi Khalil of the Izālā movement performs the same double move. Khalil argues that people do not understand the meaning of shari'ah: "They are just thinking of *ḥudūd*. People do not consider the *mu'āmalāt* (treatment of others). *Ḥudūd* is only one percent of the shari'ah. The benefits are numerous in the shari'ah system. Whoever steals should have their wrist cut off."[59]

Shaykh Rabi'u Daura, leader of the Izālā in Kaduna, also performed this double move, saying that the *ḥudūd* is *"aṣl al-shari'ah"* [the foundation of the shari'ah]." Yet he added, directly after making this statement, *"al-ḥadd fī sharī'at al-Islām tawkhīf"* (The function of *ḥadd* punishments in Islam is to frighten people).[60]

CHAPTER THREE

Origins of the Stoning Punishment

The deepest layer of the sunnaic paradigm lies in the Islamic legal history of the stoning punishment. To review, the cultural power that Nigeria draws upon to re-enliven the shari'ah can be mapped according to the following dialectical triad, the first two layers of which I examined in the previous chapters: (1) the existential concerns of Nigeria's present; (2) the Sokoto Caliphate and the *jihad* leaders who established it, to whom the contemporary proponents of shari'ah referred; and (3) the subject of this chapter, the classical period of Islam that was referred to by the Sokoto *jihad* leaders (as well as in Nigeria's present, thereby strengthening the dialectic) through *ḥadīth* works and hagiographical biographies *(sīra)* of the Prophet Muḥammad.

Chapter 1 traced the deep social structure that set the stage for the reintroduction of full shari'ah penal codes in thirteen northern states. I argued that "idealized" shari'ah addressed a demand for social order in a country contending with various forms of chaos. In this context, I postulated that the stoning punishment is imbued with a "legitimizing horror"; though no Nigerians I spoke to were keen on stoning as such, they defended its presence in Islamic law, not only based on the tautology that it is part of Islamic law, but also because such harsh punishment engendered the threatening environment necessary to compel the corrupt elite to follow the laws of God where the laws of man had failed.

Chapter 2 traced the history of the revered Sokoto Caliphate in Hausaland, excavating why that history carries such potent symbolic power for Nigerians today. One reason for that symbolic power is the caliphate's self-conscious understanding of itself within Prophetic history, as evidenced by the form and content of the caliphate's polemical literature. But to place a contemporary society within the symbolic field of the Prophet's "perfect society" (in fulfillment of the sunnaic paradigm) is not simply a symbolic ideal. Once shari'ah law is imposed, or "enlivened" (to use the verb preferred by a Nigerian interlocutor and legal scholar), I argue that, to some degree, a contemporary society takes on the sociological particularities and intellectual idiosyncrasies that characterized the birth of that law. This idea is controversial for those invested in a more existential reading of present events, but I believe that *some* semblance of the "spirit of the law" holds throughout time, so long as that law is divinely overdetermined. This chapter, therefore, explores those "spirit of the law" conditions—the moment in Islamic legal history before stoning became reified and considered always already stable. Against this anachronistic notion of "divine stability" that we so often see in postmodern/postcolonial societies that introduce Islamic law, I argue that the same contingencies that characterized the production of a given law—the stoning punishment in this case—make themselves manifest today when that law is resurrected, some five and a half centuries after it was codified.

To begin with, the stoning punishment does not originate with Islam, but in the Ancient Near East, making an appearance in Mesopotamian, Roman, Judaic, and finally Islamic texts. In Islamic history, the punishment has hardly ever been applied since it was codified; and if Islamic legal methodology were followed closely, *zinā* would be nearly impossible to prove. The ease with which the stoning punishment seems to be meted out in our contemporary, postmodern period is therefore largely a function of the abandonment of traditional jurisprudential methods. Indeed, stoning in Islam is a postmodern phenomenon.

While stoning as "legitimizing horror"—both in nineteenth-century Sokoto *jihad* literature and in the contemporary period—depends on the assumed historical, hermeneutic, and ethical "stability" of the punishment, this chapter shows that, insofar as the difficult-to-contextualize early source material allows us to draw tentative conclusions, stoning's genesis in the Islamic tradition was fraught, contingent, anthropomorphic (i.e., originating from a human, rather than divine, source), and borrowed. This chapter, therefore, does not attempt to ascertain the precise nature of the stoning punishment's entrance into the Islamic tradition; rather, it attempts to show that (1) experts who have examined the material disagree strongly about basic questions of stoning and of Islamic law's provenance and (2) the stoning punishment is represented in the tradition itself as a problematic and contingent punishment. This ambivalence is evident both in contemporary northern Nigerian societies' discourse about stoning and in the trial of Amina Lawal, which I analyze in depth in chapter 5.

With respect to the question of agency, causality, and scripturally sanctioned punishments, my analysis of the deep structure of Nigerian societies' grassroots demands for shariʿah law has convinced me that there is no direct causal link between being a Muslim and performing the stoning punishment, despite the fact that stoning as a punishment for married adulterers is "on the books" in all major Sunni and Shiite schools of law. To actually perform stoning—or, one might argue, any aspect of Islamic law—necessitates sociological and political maneuvering in the public sphere. In much contemporary Islamic and Western discourse, however, stoning is misattributed as following directly and inevitably from "Islam." This denial of the messy sphere of politics, of human subjectivity, and of historicism renders Islam and Muslims outside of the normal processes of human action—a fantastical move that serves the purposes of particular agendas in both the Muslim majority and Western worlds. It is much more difficult to malign Muslims or Islam—or, conversely, to claim religious and political authority over its powerful mantle—if contingency, subjectivity, and ambivalence are admitted into the equation.

In regard to the Islamists seeking power in Nigeria, I argue that something in the horror and absoluteness evoked by the stoning punishment functions as an important source of political legitimacy for these would-be leaders. Islamic law would be a no-nonsense system, and its leaders, who present themselves as simply following the laws of God and his Prophet, must therefore be obeyed without question. Still, these political optics do not fully answer the question of why Amina Lawal was sentenced to death by stoning and later acquitted in an Islamic court. To do so, one must probe the extant source material and intellectual history of the stoning punishment in the Islamic tradition. In chapter 4, I analyze the legal mechanisms by which Islamic law was interpreted in a spare and reductionist way that turned away from classical jurisprudence—making the stoning punishment much easier to mete out in twenty-first-century Nigeria.

STONING AS STABLE AND UNCONTESTED IN CONTEMPORARY NIGERIA

The stoning punishment is part of a larger Islamic tradition that northern Nigerians have consciously sought to resurrect, precisely because of this classical tradition's (imagined) stability. Take, as a case in point, a conversation I had with Aliyu Musa Yauri, an attorney in Abuja and one of Lawal's lead attorneys, on the topic of stoning. His demeanor was strange. I told him some of the Islamic arguments against stoning, because he had mentioned, a bit nervously, that "Some say it's not in the Holy Qur'an." I said, "Yes, this is the case."

He said, "But it is all over the *ḥadīth* of the Prophet, and in Sahīh al-Bukhāri [the most authoritative compilation of *ḥadīth*]. Then he added, tentatively, "Do you think some of these are forged?"

I said, "Some are weak, yes, but the point is, the early *fuqaha'* [legal scholars] used *takhsīs* [specification] and *naskh* [abrogation] to resolve this contradiction."

He replied, "I am very proud of Islam and I am willing to ignore all of this. It is just academic."[1]

Saudatu Mahdi, secretary general of the Women's Rights Advancement and Protection Alternative, helped me interpret this conversation. She said of Yauri: "He's using the legal system to do what he can, but a lot of people are afraid of scholarship and reluctant to challenge the laws themselves. One focuses on interpretation and education because the actual text is a 'no go' area and absolutely off the table."[2] Even my attempts to explain the instability of the early Islamic texts from a scholarly perspective led Yauri to abruptly change the subject.

The twenty-first-century need to understand Islam as always triumphant gives contemporary Muslims strength in the face of daunting odds. The triumph of the Prophet Muhammad and his companions over their military and ideological enemies is central to Islamic cosmology. While these victories are represented as divinely assisted in hagiographical Islamic accounts, they are also often represented as quotidian military affairs. The Battle of Badr (2 A.H./624 C.E.), in which the Muslims, with 313 fighters, triumphed over the Quraysh (an Arabian tribe of idolaters that was hostile to Muhammad), who had ten thousand, can be historically dated. Vivid images of Mu'āwiyah's[3] army on horseback raising hundreds of spears with copies of the Qur'an on the tips in an attempt to stave off Alī ibn Alī Ṭālib's (d. 40 A.H./661 C.E.) army in the Battle of Siffīn (36 A.H./657 C.E.) are conjured by lay Muslims and artists. No miracles were represented to have been manifested in these battles, except perhaps the triumphs themselves. Adding to the lore, a small band of Muslims are represented as having gone on to build a lasting civilization. This flattened, miracle-free account is a "rationalist" representation of these events, which I believe may have been in circulation around Uthmān Dan Fodio's time, particularly in light of evidence that suggests that Dan Fodio drew inspiration for his *jihad* from the nascent Waḥḥābī movement in the northeast.[4] Thus, there is a sense in which actual power can be derived from the understanding and internalization of this notion of the past triumph of a group of men to which contemporary Nigerians, in some sense, belong—allowing perhaps a deeper understanding of the motivations and stakes involved in reifying the past. It is, in part, from within this nexus of "proven" power that the authority of the classical period stakes its contemporary claim.

The stoning punishment for adultery, found in the *ḥadīth* collections, differs from the Qur'anic punishment (flogging) for a crime that can be thought of as functionally the same. Islamic intellectuals in the classical period also developed devices such as *naskh* (abrogation), a particular form of which is applied to the stoning punishment.[5] These factors point to a tradition whose construction includes human subjectivity and idiosyncrasy, in contrast to the form of idealized shari'ah expressed in contemporary northern Nigeria.

EARLY SOURCE MATERIAL

Stoning as a legal punishment predates Islam by at least three thousand years. The argument therefore cannot be made that stoning is uniquely Islamic in any practical, legal, or ethical sense. It was meted out in the Ancient Near East for a variety of crimes, including adultery, before making its way into the Islamic *ḥadīth* literature. Pavel Pavlovich aims to ascertain how stoning traditions spread in the second and third Islamic centuries, in an attempt to work out precisely how the stoning punishment should be understood to have entered the tradition.[6] As Pavlovich makes clear from the beginning, the debate about the establishment and treatment of stoning is limited by conflicting accounts of its provenance. This observation is not surprising, as methodologically navigating these conflicting accounts has been a dominant preoccupation in Western scholarship since before Joseph Schacht's *Origins of Muhammadan Jurisprudence* (1950), which critically examined the traditional

Islamic methodology of *isnād* (chain of transmission) analysis. Following the general trend in Islamic studies since, Pavlovich adopts Harald Motzki's *isnād cum matn*[7] method, theorizing that the "general textual stability of the tradition suggests that it goes back to a single source whose identification with ʿAbd al-Razzāq is beyond doubt."[8] Pavlovich traces the earliest tradition devoted to voluntary confession to *zinā* (adultery) as reaching back to the first quarter of the second Islamic century (718 C.E./43 A.H.). Pavlovich theorizes that by the end of the second century A.H. the tradition's volume had grown, including now a discussion of the offender's marital status and mental sanity.

In pre-Islamic Near Eastern legal codes, adultery was considered a property crime against husbands or fathers, depending on circumstances—women, for all intents and purposes, had no legal identity. Whether and which ancient Near Eastern legal codes influenced Islamic law is the subject of a debate that has been fundamental to Western scholarship for at least fifty years. Ignaz Goldziher (d. 1921 C.E.) assumes Islamic law to have grown out of Judaic law, an argument Patricia Crone describes as "hasty."[9] Against this view, Walter Young surveys nearly all Mesopotamian societies, showing that they considered adultery a capital crime by comparing mnemonic phrases and the assorted epigraphs, tables, and documents that reveal what we know of ancient Near Eastern legal codes.[10]

Young notes that Urukagina (2400 B.C.E.), who was the ruler of the city-state of Lagash in Mesopotamia, provides the most direct example of the stoning punishment's use as a punishment for adultery in ancient Near Eastern legal codes. The Urukagina legal reforms—thought to be the first in human history—brought a new prohibition on polyandry, ending the custom of women taking two husbands by making the practice punishable by stoning.

Mesopotamian legal codes continued the practice of criminalizing adultery. The code of Ur Namma (r. 2195–2010 B.C.E.) called for punishment by (an unspecified) death for a man who deflowered another man's virgin wife. Death was also the punishment for a wife who initiated adultery, whereas her paramour was acquitted.[11] Similarly, in the laws of Eshnunna (ca. 1800 B.C.E.), the wife receives an unspecified death for initiating adultery, though the paramour's fate is not clear.[12] By the time we reach the 1750 B.C.E. legal code of Hammurabi, both the wife and the paramour were killed by being bound and cast into a river; a wife of a captive man who escaped that marriage for another man also faced drowning. A man who committed adultery with his living brother's wife was put to an unspecified death according to Old Hittite laws (ca. 1650–1500 B.C.E.); the same for a man who, while in Hittite lands, frequented "foreign" women.[13] Finally, Middle Assyrian laws (ca. 1076 B.C.E.) sanction unspecified death for committing adultery in the paramour's house, and an unfaithful wife was thrown to her death from a tower in certain Babylonian law reports.[14]

JUDAIC ORIGINS

W. H. Bennett notes that "stoning seems to have been the most usual mode of capital punishment" among the ancient Hebrews.[15] Adultery in the Hebrew Bible is construed as a property crime against a husband or father, with the property construed as the wife or daughter in question. Expanding on this theory of stoning, J. Poucher writes:

> Stoning was the ordinary formal and legal mode of inflicting punishment in the earlier history of the children of Israel, and was in vogue before the departure from Egypt (Ex. 8.26). Even beasts might be the victims, evidently as a spectacular example (Ex. 19.13, 21.28, 29, 32). Stoning was the penalty for taking "the accursed thing" (Jos. 7.25); for adultery and unchastity, the death sentence being pronounced in Lv. 20.10, and the means of carrying it out stated in Dt. 22.21, 24, Jn. 8/5.7; for blasphemy (Lv. 24.10–24) ... for divination (Lv. 20/6.27), idolatry (Dt. 13.10); dishonour to parents (Dt. 21.21), proselytizing falsely (Dt. 13/5.10) and Sabbath-breaking (Ex. 31.14, 35.2, Nu. 15/35.36). Doubtless other capital crimes would thus be punished, and the city of Jerusalem was so threatened as if it were an individual culprit (Ezk. 16.40).[16]

The following passages from Deuteronomy address adultery:

> Deut. 22:22: If a man is found sleeping with another man's wife, both the man who slept with her and the woman must die. You must purge the evil from Israel.[17]

> Deut. 22:23–4: If a man happens to meet in a town a virgin pledged to be married and he sleeps with her, you shall take both of them to the gate of that town and stone them to death—the girl because she was in a town and did not scream for help and the man because he violated another man's wife. You must purge the evil from among you.[18]

These passages make clear that what constitutes a crime is the violation of another man's wife; this formulation leaves little room for women as autonomous physical or legal bodies. The Judaic tradition also contains several linguistic references to stoning.

Young notes that verse 24:2 of the Qur'an, *"al-zānia wa al-zānī"* (the adulteress and the adulterer), differs in an important way from the ancient concept—both the adulterer and the adulteress receive equal punishment for committing the crime of *zinā.* Young sees a connection—or what he calls a "familial" similarity—between these constraints found in the Old Testament and "the process through which Muslim *fuqaha'* [legal scholars] developed more and more stringent witness requirements for accusations of *zinā,* nearly reaching such a point as to make application of the *ḥadd* impossible without confession."[19]

In sum, Judaic and Islamic law are conceptually similar with respect to sexual and property offenses, but differ in their details. One important difference between the two traditions is that, while in the Hebrew Bible's conception a betrothed girl could be stoned for infidelity if her parents were unable to prove her chastity, Islamic law holds that the girl would not be stoned for illegal sexual activity, and besides, the burden of proof would not be placed on her parents.

PRE-ISLAMIC ARABIAN LAW

Recent scholarship argues that the most important source for Islamic law must be Arab customary law, despite our lack of textual evidence of this from the Mesopotamian and Judaic traditions. This argument amounts to the simple claim that the reforms of the Prophet must have been determined by the customs of his own time and place. Noel J. Coulson argues this, asserting that legislation should be understood as a supplement to, and not a substitute for, existing customary law.[20] It is impossible to make the argument about precise origins of the stoning punishment one way or another, but for Young the evidence that the stoning punishment is part of "a larger Near Eastern Semitic common law" outweighs the arguments that it is not.

One of the most important sources of evidence that scholars have in determining borrowed Semitic lineages is to assess the parallel use of mnemonic devices in pre-Islamic legal codes and contemporary Islamic law. One of the most well known of these devices is *"Al-walad l'il farāsh wa l'il 'āhir al-ḥajar"* (To the [legal] bed belongs the offspring, and for the adulterer/fornicator, [belongs] the stone).[21] This means that children will be the property of the legal husband.[22]

Uri Rubin has conducted the most important study of *"Al-walad l'il farāsh wa l'il 'āhir al-ḥajar."*[23] This maxim is significant not only in its suggestion of a pre-Islamic origin for the stoning punishment, but in what it tells us about Islamic norms for governing sexuality. Rubin disagrees with the supposition (which became assertion) of Schacht and Goldziher that, since the saying is "incompatible with the Qur'an," it must be of Roman origin. Instead, Rubin argues that the *farāsh* utterance corresponds to the (unsuccessful) "Qur'anic campaign against the practice of the *di'wa.*"[24] By disagreeing with the notion that the mnemonic device *al-walad l'il farāsh wa l'il 'āhir al-ḥajar* is of Roman origin, Rubin lends credence to Young's and Hallaq's critiques of Patricia Crone's argument that Islamic law is best traced to Roman provincial codes.[25] Young argues that *'āhir* is a term synonymous with *al-zānī,* and, as such, the scholars would need to simply prove the pre-Islamic origin of the maxim to confirm an association between stoning and *zinā* in pre-Islamic Arab custom. Rubin argues that the maxim does have pre-Islamic origin: "The first to have uttered it is said to have been the famous *amthāl*-teller Aktham b. Ṣayfī." [26] Moreover, the sources describe specific occasions on which the Prophet made legal use of the *farāsh* maxim.

The first part of the dictum, concerning *farāsh* (the bed), was used in several cases where the identity of a child's father was unknown, and in most cases where the mother was suspected of immoral sexual activity. The *farāsh* maxim makes it clear that a child retains a genealogical relationship with his or her "legal" father (i.e., the man who sleeps legally with the mother), though this child may have a biological relationship with another man. This prevents the child from becoming *"walad al-zinā"* (child of illegal sexual activity), a pejorative moniker that would exempt that offspring from inheritance rights.

Importantly, Rubin argues that allegations against the morality of mothers were often made in connection with disputes about inheritance. In a famous example involving the Prophet's wife Zaynab al-Asadiyya, who sought his advice about a slave girl who was suspected of having conceived her son by a man other than her father, the Prophet examined the child's physiognomy and ascertained that he was not the offspring of Zaynab's father. The Prophet then made the following declaration: "'*inna l-mirātha lahū wa-amma antī fa-hatajibi minhu*" (He is entitled to the inheritance, but as for you [i.e., Zaynab], veil yourself in his presence).[27] This ethic is important as a blueprint for both sexual morality and inheritance rights. It is also important in that the maxim's second part, *al-āhir-l-il hajar* (for the fornicator, the stone) is clearly derived from ancient Arab custom.

ORIGINS OF ISLAMIC LAW, STONING, AND HISTORIOGRAPHICAL ISSUES

The classical period of Islamic history, composed of the Prophetic and immediate pre-Islamic period, is difficult to navigate using available source material. While scholars have left pre-Islamic scholarship on stoning to the few who are literate in ancient Semitic languages, including Biblical scholars and traditional Orientalists in the formative period of Islam (approximately first/third to seventh/tenth centuries) within which stoning entered the tradition, the punishment has been the subject of deep scholarly debate about historiography, made all the more overdetermined by the scriptural nature of the sources in question.

Arabic–Islamic sources that consider the earliest origins of the stoning punishment tend not to examine the pre-Islamic source materials.[28] These sources are probably omitted because this knowledge is not germane to the theological agenda of that era's scholars, who were primarily concerned with ascertaining God's will through an interpretation of scriptural sources. Accordingly, as the tradition developed, certain *adāb*—practices or standards of proper behavior and demeanor expected of those who conducted such studies—were adopted to regulate how the texts should be read. An example of such *adāb* is found in the introduction to an instruction manual published by Al-Azhar University in Cairo to train *fuqaha'* (legal scholars). The following must be the ideal bearing of one who seeks religious knowledge: *"an yu'tī faḥman salīman, wa 'aqlan mustāqīman, wa qalban mushārakan bī nūr al- akhlās, fī huwa bāhatha al-itijāh al-qawīm yusir fī al- tarīq' ila fahm musāḍir al-shara' wa muārduhu . . ."* (that he was given [by God] a sound understanding, and a sound mind, and a heart that is connected with the light of the eternal, for he is searching for the right path [and] for the easy way to understand the origins of the shar'īah, and the purpose of [the shar'īah]).[29] For modern scholars seeking training in Islamic law, the "way of seeing"—which is to discipline the student of the tradition into assuming a place of humility and quiescence before the text—is considered essential to its proper understanding.

NON-ARABIAN ORIGINS?

For modern scholars like Patricia Crone, this disciplining practice of early Islamic source materials can lead to inaccuracies. Crone (1987) discusses the role that Roman and provincial law (meaning the law that governed the provinces of the Roman Empire) had on their Arab conquerors. Crone contends that

> [The] Islamic tradition consistently presents Islamic law as a modified version of Arab law, virtually every legal institution being traced back to pre-Islamic Arabian practice and/or to rulings by the Arabian Prophet and his immediate successors. Even institutions rejected by Islamic law are traced back in this fashion, pre-Islamic practice being in this case presented as pagan rather than Arab, while the Prophet and his immediate successors are employed to condemn rather than to validate.[30]

Crone argues that "manipulation" of historical material is obviously doctrinally inspired, "but the tradition is in fact armed to the teeth against imputations of foreign influence."[31] For Crone, Islamic law is most obviously influenced by Jewish law, for "the shari'a and the *halakha* are both all-embracing religious laws created by scholars who based themselves on scripture and oral tradition, employed similar methods of deduction, and adopted the same casuistic approach; hence the structural similarity between Jewish and Islamic law is obvious to the naked eye."[32] Since, for Crone, Jewish law is so fundamental to the formation of Islamic law, Roman legal influence becomes that much harder to pin down—and even when it is pinned down, the possibility remains that such elements entered the Islamic tradition through Jewish law.

Furthermore, Muslims combined "the tribal legacy of the invaders" with Jewish concepts to produce Islamic law, though the Jewish concepts probably provided raw, unchanged material as well. Crone argues that what was reshaped was essentially Provincial Roman practice, which contained elements of Roman law in Syria and Egypt in addition to Sassanid law in Iraq, and also, of course, Roman law. These laws all entered the shari'ah, but the shari'ah is, nonetheless, at bottom, "indigenous law of the Near East as it had developed after Alexander. The Muslims sifted and systematized this law in the name of God, imprinting it with their own image in the process."[33]

Against this view, Young argues that Crone displays a "barely-concealed zeal" to separate Islamic civilization from the "terra incognita" of Arabia.[34] Crone characterizes Islamic law as a derivative, and therefore marginal, legal code, asserting that "the undisguised Greek nature of Islamic philosophy is the *quid pro quo* of its marginal status."[35] To underscore this assertion, Crone cites Goldziher, who wrote that "*Fiqh* was no more a product of the 'Arab genius' than grammar or *kalām;* the stubborn antagonism of Islam to the rest of the world."[36]

It is hardly difficult, therefore, to appreciate how quickly debates about the origins of Islamic law become interpolated within questions of "authenticity" and a querying of the epistemological foundations of Orientalist scholarship. My point in highlighting these debates is to demonstrate the scholarly issues at stake when attempting to understand stoning's entrance into the Islamic tradition. At the theoretical level, these hermeneutic issues and questions raised by the source material point to the punishment's historicity and sense of contingency in the Islamic tradition; at a practical, evidential level, it is clear at this stage that the punishment is borrowed—if not from Judaic or Roman Provincial Law, then from ancient Arabian custom.

Wael Hallaq is Crone's most prominent critic, disputing two of her assumptions. The first is Crone's claim that the Arabian Peninsula was, for all intents and purposes, an arid "terra incognita" when Islam was introduced, and that the Muslims themselves were "desert dwellers" who "lived an impoverished life of nomadism and tribalism" before embarking on their conquests. Hallaq believes that these presuppositions flow directly from the notion that legal institutions had to be borrowings from the "high" imperial cultures of the north, especially that of Byzantium. This view, argues Hallaq, would comport with the "now widespread perception of Muslims as 'backward.'"[37]

In view of this fraught historiographical and, perhaps, ideological debate, it is interesting to note the views of nineteenth-century European Orientalists such as Theodor Nöldeke and Friedrich Schwally, who argued in their *Geschichte des Qorâns* (1860) that stoning was inauthentic and that the "stoning verse," to which we will turn below, was invented to justify the punishment.[38] For her part, Crone maintains that stoning was taken directly from the Pentateuchal doctrine, and not from Middle Eastern practice as argued by Young. Crone believes the practice was isolated from pre-Islamic Arabs and the entire Middle Eastern milieu.[39] It has been important to trace the broad outlines of this debate in order to gain a sense of the issues at stake in the historiographical debate about Islamic law's origins: what we do know incontrovertibly is that the stoning punishment for adultery predated Islam by millennia.

ZINĀ AND (THE ABSENCE OF) STONING IN THE QUR'AN

The stoning punishment—which is not found in the Qur'an—was introduced into the Islamic tradition through *aḥadīth;* we will now examine the *aḥadīth*'s relationship to the research on the pre-Islamic origins of stoning that was presented above. The following are the verses of the Qur'an that treat adultery *(zinā).* The first is verse 4:15:

> If any of your women is guilty of unnatural offense, bring four of your witnesses to give evidence; if they testify against them, retain them in the houses until death overtakes them or God provides some other way for them.[40]

The next verse, 4:16:

> And the two who commit it among you, dishonor them both. But if they repent and correct themselves, leave them alone. Indeed, Allah is ever accepting of repentance and Merciful.[41]

This verse uses *"al-ladhāni,"* the dual form, which, Young argues, being of common gender, includes a second reference to females. Hence there is a category of female in verse 16 that is distinct from verse 15. In any case, verse 4:15 is considered to have been abrogated *(mansūkh)*[42] by verse 24:2, which is the verse therefore most cited in *fiqh al-zinā* (the Islamic law of *zinā*):

> The adulteress and adulterer should be flogged a hundred lashes each, and no pity for them should deter you from the law of God, if you believe in God and the Last Day; and the punishment should be witnessed by a body of believers.[43]

It is noteworthy that the Qur'anic injunction against *zinā* starts with the female fornicator. In the subsequent verses when the initiator of marriage is the subject of the sentence, that subject is male. Hence, the Qur'anic text clarifies that the marrying agent in marriage is the man. In verse 24:3:

> The adulterer can marry no one but an adulteress or his partner (in the act). This is forbidden the believers.[44]

The fact that an adulterer can only marry an adulteress is reminiscent of the Old Testament ruling that a rapist must marry the virgin that he has forcibly deflowered, though with important differences in the Islamic rendering—including a marked increase in gender egalitarianism. In verse 24:4, however:

> Those who defame chaste women and do not bring four witnesses should be punished with eighty lashes, and their testimony should not be accepted afterwards, for they are profligates.[45]

There does not appear to be an opportunity to defame chaste men, which reinforces the notion of men as the agents of marriage and female virgins as its passive recipient. This sense of the male as marrying agent is also found in verse 24:6–7:

> Those who accuse their wives and do not have any witnesses except themselves, should swear four times in the name of God, the testimony of each such person being that he is speaking the truth. (6)[46]
>
> And [swear] a fifth time that if he tell a lie the curse of God be on him. (7)[47]

A man is able to accuse his wife of adultery without four witnesses, provided he swears a fifth oath to God that he is telling the truth. The Qur'an is silent as to whether a wife can make the same accusation.

According to verse 24:8, a wife has an opportunity to escape punishment if she swears to God that her husband is a liar; but again, the Qur'an is silent on whether she may make a similar accusation against her husband:

> The woman's punishment can be averted if she swears four times by God as testimony that her husband is a liar.[48]

Finally, verse 24:9 asserts that she will be punished if her testimony defending herself against the accusations of her husband is untrue:

> Her fifth oath being that the curse of God be on her if her husband should be speaking the truth.[49]

A literal reading of the above verses leaves the unmistakable impression that men are the agents in marriage, while women are the passive objects of the marriage contract. The wife does have a right to defend herself against defamation, but she does not appear to have the right to make the accusation of adultery herself.

ETYMOLOGY OF THE ROOT FOR "STONING": R-J-M

Grammatical analysis as a way to gain greater insight into the meaning of the roots of words as they are used in the Qur'an is a common Islamic intellectual practice. Below are the meanings of the root R-J-M in the Semitic scriptures; R-J-M is also the root of the word *rajam* (stoning) in Arabic. *Rajam* occurs at least fifteen times in the Old Testament. With one exception, none of the mentions of *rajam* are related to adultery or fornication. The one exception is found in Ezekiel (16:40 and 23:47), where Jerusalem and Samaria are likened to "women who commit adultery and shed blood" (Ezk. 23:45). As a result, a mob "will stone them and cut them down with their swords" (Ezk. 23:47).[50] Stoning is prescribed in the Old Testament for blasphemy, disobeying God's commands, and rebellion against family authority. The root *rajam* in these contexts is found in the following verses:

1. Lev. 20:2 for sacrificing children to Molech
2. Lev. 20:27 for sorcery
3. Lev. 24:14, 16, 23 for blasphemy
4. Num. 15:35–6 for gathering wood on the Sabbath
5. Deut. 21:21 for the rebellious son who disobeys his father and mother
6. Jos. 7:25 for stealing from the Plunder.[51]

LISĀN AL-'ARAB

Muḥammad ibn Mukarram ibn Manr's (d. 711 or 712 A.H./1311 or 1312 C.E.) *Lisān al-'Arab* is the most widely cited classical Arabic dictionary of the tradition; consulting this dictionary to determine the meanings of roots found in the Qur'an continues to be de rigueur for traditionally trained Islamic scholars.[52] The entry on R-J-M explains that the sense of R-J-M as "killing" does not appear in the Qur'an: *"wa qad warada fī al-Qur'an al-rajamal-qatl fī ghayr mawḍa' min kitāb Allah 'az wa jal"* (R-J-M is mentioned in the Qur'an, [but] the sense of killing *[qatl]* is not present in the book of Allah [dear and great]). The reason the R-J-M came to take on this sense of killing, the *Lisān* continues, is because "they" (the Arabs) were stoning two adulterers, and it thus entered the lexicon. The entry goes on to provide several other meanings of R-J-M found in the Qur'an, including *al-la'ān* (cursing), as in, for example, *"al-shaytān al-rajīm"* (Satan, the accursed). Another use of R-J-M has to do with soothsaying, as in *"al-marjūm bī al-kuwākib,"* or a soothsayer of the heavens/planets. *Lisān* also gives the meaning of "to separate" or to "exile," as in the Qur'anic phrase *"l'in lam tantahu l'arjamnāka."* Another meaning of R-J-M is "supposing," or *dhann*. The most important point to note for our purposes is that R-J-M with a connotation of "killing" or "stoning to death" is not found in the Qur'an and, as shown above, is nowhere prescribed for the crime of *zinā.*

ḤADĪTH

Six *aḥadīth*[53] demonstrate that the Prophet had adulterers stoned to death for committing the crime of *zinā.*[54] There are (at least) two major ways to understand these *aḥadīth.* The first is through traditional *ḥadīth* methodology, a method of analysis that involves assessing the relative strength of the chain of transmission *(isnād)* of *ḥadīth.* The second is *matn* (analysis of the quality of the content) of an individual report, which assists us in ascertaining the authenticity of the stoning *aḥadīth* using traditional Muslim *ḥadīth* methodology. Since these *aḥadīth* make up the proof texts and referents for later legal arguments, *ḥadīth* authenticity is an important reflection of the "authenticity" of the punishment within the "orthodox" mainstream imaginary, particularly after the fourth century, when the science of *ḥadīth* became, for all intents and purposes, canonized.[55] As a source for material history, *aḥadīth* provide clues to the origins of the punishment in pre-Islamic legal systems, insofar as scholars have found linguistic and/or stylistic parallels with earlier Near Eastern codes. The relationship between *ḥadīth* reports that represent stoning as having occurred in the Prophet's time as a punishment for *zinā* and the introduction of the punishment in Islamic law is complex epistemological terrain, taking up the issue of what constitutes revelation. With many more sources to consider in a live religious tradition, the stakes of the discussion become significantly higher for both devout Muslims and critical textual historians.

The *ḥadīth* below indicates the pre-Islamic (in this case, Judaic) provenance of the stoning punishment:

> Mālik related to me from Nafi' that 'Abdullah ibn 'Umar said, "The Jews came to the Messenger of Allah, may Allah bless him and grant him peace, and mentioned to him that a man and woman from among them had committed adultery. The Messenger of Allah, may Allah bless him and grant

> him peace, asked them, 'What do you find in the Torah about stoning?' They said, 'We make their wrong action known and flog them.' [. . .] They spread it out and one of them placed his hand over the verse of stoning. Then he read what was before and after it. 'Abdullah ibn Salam told him to lift his hand. He lifted his hand and there was the verse of stoning. They said, 'He has spoken the truth, Muhammad. The verse of stoning is in it.' So the Messenger of Allah, may Allah bless him and grant him peace, gave the order and they were stoned."[56]

This *ḥadīth* portrays Muḥammad holding the Jews in Medina accountable for upholding the precepts of their own religion. The discussion of this *ḥadīth* in the *sīra* (hagiographical biographies) of ibn Isḥāq[57] and ibn Hishām[58] suggests that perhaps one explanation for the Prophet's (represented) insistence that the Jews obey their scripture was that the Prophet was motivated to be "more Abrahamic than the Jews"—he wanted to lay claim to an Abrahamic lineage in the face of Jewish opposition. This postulation is interesting for several reasons, among which is a sense, shown throughout this study, that stoning carries an important authenticating weight—what I call its "legitimizing horror" in the northern Nigerian context.

This *ḥadīth* distinguishes between *thayb* (married adulterers) and *bikr* (unmarried/virgin ones):

> Mālik related to me from ibn Shīhāb from 'Ubaydullah b. 'Abdullah b. 'Utba b. Mas'ud that Abu Hurayra and Zayd b. Khālid al-Juhānī informed him that two men brought a dispute to the Messenger of Allah, may Allah bless him and grant him peace. One of them said, "Messenger of Allah, judge between us by the Book of Allah!" The other, who was the wiser of the two, said, "Yes, Messenger of Allah, judge between us by the Book of Allah and give me permission to speak." He said, "Speak." He said, "My son was hired by this person and he committed fornication with his wife. He told me that my son deserved stoning and I ransomed him for one hundred sheep and a slave-girl. Then I questioned the people of knowledge and they told me that my son deserved to be flogged with one hundred lashes and exiled for a year, and they informed me that the woman deserved to be stoned." The Messenger of Allah, may Allah bless him and grant him peace, said, "By Him in whose Hand my self is, I will judge between you by

> the Book of Allah. As for your sheep and slave-girl, they should be returned to you. Your son should have one hundred lashes and be exiled for a year." He ordered Unays al-Aslami to go [to] the wife of the other man and stone her if she confessed. She confessed and he stoned her.[59]

This distinguishing process between the married *(muḥṣan/thayb)* adulterer and the unmarried *(bikr)* adulterer was the grist for the mill for the introduction of *takhsīs* (specification) in Sunni *'uṣūl al-fiqh* (foundations of jurisprudence). Ibn Kathīr expands upon the Qur'anic verse mandating flogging for *zinā* in the excerpt below, and he includes the line "flog them with one hundred lashes." Ibn Kathīr then moves seamlessly into a discussion of the *takhsīs* between this Qur'anic punishment for adultery—flogging—and the *ḥadīth*-based punishment for *zinā* committed by married persons, stoning:

> This honorable Ayah contains the ruling on the law of retaliation for the person who commits illegal sex, and details of the punishment. Such a person will either be unmarried, meaning that he has never been married, or he will be married, meaning that he has had intercourse within the bounds of a lawful marriage, and he is free, adult and of sound mind. In addition to this he is to be banished from his homeland for one year, as was recorded in the Two Saḥīḥs from Abu Hurayarah and Zayd b. Khaild al-Juhani in the *ḥadīth* about the two Bedouins who came to the Messenger of Allah. One of them said, "O Messenger of Allah, this son of mine was employed by this man, and committed *zinā* with his wife. I paid a ransom with him on behalf of my son one hundred sheep and a slave-girl, but when I asked the people of knowledge, they said that my son should be given one hundred stripes and banished for a year, and that this man's wife should be stoned to death. The Prophet then said:
>
>> By the One in Whose Hand is my soul, I will judge between you both according to the Book of Allah. Take back the slave-girl and sheep, and your son is to be Given one hundred stripes and banished for one year. O Unays—he said to a man from the tribe of Aslam—go to this man's wife, and if she confesses, then stone her to death.
>
> Unays went to her and she confessed, so he stoned her to death. This indicates that if the person who is guilty of illegal sex is a virgin and unmar-

> ried, he should be banished in addition to being given one hundred stripes. But if married, meaning he has had intercourse within the bounds of lawful marriage, and he is free, adult and of sound mind, then he should be stoned to death.[60]

This *ḥadīth* is mentioned in the great Nigerian *jihad* leader Uthmān Dan Fodio's important late-eighteenth-century *fiqh* work, *Ihya' al-Sunnah wa Ikhmād al-Bid'ah,* to which I referred in the previous chapter.

In the following, last *ḥadīth,* Islam's second caliph, 'Umar ibn al-Khaṭṭab (d. 26 A.H./644 C.E.), asserts that the stoning punishment actually is in the Qur'an (but did not make it into the written iteration thereof) and was practiced by the Prophet. Thus, the punishment carries the force of law. This represented speech of Umar's is an extraordinary intervention, mentioned by all *tafasīr* and *fiqh* of the stoning punishment, and therefore warrants special attention:

> Malik related to me that Yahya ibn Sa'id ibn al-Musayyab said, "When 'Umar ibn al-Khattab came from Mina, he made his camel kneel at al-Abtah and then he gathered a pile of small stones and cast his cloak over them and dropped to the ground. Then he raised his hands towards the sky and said, "O Allah! I have become old and my strength has weakened. My flock is scattered. Take me to You with nothing missed out and without having neglected anything." Then he went to Medīna and addressed the people, saying, "People! Sunan have been laid down for you. Obligations have been placed upon you. You have been left with a clear way unless you lead people astray right and left." He struck one of his hands with the other and then said, "Take care lest you destroy the ayāt of stoning so that someone will say, 'We do not find two ḥadd in the book of Allah.' The Messenger of Allah, may Allah bless him and grant him peace, stoned, so we have stoned." By Him in whose hand my soul is, had it not been that people would say that 'Umar ibn al-Khaṭṭab has added to the Book of Allah, we would have written it: "The full grown man and the full-grown woman, stone them absolutely." We have certainly recited that.[61]

The representation of 'Umar ibn al-Khaṭṭāb's role in solidifying the stoning punishment in the Islamic canon cannot be overestimated, and a much larger study is warranted of 'Umar's role in setting the sexual order in early Islam. For now, I will stop to make a few observations (and I will make more observations related to gender in chapter 6). It is clear from this *ḥadīth* that 'Umar is represented as representing himself as having special access to the practices of the Prophet. It is indeed on the basis of this *ḥadīth* that many jurists uphold the stoning punishment for married adulterers, despite the presence of another punishment for the same crime in the Qur'an. As I discussed earlier, the divine injunction to stone adulterers to death for adultery is an abrogated *(mansūkh)* verse that the second caliph 'Umar was instrumental in introducing to the tradition. The evident difference in scholarly concern with the two issues might even lead us to postulate that questions of spiritual and political authority during this intellectual period in this discourse were decidedly secondary to satisfactorily sorting out the theological difficulties presented by verses, which are divine by definition, that did not make it into the Qur'an.[62]

Hence, traditional sources suggest that 'Umar's influence upon divine revelation was not considered a theological problem at the time the scholars wrote about it. As Avraham Hakim argues, this could be because the construction of the Prophet as the sole lawgiver resulted from a process of scholarly consolidation of norms and sources, and so 'Umar's law-giving capacity could not have been directly and self-consciously represented.[63] That 'Umar's influence on revelation, and hence potential rivalry with the Prophet, was not considered a problem suggests that during a certain period of Islamic intellectual history a more oligarchical conception of authority was acceptable than in later periods, when the tradition had further congealed. Burton argues that the omnipresence of 'Umar in these *ḥadīth* narratives is significant for several reasons, including the consideration that 'Umar was known to "insist forcefully" on adherence to the Qur'an for matters of ritual and worship, leading to policies adopted by newly conquered garrison towns under 'Umar's command. These policies became customs and these customs later became integral to the law.[64] This impression of

'Umar's epistemological predilections, when combined with his law-giving authority, lends credence to the theory that 'Umar's authority was responsible for the *shaykh* and *shaykha ḥadīth.*

The dominance of 'Umar in the early stoning reports suggests that there was an anthropomorphic element to the orthodoxiation process of divine law in the classical period. 'Umar's idiosyncrasies with respect to the control of female sexuality are represented as granting authenticity to *aḥadīth* that prescribe stoning; and his dominance in actual *ḥadīth* reports, as well as the importance of his son ibn 'Umar, as a transmitter of *ḥadīth* mandating stoning, highlights the importance of companion *ḥadīth,* which were considered as authoritative as prophetic *ḥadīth* before Shāfi'ī.[65] According to John Burton, the purpose of these *aḥadīth* is to clarify for us that, since the time of the Prophet, Muslims had continuously stoned in cases of adultery.

Scott Lucas examined the stoning *ḥadīth* as compiled by Abu Bakr Ahmad b. Husayn b. 'Alī b. Moussa al-Khosrojerdi al-Bayhaqi (d. 458 A.H./1066 C.E.), who identified the stoning *aḥadīth* that appear in the canonical collections of Al-Bukhārī and Muslim *(al-sunan al-kubra),* which number only eight.[66] These eight can be categorized, according to Lucas, by the following criteria:

1. 'Umar's insistence that the "verse of stoning" existed and that the Prophet stoned "on the basis of testimony, pregnancy, or confession" (Bayhaqi 1999, bab 2).

Here the authority of the *ḥadīth* is buttressed by 'Umar's insistence that the Prophet stoned, signaling that a law-giving authority was attributed to 'Umar, which I will turn to in more detail below.

2. Ibn Mas'ud's previously mentioned report that Muhammad said "The blood of a Muslim may be shed in only three possible cases—the married person who commits adultery; a life for life; and a person who abandons his religion and separates from his community" (Bayhaqi, bab 4).

This criterion shows that adultery is among what are known in the tradition as *al-kabā'r* (the biggest of) sins.

3. The version of the Unays story that Muhammad ordered 100 lashes and a year of exile for the never-married fornicator and lapidation for the adulterer who confesses, transmitted by Abu Hurayra and Zayd b. Khalid (Bayhaqi, bab 4).

These *ḥadīth* form part of the basis of the specification *(takhsīs)* that would resolve the contradiction between the Qur'anic verse that mandates flogging and the *aḥadīth* that mandate stoning.

4. Abu Hurayra's version of the Ma'iz story which mentions the quadruple confession, Muhammad's inquiry into his sanity and marital status, and his verdict to stone him (Bayhaqi, babs 4, 10).

This *ḥadīth* establishes quadruple confession and inquiry into the sanity and marital status of defendants.

5. Jabir's version of the Ma'iz story, which adds the detail that Muhammad did not perform the funeral prayer over Ma'iz's stoned corpse (Bayhaqi, bab 9).
6. Ibn 'Umar's version of the story of the two Jewish fornicators whom Muhammad stoned on the basis of the "stoning verse" found in the Torah (Bayhaqi, babs 4, 37).
7. Ibn Mas'ud's report of Muhammad's forgiveness, on the basis of Q. 11:114, of the man who confessed to engaging in everything short of sexual intercourse with an unrelated woman (Bayhaqi, bab 33).
8. Abu Hurayra and Zayd b. Khalid report the Prophet's statement regarding the master's right to flog his fornicator slave girl and his advice to sell her "even for [the value of] a rope" if she continues fornicating (Bayhaqi, babs 34, 35).[67]

Lucas points out that these *ḥadīth* are poorly disseminated, "with the noteworthy exception of the story of Ma'iz."[68] Lucas wonders how it could be that

> Only ibn Mas'ud has heard the Prophet declare that the death penalty is applicable in only three cases? Why is 'Umar the only Companion who insisted that a "verse of stoning" existed and was then excised from the Qur'an? How could only Abu Hurayra and Zayd b. Khalid have known the story of Unays? It is difficult to see how any of these reports, save the story of Ma'iz, can be relied upon to serve as decisive legal proofs regarding the multiple penalties for illicit intercourse.[69]

These curiosities, together with other features of the *ḥadīth* texts,[70] draw Lucas to conclude that the Prophet is represented as possessing "an extreme reluctance to apply the stoning penalty."[71] Lucas discusses one additional story to buttress this point: that of a man who confessed to the Prophet that he had done everything short of intercourse with a nonlegal woman, whereupon the Prophet received/recited the Qur'anic verse "Establish worship at the two ends of the day and in some watches of the night. Lo—good deeds annul ill deeds. This is a reminder for the mindful" (Q. 11:114) and sent him away (Bayhaqi, bab 33). As Lucas remarks, "How far we are from the modern religious courts of some Muslim countries that sentence people to flogging for significantly lesser offenses!"[72]

HISTORIOGRAPHICAL ISSUES

Jurists and exegetes found themselves confronted with Qur'anic verses and *aḥadīth* that prescribed two different punishments for what can be construed as the same crime of adultery.[73] The Qur'an mandates flogging one hundred lashes for adultery, while the *ḥadīth* calls for the stoning of married adulterers. These two different punishments for the same crime produced a clear legal problem. In response, hermeneutic devices such as *takhsīs* (specification) and *naskh* (abrogation) were developed to reconcile this problem. For example, jurists could settle the issue by means of specification as follows: a married adulterer *(thayb/muḥṣan)* would be sentenced to death by stoning, mirroring the language of the *ḥadīth,* while unmarried adulterers *(bikr)* would be sentenced to flogging as mandated in the Qur'an. This distinction between *thayb* (married) and *bikr* (unmarried/virgin) was reportedly made by the Prophet himself.

NASKH AND THE LEGACY OF SHĀFIʿĪ

Al-Shāfiʿī, who developed Islamic law's principles of jurisprudence *('uṣūl al-fiqh),* reconciled the stoning punishment with Islamic law, leaving the single most powerful jurisprudential legacy for subsequent scholars to reckon with. Shāfiʿī held that sunnah, including *ḥadīth,* couldn't abrogate Qur'an. This rule was circumvented to legalize stoning though several means. One was ʿUmar's *ḥadīth,* discussed above, claiming the existence of a verse that did not make it into the book of God, but that had nonetheless been recited. This "hidden verse," located in what Jalāl al-Dīn al-Suyūtī (d. 910 A.H./1505 C.E.) calls *"al-lawḥ al-mahfūẓ,"* was abrogated in its recitation but not in its value as a legal maxim, in a form of abrogation called *"naskh al-tilāwa dūn al-ḥukm."*[74] I have not seen counterevidence for the assertion that Shāfiʿī developed this form of abrogation to legalize the stoning punishment in particular. As Burton says, "Of all the disputed questions in the *fiqh,* and especially in the *'uṣūl,* none is richer in variety of treatment, or fuller in its appeal to Qur'an and Sunnah sources, or more acute in tension as to the relative weight that the *fuqaha'* were alleged to have accorded to each of the sources than that of the penalties for fornication and adultery."[75]

Mālik ibn Anas (d. 179 A.H./795 C.E.), however, was explicit in his assertion that sunnah does supersede the Qur'an on the issue of stoning. According to Mālikī jurist Abu ʿAbdullah Al-Qurtubī (d. 671 A.H./1273 C.E.):

> Mālik admitted this principle [sunnah superseding Qur'an], but Shāfiʿī denied it, although the *fuqaha'* all admit, in the instance of the penalty for the adulterer, that the flogging element of Q 24:2 has been allowed to lapse in the case of those offenders who are condemned to death by stoning.

> There is no explanation for the abandonment of the flogging element other than that the penalty all now acknowledge is based on the Sunnah, i.e. the practice of the Prophet.[76]

Though *naskh al-tilāwa dūn al-ḥukm* is a Shāfi'ī doctrine, other *madhāhib* began to argue that instances of Quranic verses that were "missing" were located in "another" Qur'an *(al-lūh al maḥfūz)*. Hence, the introduction of the Platonic notion of the "perfect" Qur'an in the heavenly sphere that cannot escape comparison to the presumably imperfect one on the earthly sphere. Burton takes this to suggest that the *madhāhib* worked in dialectic relation during the period of their formation.[77] More specifically, Burton believes that the concept was solidified in the period between Ṭabarī's (d. 310 A.H./923 C.E.) and Zamakhsharī's (d. 537 A.H./1143 C.E.) elaborations on the concept. Burton describes this difference as essentially a battle between Shāfi'ī and Mālik as to whether *ḥadīth* can abrogate Qur'an. While Shāfi'ī denies that this happens in the case of stoning, Mālik acknowledges that this is what has occurred. This epistemological debate, among other reasons, makes stoning perhaps the most controversial of *ḥadd* laws.[78]

Burton notes that Shāfi'ī's move to abrogate the Qur'an with a *ḥadīth*—even if that *ḥadīth* gestures toward a "hidden" Qur'anic verse—marks a strange departure from the ordinary rules of abrogation: to abrogate a verse in the Qur'an with another verse, in keeping with the traditional principle of reading the Qur'an with the Qur'an. Speaking of abrogation more broadly, Burton asserts that anxiety over what looked like conflicting statements in the Qur'an "spurred the scholar to discover a way of removing embarrassment and problem at one and the same time. The concept of naskh was the Muslim's ingenious response to the stimulus of embarrassment.... But the stubborn fact remained obvious to everyone with eyes to see: that earlier punishment had been established by the Qur'an in Q. 24:2."[79]

According to early *ḥadīth* scholar ibn Shihāb al-Zuhrī (d. 124 A.H./741 or 742 C.E.), learned jurists themselves often are unaware of the abrogator and abrogated in *ḥadīth*.[80] When chronological order is not possible to ascertain, then recourse is made to rules of preference *(al-tarjīḥ)* to determine which of the two is stronger and therefore preferable. The primacy of chronological order as a rule governing abrogation (i.e., whichever verse was revealed later takes primacy) itself raises profound theological problems, as all verses are supposed to be equally divine because they were revealed by God. Andrew Rippen points out that the notion that Qur'anic verses follow in a linear subsequence is "remarkably underplayed in classical Muslim testaments."[81] Because latter-chronological supremacy is actually not accounted for in the sources, Rippin argues that "The real key to understanding *naskh,* then, is to realize that it, in fact, resolves conflicts between *fiqh* and the other two sources rather than conflict within the Qur'an and Sunnah, at least when the exegesis of these two is not approached with the baggage of the *fiqh.*" Stoning, which, using normal rules of abrogation, cannot be legalized, is the prime example of what makes abrogation problematic as a practice and concept.

Abrogation theories that rely on the valorization of mortal, linear time to determine stoning's legality suggest that, for Islamic exegetes, revelation's essential historicity was understood. Burton argues that the emphasis on abrogation among the early exegetes and jurists suggests the presence of a secondary science, *'uṣūl al-fiqh,* since jurists acknowledged the stoning penalty, differing only in regard to its source. Since abrogation involves contentious propositions such as "suspending" Qur'anic rulings, the most expedient route to legalization would be to ground abrogation theory in Qur'anic verses.[82] This is precisely what happened.

SUNNAH

The second method by which the Islamic origins of the stoning punishment can be accounted is by understanding the concept of sunnah as a vehicle through which, as Robert Hoyland argues, "the practice of the tribe meets tradition."[83] The term *sunnah* connotes exemplary modes of conduct, and the perfect verb *sanna* connotes "settling or fashioning a mode of conduct as an example for others to follow."[84] Here, the notion that Prophetic practice informs the behavior of subsequent generations of Muslims raises an important methodological question: How can the Islamic intellectual past be accounted for in the postmodern Nigerian present? The concept of sunnah connotes a perfect society to be emulated throughout history. Mālik described Islamic law itself as the intellectual outcome of Medina's historical links back to the perfect society of Prophetic times. In the formative period of Islamic law, sunnah comes to be understood as the generally accepted doctrine of the Mālikī school, whereas from Shāfi'ī onward, sunnah is considered the exclusive legacy of the Prophet.[85] I found this notion of the "perfect society" to be essential for northern Nigerians struggling with their own societies' challenges—the Medinan model offers a hopeful, divinely assisted benchmark for progress. This perception of the Medinan model is one of the key reasons this makes up the deepest layer of the sunnaic paradigm.

Joseph Schacht conceptualizes sunnah as the practice in pre-Islamic Arabia that first rejected Islam, then absorbed it. The concept then "reasserted itself" as central to Islamic law. The first Islamic *sunnan* (plural form of *sunnah*) were less legal and more political, regulating the business of the caliphate. For Schacht, when the sunnah of the Prophet gained ascendancy through the work of Shāfi'ī, a doctrinal link was established "between the sunnah of Abu Bakr and 'Umar and the Koran."[86]

Sunnah's provenance, for Wael Hallaq, was in the first instance "secular," composed of the "time-honored communal and tribal" practices of the Arabs in addition to the examples of Abraham, Ishamel, and Muḥammad himself. The Companions also had their own *sunnan;* their authority, along with the other Companions of the Prophet, was not, Hallaq argues, exclusively secular, but rather both tribal and religious:

> [I]n the sense that the model conduct they provided was due not only to the fact of their charismatic and influential leadership, but also because their conduct was viewed as having been in line with the principles of the new religion—principles that they absorbed by virtue of their intimate knowledge of what the Prophet and his religion were all about.[87]

This understanding of the theological and emotional value of sunnah as it developed in the Islamic tradition may help explain how, in a post-modern legal context—in which the nuances of jurisprudence were, in a sense, purposely abandoned—the stoning punishment was seen as authoritative and meted out accordingly, with relatively little hesitation.

CONCLUSION

The contingent introduction of the stoning punishment into the Islamic tradition foregrounds the elements of anthropomorphism in the divine tradition's development. The punishment's provenance in pre-Islamic legal systems, from the Mesopotamian to the Arabian to the Judaic, places the Islamic tradition that adopted it in temporal and geographic context, bringing into view the fundamental historicity of the process of "divinization" of the stoning punishment. Epistemological devices such as *takhsīs* and *naskh* show the role played by Islamic jurists and philosophers in the construction of a harmonized tradition. Stoning, a punishment in some ways anomalous and even contradictory to the Qur'an, had to be aligned with the imperative to maintain an intellectually consistent terrain for rapidly emerging Islamic socialities during this formative period.

Can the ambivalence found in northern Nigeria about the stoning punishment be attributed (in any or all measure) to its status in the tradition as an always exceptional, always controversial punishment? In his essay on the Prophet, sunnah, and charismatic authority, Jon Brockopp argues (following Max Weber) that when a history is imbued with a notion of the divine, its recipients suppose that reproducing that divinity is a matter of repeating those same acts.[88] Something similar can be said for the stoning punishment in a northern Nigerian society that craves a radically ordering legal system. By focusing on the stoning punishment, this chapter has suggested that such a legal system, at its barest roots, never existed.

CHAPTER FOUR

Colonialism

Then and Now

There are no Nigerians.
Shaykh Sanusi Gumbi

By 2035, Nigeria is projected to have the fifth-largest population of Muslims in the world (an estimated 116,832,000).[1] Dr. Aliyu Ibrahim, a professor of Islamic law at Zaria University whom I visited one day in March 2010, was, along with his colleagues, quite proud of this statistic, believing that Western concerns about a Nigerian population explosion are a conspiracy designed to weaken Nigeria. Pointing to China's use of their burgeoning population as a means to develop and strengthen their economy, Ibrahim believes that there is plenty of room in the arid deserts of northern Nigeria for more people. "This is our land," he added, "it has been colonized, and we will not let that happen again." His implication was that it is essential to occupy Nigerian land with free Nigerians.

For Ibrahim and his comrades and colleagues, the history of colonialism marks the defining moment of deep cleavage in northern Nigeria, a cleavage that the shari'ah revolution of 1999 was, in part, trying to repair. This chapter describes the history of colonial military interventions in Hausaland and analyzes the effects of colonialism on Islamic law. In large part, colonialism gave rise to the sunnaic paradigm, for without it the instinct to reach aggressively back into history to cleanse and preserve Nigerian society would be far less acute.

Dr. Ibrahim and many other northern Nigerian intellectuals I met dismissed the federal structure of Nigeria as little more than a colonial innovation. It must be noted, however, that this statement serves a rhetorical function; this sentiment was nowhere near as popular when northern Muslims themselves dominated federal politics. That changed in 1999, when Olusegun Obasanjo became the first Christian president to be elected in Nigeria. Distancing Hausaland from the federal structure can thus be understood as a metonymy for giving up on Nigeria altogether. I asked Salisu Bala, director of the Awera House, a research institute in Kaduna, for his view on a refrain I had heard from both southern and northern Nigerians alike that the Hausa were "in love with power." He did not deny it, describing to me the deplorable state of education in Kaduna State, and ending with a flourish: "What else do we have? All of the resources are in the south!"

Amid the chaos that has plagued Nigeria since its independence, starting with the Biafra civil war (1967–70), successive military dictatorships, the devaluation of the naira in 1992, and a transition to democracy that only seemed to increase the corruption—many in northern Nigeria have sought forbearance in their Hausa identity, an identity that precedes this turmoil both temporally and theoretically. Shaykh Khalidu of Jos, who leads a mosque that houses Muslim refugees from increasingly frequent sectarian massacres, remarked that one of Nigeria's problems is the use of English to conduct official affairs: "If Ajami [Hausa written in the Arabic script] had been allowed to exist, we could have been like India or Iran—people who function in their own language."[2] The fact that Hausaland did not develop in this manner is experienced as a tragic loss.

Not all perspectives in northern Nigeria consider homogeneous identity the key to preservation of society. Shaykh Sanusi Gumbi of Kaduna calls himself a practical man. Though fully aware that the ties that bind a body called "Nigerians" are often tenuous, he argues that, ultimately, "nobody wants to split northern Nigeria off from the rest of the country." An article I came across in a Nigerian newspaper in 2010, penned by then leader of Libya Colonel Muammar Gaddafi, advocated for just this split, prompting Nigerian authorities to expel Libya's ambassador. However, I came to understand that threats to split the country were macabre fantasies that were ritually enacted in the Nigerian press, perhaps to nurture a comforting notion of a "nuclear option"—splitting Nigeria—if the situation of the country continued to decline.

With these tensions and possibilities always in his mind, Shaykh Gumbi believes that the fact that there are multiple religions in Nigeria should essentially end the discussion about shari'ah. He elaborates: "For the majority of Muslims, if you say 'shari'ah,' you have to then define, 'what is shari'ah?' Nigeria has a constitution. It is impossible to have Islamic law in the state, Muslims for the mosque and Christians for the church." Shaykh Gumbi supports the federal system and does not want a form of law that is for Muslims or Christians only. He implores the powerful to "start shari'ah on yourself first" before attempting to impose it on other people.[3] Dr. Asmau voiced a similar criticism, arguing that Nigeria is not one hundred percent Muslim or Christian in any state, and therefore it is improper to impose the criminal aspects of shari'ah in any state.

Some, like Mustapha Guadebe, are offended by what he describes as the open cynicism of the shari'ah experiment: "They promise the Messiah will come, and we will live in peace. This is so cynical. They don't know God—only cults and juju."[4] Guadebe reflects an attitude I heard often among those who follow Nigeria's negotiation of religion and politics—namely that everything is political, from stoning to shari'ah. Indeed, Guadebe believes that shari'ah has been politicized since the *jihad* of Uthmān Dan Fodio, reflecting Northern Elements Progressive Union founder Aminu Kano's arguments that the emirate system was a corruption of the *jihad*'s original egalitarian spirit and that Ahmadu Bello, Dan Fodio's son, who opposed the emirate system, was fighting to preserve that original spirit.

It must be noted here that I found the refrain that the "shari'ah" is (totally) "political" was an overwhelmingly elite discourse, while the more popular notion was that shari'ah and social justice are essentially the same concept. An acquaintance I met in Kano understands the matter more straightforwardly: "I can't cross either Nigerian or shari'ah law." His simplified understanding of Islamic law holds that Amina Lawal should have been killed, but she got off because of politics. Professor Auwalu Yadudu writes on whether stoning is barbaric:

> It is a matter of value judgment. Those who say you shouldn't kill, stone someone to death for committing adultery, are making judgments based on their convictions. They don't think that it is right but the same people will say if you commit murder, you can be killed. Maybe they will say killing someone by lethal injection is more humane. But I think that it is the person who is the victim of the death sentence who will judge ... who carried it out on him. But I will tell him that well I believe in it, and I have faith in it and I don't see it as barbaric. All the safeguards and the procedural safeguards that shari'ah has put in place and complied with and maintained, the Moslems need not be told that there is some way of taking the life of someone which is more humane than some others.[5]

I spoke to Professor Yadudu eight years after he wrote this article, while he and his fellow northerners were in the thick of the shari'ah experiment. I don't think he had generally changed his mind that moral outrage about one form of death penalty over the other is relative, but the degree to which the shari'ah experiment had been politicized had clearly dampened his enthusiasm for it. This change of heart in the face of the politicization of the process was a common theme that prompted me to ask several people if they thought shari'ah, as of 2010, was still alive or dead.

Khadija Asaiko, a women's and children's rights activist in Jos, thinks it is dead, with the politicians extending their corruption to even the most sacred of topics—God's law—and bringing a new level of despair to Nigeria. Hamidu Bobboyi believes that "there is no more political capital for shari'ah. People's beliefs are at a personal level." Attorney Ahmed Garba of Jos thinks it's dead: "The shari'ah benefit to the common man has been negative. People originally thought shari'ah would make their problems disappear. It was implemented mostly due to pressure and to gain political support; people are not enthusiastic anymore." Garba continued: "The shari'ah is very political now; a way of reducing opposition. Shari'ah does not govern contracts, it's limited to shari'ah commissions and distributions of *zakāt.*" Dr. Abdulkareem Sadiq thinks it's dying, saying, "If you follow shari'ah strictly, folks in the government would be against it. That's why it has fizzled out and the demand has died down." A vendor of watermelon I spoke to while waiting for an *achaba* (motorcycle) in Sokoto put it this way: "The thing wasn't thought through; we all bungled along. We did not give serious consideration to what is being done. Maybe it could not have been done any other way."

On the other hand, a shaykh I met who led a mosque in Abuja told me, *"Allah nazala al-shari'ah, Muhammad salla Allah alayhu wa salama tahakuha, wa ana tahaktuha fī zārīa"* (God brought down the shari'ah, Muhammad, may God have mercy on him, enacted it, and I enacted it in Zaria). However, despite his use of poetic alliteration in Arabic, and despite the simplicity of the sentiment, the shaykh quickly complicated his statement by saying this: "Shari'ah attacks the conditions that lead to stealing and *zinā,* not the offenders themselves. This is the idealized form of shari'ah many support." He left unsaid the plain fact that the conditions underlying shari'ah's implementation had not been met.

People regularly wondered aloud to me, with astonishment, how it could be that no one, up to that point, had challenged the constitutionality of the shari'ah in federal court. This would have exploded the shari'ah issue in a country that is firmly divided on its constitutionality, quite possibly leading to violence. At issue is article 39 of the Nigerian Constitution, which guarantees freedom of religion for all Nigerians. Northerners (roughly) interpret this as the right to establish shari'ah courts, while southerners (roughly) believe that precisely the establishment of such courts is in violation of their freedom of religion. Former chief justice of the Supreme Court of Nigeria Mohammed Uwais reportedly prayed that he would never be called upon to legislate the constitutionality of shari'ah. This legal ambivalence has had terrible consequences for up to hundreds of accused criminals who have been sentenced to *ḥudūd* punishments and who are simply sitting in custody today, waiting to be stoned or amputated, which is not likely to happen. Governors of those states will not sign off on their punishments, sensing society's lack of appetite to see poor and unprivileged people punished in a manner that outweighs the crime.[6] While some believe that these sentences will eventually "moderate" themselves, these unfortunate victims are caught in a judicial and political purgatory in the meantime. Echoes of this legal ambivalence were found in President Obasanjo's orders not to "crack down" on shari'ah.

By the time I left the field in 2010, it was clear to me that most people understood post-1999 shari'ah to have been little more than a strategic tool to aid Ahmed Sani Yerima's reelection campaign. The desperation and idealism that prompted many to support shari'ah have made this creeping conclusion very disillusioning for northern Nigerians. While the *hisba* are empowered and shari'ah laws are on the books, it has become clear to many that, as a woman in Kaduna from whom I frequently bought food put it, "You can't starve the people and punish them." Punishment without justice is not the shari'ah upon which people place their ideals, but a newer, crueler form of betrayal.

"THE OTHER": CONSTRUCTIONS OF COLONIALISM AND THE WEST

Several men gathered in Ibraheem Sulaiman's cozy Zaria office to sit in on our conversation about shari'ah in Nigeria. I didn't get the impression that they were gathering for the special occasion of meeting with me, but rather that this familial-feeling meeting of men, full of warm camaraderie—a room full of academics, journalists, Islamic activists, and their students—was a frequent, if not daily, affair that was complete with tea, snacks, and genuinely funny jokes I felt a bit shy laughing at. I was perched by myself on the lone, long couch, since the men were polite enough not to sit next to me. In the course of the conversation, Dr. Sulaiman said to a chorus of approval: "Every society is responsible for itself. Shari'ah in the north is merely an expansion of an existing system. And one day, the United States will turn into a Muslim-majority society."[7]

Post-1999 shari'ah should be understood as a globalized phenomenon. It is about not only domestic Nigerian strife, but also the geopolitical causes of domestic Nigerian strife. The post-1999 shari'ah story does not follow from a strictly linear understanding of Nigerian history; rather, it is interpolated within Hausaland's actual interaction with their British colonial masters, and within northern Nigerians' contemporary memory of that chapter in its history. Shari'ah is not simply an outcome of the animus and competition over power and wealth between northern and southern Nigeria; it is also a response to a deeper clash of epistemologies between two regions whose origins can be traced to colonial powers that privileged the south with respect to Western education and the job prospects and wealth that followed.

With this set of anxieties in mind, one can better understand the widespread distrust of the study of Islam in English in northern Nigeria. According to attorney Ahmed Garba, the phrase "Western world" is used "without really understanding what it means"—most of the time the phrase denotes "the British" (meaning nineteenth-century colonial Britain) and America, but the larger connotation is the cultural, political, and economic complex that northern Nigerians perceive to be repressing them.[8] Ibraheem Sulaiman points out that "Most of Africa is composed of European imperialism and Muslim [resistance] politics: Muslims are determined to maintain their identity, they refuse to surrender. For example, it is an insult to speak to an older person in English."[9] Dr. Mustafa Ismail proposed that the youth think Amina Lawal got off because of international politics, which makes the equation seem like a simple one of "Islam vs. non-Muslims." This, according to Ismail, is tied to the Palestinian problem, and thus, he believes, the "temperature will come down once that problem is solved. The elections in Gaza and Algeria exposed the elections' hypocrisy."[10] These sentiments suggest that post-1999 shari'ah can be understood not as a simple return to "Islam," but rather as a response to negative external factors that, at this point, could only be redeemed through the language and discourse of "Islam."

Aliyu Musa Yauri, one of Lawal's lead attorneys, whom I mentioned earlier, believes that the West is trying to destroy Islam. Ironically, Yauri himself was accused of being paid to defame Islam when he took up Lawal's case. He reflected: "The common man is in a state of desperation because of the level of corruption. The Islamic legal system is just, and it would do him proud if something outside the West is applied in his own land. He would have ownership over that and see it as his 'own' system."[11] The return to an Islamic system, one northerners can call "their own," is framed in the same breath as a reaction against the West—the two instincts are not separate. Yauri continued:

> I am very proud of Islam. And America is against the Muslims, especially with the Palestinians losing their land and getting slaughtered and America turning a blind eye. And all the other massacres of Muslims. There are some honest Nigerians, some ingenious Nigerians, but they have mostly been disabled. It is only money that gets you anywhere, only money that gets you an office, a job, or respect. It is not merit. Whatever little money I make I must share with my younger brother and my aunt. This is how we are.[12]

This narrative of a globalized Muslim victimization contains data points familiar to those who study the contemporary Islamic world: the Palestinians, Iraq, Afghanistan, and the treatment of Muslims in the West. I was therefore surprised when Yauri's tone shifted from the satisfied complacency that can accompany grand narratives such as this to a sharper register that held more acute pain as he spoke of the difficulties in Nigeria: "Everything is money, there is no merit. He who has an office, an education, connections, this is because of money. Why doesn't the West do something to stop this corruption!"[13]

Yauri's animus toward the West does not lead him to call for America to withdraw from Nigerian affairs, but rather consists of complaints that America is not more engaged. Yauri argued that Americans are only interested in helping others when they themselves feel a bit down; but then, in a surprising twist, he said, his passion rising: "America should come in and tell these Nigerians on top to stop being so corrupt! We need a level playing field!"

I asked, "But do you think there is a solution to this problem of corruption that Nigerians themselves can come up with?"

Yauri replied, "I don't think so, because Nigerians today are sycophants. They can all be bought. Everything is money." [14]

And so the need for the West's help persists. Societal decay is understood by northern Nigerians to originate from a top-down corruption that is not so much caused by the West as tolerated by it. Why else might billions of dollars be kept in offshore European bank accounts? Why would the West do business with those who oppress their people so garishly? A power greater than Nigeria has a responsibility to restore justice to this intolerable situation, and the West—with its forked tongue, hypocrisy, invasive non-governmental organizations (NGOs) focusing on the wrong issues, and inevitable self-interest—was not the answer.

Yauri said something else that struck me as odd: "If the southerners really cared about this case, why didn't one of them challenge it in common law court?"

I said, "But that would have meant challenging shari'ah itself, right?"

Yauri was silent.

THE ARAB WORLD AND THE ARABIC LANGUAGE

The rhetoric around northern Nigerians' relationship to the Arab world is complex, combining a clear desire to identify with the Arab word's powerful Islamic epistemic tradition and modern political and cultural power, while at the same time exhibiting a fierce independent streak, which is fueled in part by collective memories of Arab racism and what is seen by some as the Arabs' political and intellectual capitulation to the West.

Northern Nigerians have always been part of the Muslim world, I was often told, so it would be a mistake to understand the post-1999 "re-enlivening"[15] of shari'ah as a "rediscovering." After all, it was said with pride, Islam came to the Borno Caliphate five hundred years before the rest of Hausaland, which is around the same time Islam came to Egypt. There is a historical connection between North Africa and West Africa that runs deep; Sokoto *jihad* leader Uthmān Dan Fodio exhibited the fluidity of this exchange by arguing that Hausaland could borrow whatever they wanted from any legal code. In modern times, the *sardauna* of Sokoto, Uthmān Dan Fodio's grandson, was the vice chairman of the Organization of Islamic Countries, and the *sardauna* had cooperated with Egypt, Saudi Arabia, and Kuwait on various initiatives. The fact that books written by Uthmān Dan Fodio brought Zaki Badawi to tears was a point of pride.[16]

I asked Shaykh Khalidu why Islam was considered so absolutely legitimate as an "authentic" identity for Hausaland when it had been brought by outsiders—Arab traders in the eleventh century. His eyes lit up at this question, and he was quick to answer that Islam was considered legitimate because it was spread through trade with Africans—not through violence. The prevalent understanding in northern Nigeria is that shari'ah was spread in the same peaceful manner.

I was sitting in the research library, bent over an Arabic manuscript at the Arewa House in Kaduna one afternoon, when one of the staff members, a lovely woman who always gave me a warm smile when I walked in, put her hand on my shoulder and bent over to see what I was doing. She exclaimed, "Oh, you read Qur'an!" I smiled and asked her if she, too, read "Qur'an," and she replied that no, she was a Christian from a small tribe, but that she was nonetheless impressed with what she clearly thought was an extraordinary ability. As Khadija Asaiko put it, "People here [in the north] are in love with the Arabic language," which is considered a liturgical language. When the naira, the Nigerian currency, was printed with, for example, "Ten Naira" in Arabic, people were reportedly confused to see the language written for secular purposes. In another story Hamidu Bobboyi told me, Nigerian Christians who went to Jerusalem on a pilgrimage were reportedly stunned to meet Arabic-speaking Palestinian Christians. The category of "Christian" and "Arabic speaking" was one that Nigerians were utterly flummoxed by. Asaiko added that people are conscious of religion and preach against the West in the same breath, as if these two activities are synonyms. This indicates a lack of awareness that there are a significant number of Muslims in the West. Ahmed Garba expressed a similar fascination when he saw me write something in Arabic in my notes. He told me that people longed to go directly to the sources because of the failure to codify the laws. The sense is that, if the laws are not going to be codified, then interpretations have to be left to the individual. Fluency in Arabic is a great legitimizer in northern Nigerian society.

I often heard criticism of the shari'ah court judges' level of intellectual sophistication. "The *qādīs* are not very knowledgeable on 'Arabic,'" said Dr. Guando in Sokoto with some scorn. "They are run of the mill; secondary school—they have diplomas in Arabic and Islamic studies."[17] Judges who have an educational background in Arabic are often considered qualified to serve as Islamic legal authorities—the chief *qādī* of Kaduna was cited here as an example. He has a PhD in Arabic, not Islamic law. Garba believes that this fetishization of the Arabic language can cause northern Muslims to trivialize Islamic law, and this adds to what he describes as the naïveté and easily manipulable quality of northern Muslims. Garba added that *taqlīd* (imitation) is very prominent in Nigeria: "If you can dress like an *'ālim* (learned person) dress like an Arab, people will believe you without objection."[18]

The Arab world also came under significant critique. Aliyu Ibrahim and Ibraheem Sulaiman both spoke with amazement of former Tunisian president Habib Bourguiba's move to cancel fasting during Ramadan in the 1980s. This story fuels a narrative among some circles in northern Nigeria that Arab Islam is "weak." As Ibraheem Sulaiman put it: "The Arabs use elite readings of the text to throw away Islamic values, such as polygamy. In northern Nigeria, we ask: 'What is the law?'"[19] A couple of questions should be asked here. First, what are the societal conditions that lead a society to prefer a strict-constructionist version of Islamic law? I hope to shed light on this question in the course of this book. Another important question: Why is polygamy—and its relative lack of popularity among the Arabs—considered a particularly vexing problem for these northern Nigerian men? This could be because, while the Arabs are generally admired for bringing the world "Islam," polygamy is a Hausa practice that predates it and one that Hausa society (in particular most of its men) are not prepared to challenge. This is just one of many examples of "Nigerian (Hausaland) Islam."

Along these lines, Aliyu Ibrahim proudly recounted that Nigerians are the only people who are opposed to various United Nations commissions because they will not accept laws that are contrary to the shari'ah. This literalism that is present in northern Nigerian society is often attributed to the coherence of the Sokoto Caliphate, which aligned Hausaland with the wider Arab–Islamic civilization complex while at the same time asserting, as Dan Fodio did in his book *Bayān wujūb al-hijra 'ala 'l-'ibad*,[20] "You can't bring your Arab customs here."[21]

Despite these criticisms, however, it was clear that this same group held Saudi Arabia as a model Islamic country. During a conversation in which Aliyu Ibrahim decried the necessity of abiding by the Nigerian constitution, he said, "One acts in accordance with the constitution because I can't do otherwise, but I don't respect it." Then he added, "I wish Nigeria could be like Saudi Arabia."[22] Saudi Arabia was considered the nucleus of shari'ah, more politically significant than its size would suggest. I believe that Saudi Arabia's wealth, which is felt in northern Nigeria through its contributions to Nigerian mosques and Islamic organizations, is an important contributing factor in this admiration.

LIBERALISM AND OTHER "UNIVERSAL" HUMAN RIGHTS DISCOURSES

As we have seen thus far, the clamor for shari'ah is a piece of a larger protest over Nigeria's and, especially, northern Nigeria's place in the geopolitical order, today dominated by Western powers. Though at the first-order level the call for shari'ah is cloaked in the rhetoric of a Muslim's duty, which glosses the movement with a veneer of ahistorical inevitability, it was never long in almost any conversation before wider concerns about Nigeria's corruption—which led to speculations about the causes of that corruption—implicated the West in various guises. Aliyu Ibrahim, for example, believes that the West uses the excuse of "terrorism" and "extremism" to "root out Islam."[23] But, because he and his colleagues do not have enough access to the information network in English—and because these conversations are not, by and large, happening in Hausa—they feel they cannot adequately respond to these "mischaracterizations."

At the more theoretical level, I found a critique of liberalism. Christian Obo, the head of the Yoruba community in Kano, shared his thoughts with me one morning at Kano's shari'ah commission. He reflected on how the political history of Nigeria renders Nigerians ill equipped for "liberalism," defined here as "liberal ideas": "The bulk of the time under military command, here in Nigeria, this was a military area. The country was governed by decree, and people aren't versed in the art of lawmaking. If liberal ideas come after a period of military control, people go crazy."[24] Dr. Muzzammil Sani Hanga of the Kano shari'ah commission added that there is evidence that Westerners themselves are tired of liberalism in the ascent of the Church of Scientology, the Hari Krishna movement, and Christian revivalist churches.[25]

Western soft power is felt on the ground in Nigeria mainly by way of NGOs funded by Western governments and foundations—and these NGOs are extremely widespread. Dr. Sadiq points to the NGOs as a major political player in the way shari'ah cases are adjudicated: "Out of a hundred cases, the West only concentrates on one case of a woman who committed adultery. The NGOs use this sentiment to get money. The NGOs talk nonsense." This is a common refrain on the topic of

Amina Lawal and her case. When Dr. Sadiq says that "the West only concentrates on one case," he is collapsing Nigerian attorneys, human rights organizations, and their supporters into the category of "the West" without making any distinctions.

The perception that accepting Western money in any capacity soils the cause associated with those funds results in one of the largest cleavages in northern Nigerian society. Journalist and prominent Kano activist Bilkisu Yusuf, who is a founding member of the Federation of Muslim Women's Association and who has been its national president for the past four years (as of 2010), scoffs at the notion that her acceptance of money from NGOs compromises her causes.[26] She says,"I can't wait until money comes from the federal government!"[27] She would welcome the transparent funding of issues dear to her, like maternity rights and treatment for vesico-vaginal fistula (VVF), a widespread problem in northern Nigeria whereby women's vulvas are torn, leading to leakages of fecal matter—often due to sexual intercourse at a young age. I told Yusuf of some of my conversations with more conservative Islamist activists who attacked her efforts largely because of her acceptance of NGO money. Her reply: "These guys don't like that I take NGO money? Bring King Fahd's money! I have child mortality to deal with!"[28] The implication here is that these Islamist critics regularly accept funding from Saudi Arabia and other Gulf states. Therefore, for Yusuf, if those actors have a source of funding, she needs some as well.

Northern Nigerians are particularly suspicious of NGOs with the word "Islam" in the title. I believe this is, at bottom, a concern about who "funds" Islam in Nigeria. Since the vastness of the Islamic tradition allows for interpretations that span the contemporary political perspective from "progressive" to "traditional," it is entirely possible that whichever position finds itself with more capital can have greater influence over the general culture. Playing on the identification with the larger Islamic civilizational complex described earlier, the traditionalist camps—which regularly accept money from Arab countries of the

Persian Gulf and champion a literalist, more commonsense-sounding approach to sacred texts—currently occupy the moral high ground. In Nigeria today, mere association with Western sources of funding is more than enough to discredit whatever ensuing, progressive religious ideas might result from those collaborations. At the same time, those advocating progressive readings of texts are often doing so in an attempt to gain greater reproductive rights and marriage rights for women; as such, women and their male supporters are the main constituents for these interpretations. Yet women are not a powerful segment of northern Nigerian society, and their livelihood continues to depend, to a large degree, on their husbands and other male guardians.

Furthermore, the Izālā movement—one of the most powerful Islamic groups in northern Nigeria—veers considerably from the ethos and intellectual persuasions of the Sokoto Caliphate, which is one of the major "authenticating" pillars in northern Nigerian society. These sets of dynamics convince me that the version of Islam considered "authentic" in today's northern Nigeria has much more to do with the alchemy of social, economic, and political factors on the ground than with which scholarly interpretation of Islam is more "true" to the tradition.

There are actors in the northern Nigerian NGO scene that overplay this hand. I had a disquieting experience at the office of an NGO with "Islam" in the title whose mandate was to align "Islam" with international human rights norms. One employee of this organization said to me:

> The people who are called extremists are not really students of Islamic studies or Arabic. They have a zeal for religion but they don't understand the religion. When shari'ah was introduced a number of women were arrested and accused of adultery. Islam, many centuries ago, had already spoken of human rights along these lines—he wrote a chapter dedicated to women in the Qur'an. A number of human rights were denied women before Islam during the *jāhilīyah*. Girls could be buried alive, but after Islam you have the right to choose your husband, inherit, and receive alimony. These aspects of human rights are shared with men.[29]

It became obvious to me throughout the course of this interview that a lot of emphasis was put on gender inequality for my benefit, because the employee perceived me to be a Western researcher and perhaps because of my lack of *hijāb* and my positionality as an American Muslim—a feminist. Certain sentiments, cultures, and traditions in the region were described as "primitive" in a manner that gave me the uncomfortable feeling that I was presumed to agree with that particular choice of words. The examples provided for these "primitive" practices were "denying a woman the right to inherit" and "denying women civil rights." The meeting ended with him saying that he was interested in bringing American Muslim researchers (such as myself) to the organization, as "there are a lot of opportunities to study women and shari'ah. Do you have a woman researcher who would be interested?"

The other side of the spectrum is represented by some of the views of Aliyu Ibrahim. He was extremely critical of all NGOs in Nigeria, while at the same time championing Saudi Arabia and its financial generosity, aimed at strengthening Waḥḥābī interpretations of Islam. When I asked him about the widespread problem of VVF infections among young girls (described above), which often leads to divorce, Ibrahim replied that "VVF is propaganda. Girls can get pregnant by age twelve in Europe."[30] Dr. Ibrahim cited fertility in Europe because he sees Western-funded NGOs that attempt to battle the condition as an unwelcome attempt by the West to intervene in Nigerian affairs. Dr. Ibrahim described NGOs as "all about money" and believes they bring imperial interests to their work. It is Dr. Ibrahim's perception that the NGOs are not doing anything about election fraud, but instead focus on issues like reproductive rights, about which he said with a sarcastic laugh: "Reproductive rights! Ha! *Alhamdulallah,* the 'Nigeria factor,' extends to NGOs—these guys won't accomplish anything!" The "Nigeria factor" is the corruption that makes it difficult to accomplish a project to its end—frustration with which is, as I've argued, a leading cause of the revolution that brought post-1999 shari'ah to Nigeria.

STONING PUNISHMENT AND EUROPEAN INVASION (1879–1894)

Throughout this book, I contend that the formulation of opinion about Nigeria's colonial legacy—or, really, any historical topic—is a combination of one's subjective view of the past and, I insist, a certain kernel of truth (a theme, a trope) that also travels from the past. So we are left with two balls to juggle: one's subjective rendering of the past based on factors in the present, and a tradition that also shapes the present.

In the first half of the nineteenth century, contact between the Sokoto Caliphate and the Europeans was infrequent, limited to sparse trade.[31] In 1833 the British increased their presence by establishing the Inland Commercial Company, their first commercial establishment, which sent an expedition to the Niger–Benue confluence that same year. During that period, British enterprise within the caliphate was confined to the Niger–Benue waterways. Between 1857 and 1859, Lokoja was made the center of British activities. By 1867 British interests were firmly established, after a period of intensive trade.

As for the attitude of the caliphate toward these European adventures, R.A. Adeleye argues that they remained stable throughout the nineteenth century. While trade with Europeans was welcomed, often enthusiastically, any indication that the Europeans wished to engage in political activities prejudicial to the sovereignty of the state was vehemently resisted. Distrust was on display in the reception Muhammad Bello gave to British businessman Hugh Clapperton in 1824 and again in 1826–27. Clapperton was received warmly at first, but he later met with stiff resistance as Bello became suspicious of his warm relations with Sokoto's long-standing enemy—the Bornu Empire. Clapperton himself wrote in his journals that he was regarded as a spy, and there were rumors throughout Hausaland that he wanted to take Hausaland as the British took India.[32]

As the century progressed and the United African Company was formed in 1879, rivalry for influence in the region between British firms was replaced with rivalry between representatives of Britain, France, and Germany. The Europeans lavished African rulers with gifts, sought treaty relations with them, and promised to do whatever necessary to ingratiate themselves to them, even as they established post after post in their territory. The European attempt to secure a trade monopoly with African leaders inevitably led to attempts to control those territories politically.

But Adeleye believes that the treaties, in the final analysis, "had no relevance to the eventual loss of the sovereignty of African states to Europeans except insofar as they determined which particular European nation was to take over which particular African state."[33] For Adeleye, the caliph and his emirs were (too) slow to realize that the Europeans were slowly but surely pursuing a policy of political and economic control of the caliphate. The caliphate continuously treated extra-treaty claims that gave Europeans political control as mere "technicalities":

> Realization of the real import of the commercial relationship with Europeans was not grasped until almost on the eve of European wars of conquest. Even in individual Emirates the full danger posed by Europeans to their independence was not realized until the British conquest of Nupe and Ilorin in 1897.[34]

The troubles would continue. The last decade of the nineteenth century was riddled with setbacks for the Sokoto Caliphate. On the first day of 1900, the British administration of "Northern Nigeria" was formally inaugurated at Lokoja by F. D. Lugard, the British colonial envoy to the region. With this declaration the British abandoned their previous policy of maintaining amicable relations with the caliphate as a form of "soft power" to secure their commercial interests. Now the British goal was formal rule of the region, which they would pursue through peaceful negotiation or, if necessary, by force.[35]

I mentioned earlier that individual emirates were responsible for their own security. Hence, while the caliphate was unified up to the eve of its overthrow, it could not remain united, because of the individual relationships the caliph had with the emirs and the independent relationships the emirs had with the Europeans. The caliphate thus began to unravel. The southern emirates were the first to be captured, which served to further reduce the caliphate's capacity to resist. The northern emirates were so concerned with the French at their rear that they did not pay sufficient attention to the British encroachment on the southern territories. For their part, the British struck intermittently, taking many emirates by surprise because the northern emirates did not have precise knowledge of British intentions. This may be due, in part, to the fact that between 1900 and 1902 Lugard put a friendly face on the British presence because they were not yet ready to engage militarily.

But that day came in October 1902, when Lugard found a casus belli to intensify the attack on Sokoto—the murder of British officer Captian Maloney at Keffi. Maloney's murder was widely seen as a pretext to sell the invasion of Sokoto to the British public, as Maloney was hardly the first British officer to be killed in the region. Kano fell in 1903, Katsina surrendered in the same year, and a strong British force took up arms at Argungu under Captain Merrick, where they were ready to attack Gwandu or Sokoto at any moment.

Sokoto was captured in March 1903, sounding the death-knell for the Sokoto Empire. Adeleye calls the decision of the emirate armies to fight the British in open battle, instead of from behind city walls, "a fatal tactical blunder."[36] Lugard installed Muhammadu Attahiru I (d. 1903) in October 1902. Attahiru was given a turban and a gown, the same way a caliph appointed his emirs in the caliphate, but this time it was Lugard who outlined the sultan's duties. The sultan was deprived of political control over the emirates, and the right to appoint or depose emirs was also transferred to the British. The position of sultan would become more honorific than functional, which remains the case today.

Foreshadowing what was to come in northern Nigeria in the twentieth and twenty-first centuries, an excerpt from a letter by Caliph 'Abd al-Rahman to Lugard, received around early May 1902:

> From us to you. I do not consent that any one from you should ever dwell with us. I will never agree with you. I will have nothing ever to do with you. Between you and us there are no dealings except as between Musulmams and Unbelievers *["Kafiri"]:* War, as God almighty has enjoined on us. There is no power or strength save in God on high. This with salutations.[37]

Faced with the encroachment of a foreign power, the official narrative becomes a struggle between Muslims and *kuffār* (unbelievers).

LORD LUGARD OUTLAWS PUNISHMENTS "REPUGNANT TO NATURAL JUSTICE AND HUMANITY"

In 1900, Lugard issued a document known as the "Native Courts Proclamation," an event that many people recalled to me. I got the feeling that the grievance against Lord Lugard was both deep and recently enlivened because of the shari'ah debate.

Section 8 of the proclamation reads:

> The native law and custom prevailing in the territory over which a native Court has jurisdiction shall, subject to any Proclamation enacted for the Protectorate, be administered by such Native Court provided that no punishment, involving mutilation, torture or grievous bodily harm, or repugnant to natural justice and humanity, may be inflicted. (Given under my hand and the Seal of the PROTECTORATE OF NORTHERN NIGERIA this First day of January in the year of our Lord One thousand nine hundred. F. Lugard, High Commissioner.)[38]

Since stoning is clearly labeled by the Native Courts Declaration as "repugnant to natural justice and humanity," I became interested in the types of punishments, by contrast, that British authorities considered legitimate. In the penal code introduced by the British High Commissioner to the Protectorate of Northern Nigeria in 1910, the following is found in the section labeled "Punishments":

CHAPTER IV.—Punishments.

Kind of Punishments.

17. The punishments which may be inflicted under this code are as follows: death; flogging; whipping; stocks; field punishment; imprisonment; fine; deportation; finding security to keep the peace and be of good behviour; or to come up for judgement; payment of compensation.

18. In the construction of the provisions of this code it is to be taken, except when it is otherwise expressly provided, as follows:—

19.

(1.) The punishment of death is inflicted by hanging the offender by the neck until he is dead.

(2.)

(a.) The sentence of flogging, in cases where a person is convicted of an offence legally punishable by flogging, [requires that the person] be flogged once or twice. Such flogging shall be with a pattern approved by the Governor, and the sentence shall specify the number of strokes, which shall not exceed twenty-four strokes in all under any one or more sentences passed in respect of distinct offences legally punishable by flogging, of the commission of which any person has been convicted at one trial.

(b.) Whipping shall be with a light rod, or cane, or birch of tamarind or other twigs, and the number of strokes shall be specified in the sentence, and shall not exceed twelve under any one or more sentences passed in respect of distinct offences legally punishable by whipping, of the commission of which any person has been convicted at one trial.

(c.) A sentence of flogging or whipping shall be carried into execution at such place or places as the court may direct.

(d.) No sentence of flogging or whipping shall be passed upon a female of any age.

(3.) The punishment of stocks is inflicted by placing the offender in the stocks in a market place or some other public place for the period of one hour on three successive days, and the sentence shall specify the time and place or places.

(4.) When an offender is sentenced to field imprisonment, he may, during the continuance of his sentence, be punished as follows:

(a.) He may be kept in irons, i.e., in fetters or handcuffs, or both fetters and handcuffs, and may be secured so as to prevent his escape;

(b.) When in irons he may be attached for a period or periods not exceeding two hours in any one day to a fixed object in such manner that he must remain in a fixed position, but he must not be so attached during more than three out of any four consecutive days, nor during more than twenty-one days in all;

(c.) Straps or ropes may be used in lieu of irons;

(d.) Every portion of such punishment shall be inflicted in such a manner as is calculated not to cause injury or to leave any permanent mark on the offender; and such punishment shall be discontinued temporarily or permanently upon a report by a responsible medical officer that such punishment, if continued, would be prejudicial to the prisoner's health.

[Skipping to] (15.) No sentence of imprisonment or flogging passed by virtue of the powers given under the code or any other Proclamation, by any court on any chief of the first, second, or third class shall be carried out without the previous consent of the Governor, who may in his discretion fine or depose the said chief in lieu of the sentence of the court.[39]

Notably, the punishment for treason against the British authorities, described as "offences against public order," is death:

PART II.—Offences against Public Order.

CHAPTER IV.—Treason and other Offences against the Sovereign's Authority.

36.

(1.) Any person who levies war against the Sovereign, in order to Treason *[sic]*, intimidate or overawe the Governor, is guilty of treason, and is liable to the punishment of death.

(2.) Any person conspiring with any person, either within, or without of the Protectorate to levy war against the Sovereign with intent

> to cause such levying of war as would be treason if committed by one of His Majesty's subjects, is guilty of treason, and is liable to the punishment of death. Provided that nothing in this section prevents any act from being treason which is so by the law of England as in force in the Protectorate.

Finally, in the section on Native Courts administration, the final authority for all cases of capital punishment is explicitly lent to the colonial authorities:

> PART XVI: Native Affairs.
>
> CHAPTER LVI.—Native Courts.
>
> 11.
>
> (1.) A native court having jurisdiction over capital sentences shall as soon as possible after passing a sentence of death, send to the Resident of the province a report upon the case, together with all documents, minutes and notes of evidence taken in the case.
>
> (2.) The Resident shall immediately submit to the Governor a precis in writing of the facts of the case together with such report, documents, minutes and notes of evidence taken, and shall record his reasons in support of the sentence or otherwise.
>
> (3.) No sentence of death passed by a native court having jurisdiction over capital offences shall be carried out until it has been confirmed by the Governor. (10 of 1908, s.2.)[40]

On the surface—perhaps particularly to contemporary ears—punishments like stoning and flogging might reasonably fall under the rubric of punishments "repugnant to natural justice and humanity." Some may hold this opinion while supporting the death penalty by lethal injection or so-called "wars of necessity." When we examine the British penal code that replaced Islamic criminal law, declaring Islamic law "repugnant" to a suddenly universalized "natural justice and humanity" reveals a different theory of the motivations of colonial authorities. Whether British colonial punishments such as hanging, flogging, whipping, life imprisonment, punishment by stocks, or being chained by irons—all, with the exception of flogging, unknown to Islamic criminal law—are less "repugnant to natural justice and humanity" than stoning is a subjective evaluation and, at best, a matter of speculation. It is also important to mention here that the crime of adultery is nearly impossible to prove in the Islamic tradition (until, I argue in the next chapter, the postmodern period). It is also important to note that in fourteen hundred years of Islamic history, the stoning punishment has been exceedingly rare. The Abbāsid historian al-Athīr writes, in his massive history *al-Kāmil f'il Tarīkh,* that the stoning punishment had not been seen during the entirety of the Abbāsid Empire. During the Ottoman period there is only one, or at most two, recorded stoning cases throughout the six hundred years of the dynasty. The most famous case is that of Bayazizadeh, who was the chief *qāḍī* of the empire and who presided over a case between a Muslim woman and a Jewish man. His meting out of the stoning punishment actually cost him his position. Interestingly, the punishment took place when the Kadizadeli—the anti-Sufi and puritanical group of preachers—were active in the Empire.

A careful examination of British penal law in Nigeria during the colonial period therefore reveals a regime concerned more with control than with protecting notions of "natural justice." Procedures were put in place that compelled local authorities to seek clearance from British authorities before dispensing justice in the all-important area of criminal law. This move, repeated over decades, would surely engender a practice, and perhaps a mentality, of servility to European masters. Moreover, the details of the punishments in the British codes are curious: what is significant about "twenty-four strokes" as opposed to the *ḥudūd*-mandated ten to one hundred, depending on the crime? Detailing the type of switch that must be used for flogging—limited to light rod, cane, or birch of tamarind or other twigs—seems designed to further delimit the boundaries of the actions of local authorities. Finally, in this complex hierarchy of punishments, the only one that is not found acceptable in some form by British authorities is stoning—which, compared to the rest of Islamic history, is prodigiously sentenced in northern Nigeria today.

LEGACY OF THE ISLAMIC PENAL CODE IN NIGERIA (1958–1999)

The colonial measures discussed above continued with the enactment of the Northern Nigerian Penal Code and Criminal Procedure Code on the eve of Nigeria's independence in 1959. This placed northern political leaders under great pressure by staking independence itself on the adoption of these codes. Other northern Nigerian scholars also place the death-knell for traditional Islamic law in a 1958 panel of jurists known as the Rannat Panel. The chief justice of the Sudan was the chairman of the panel, and the other members were a retired justice of Pakistan's Supreme Court; J. N. D. Anderson of the United Kingdom's School for African and Arabic Studies; and Nigerian legal experts Sir Kashim Ibrahim, Alkali Musa Bidda, and Mr. Peter Achimugu. This combined group of British and Nigerian legal scholars visited the Sudan to observe how a nation with a similar religious makeup as Nigeria applied Islamic law alongside the English criminal code. In the process, colonial authorities argued that this adoption was necessary "if the self governing region was to fulfill its role in the federation of Nigeria and command respect among the nations of the world." Refusal to implement these laws, moreover, "was bound to jeopardize the region's commercial and industrial interests financed by capital from abroad."[41] The decisive moment in the transformation of Islamic criminal law in northern Nigeria came in 1959, with the adoption of the penal code. The conflicts between Islamic law and the criminal code intensified.

The final recommendation of the Rannat Panel was to eliminate criminal Islamic law and to import wholesale the Sudan Penal Code, which was essentially a British code used in the Sudan and the Indian subcontinent. Some of its provisions accept principles of Islamic law concerning alcohol and adultery, a move that contemporary Nigerian scholars see as a concession to Muslim sensibilities that appeared to respect essentially superficial matters, which, in any case, would only affect the least powerful in these Muslim societies under colonial rule.

This proposal was reluctantly accepted by the regional legislature of northern Nigeria. According to Yadudu, "The Minorities Commission and the Abu Rannat Panel were in effect used as a smokescreen by the departing colonial administration to give local legislative legitimacy to a decision which had long been officially entertained."[42] The principal means by which to do this, according to many Nigerian scholars I interviewed, was to codify the formerly more fluid penal code. The result of this was a vastly reductionist Zamfara penal code, enacted on January 27, 2000, that reads as follows:

> Criminal law falls in the shar'ia under three separate headings:
>
> 1. Qur'anic offenses and their punishments.
> 2. The laws of homicide and hurt.
> 3. Other crimes punishable at the discretion of the judge *(ta'zir, siyasa).*
>
> Qur'anic offenses, *ḥudūd:*
>
> 1. Unlawful sexual intercourse, *zinā.*
> 2. Theft, *sariqa.*
> 3. Robbery, *hiraba.*
> 4. Drinking alcohol, *shurb al-khamr.*
> 5. False accusation of sexual intercourse, *qadhf.*
>
> Punishments:
>
> *Zinā* punishment: Stoning to death for persons who are already married or who have ever contracted a valid marriage. For those who have never contracted marriage, the punishment is 100 lashes, and in addition, banishment for men.
>
> Theft: Amputation of the right hand.
>
> Robbery: Death if a life has been taken, by crucifixion if both lives and property have been taken, and banishment if there was a 'hold up' without further aggravation.
>
> *Qadhf* and drinking alcohol: 80 lashes.[43]

In the end, the real reason for these reforms, according to Nigerian critics, was to render Islamic law subservient to English common law.

Zinā is defined as unlawful sexual intercourse, which is punishable by death by stoning for an adulterer who has currently or in the past contracted a marriage. Unmarried adulterers are subject to one hundred lashes. Additionally, men are punished by imprisonment for up to one year. Sodomy—anal penetration of a man or woman—is punished by one hundred lashes; the Kano and Zamfara codes do not stipulate that the punishment is only for men. The Niger penal code does not mention imprisonment.[44] The brevity of this code is partly responsible for the ease with which the stoning punishment can be meted out—jurists reckon with fewer injunctions and contingencies.

CONTEXT: EARLY MODERN EGYPT AND NIGERIA (HAUSALAND)

It is useful to broaden our scope at this point to examine how colonial law affected other Islamic political entities. Amira Sonbol's work on Ottoman-era court records before the era of European colonization gives a larger historical view of similar dynamics—whereby Islamic law is only in effect in civil matters, often concerning women and children—in other British colonially administered areas in the late nineteenth and early twentieth centuries. Sonbol makes the critical distinction between shari'ah and *fiqh* in her discussion of late Ottoman Egypt and Palestine:

> Shari'ah is the sum total of religious values and principles as revealed to the Prophet Muhammad to direct human life, and should not be confused with fiqh, which is the product of the efforts of the fuqaha over the centuries to derive concrete legal rules form the Qur'an and the Sunnah. These fuqaha did not work in a vacuum but rather through their cultural and social lenses and experiences in an effort to try and find a way to reconcile the customs and conditions of their age and place with rules dictated by the Qur'an.[45]

It seems to me that this distinction Sonbol makes provides one of the reasons jurisprudence was sidelined in Lawal's proceedings. As I demonstrated in our discussion of idealized shari'ah, northern Nigerians are precisely interested in a reduced, "silver bullet" solution to difficult problems, and as such are less interested in promoting the nuances of jurisprudence. It is an extreme case like the stoning punishment that draws out the instincts toward nuance, but even here, to be most effective in the court of law and the court of public opinion, the arguments in Lawal's defense are best made with perfunctory allusions to primary sacred texts like Qur'an and *ḥadīth.* Ottoman-era court proceedings in Ottoman Egypt and Palestine reveal a society in which law figures prominently in everyday life; women, in Sonbol's study, regularly went to court to litigate real-estate purchases, sales, and rentals; dispute ownership of property; register loans they made to others; deal in goods; contract their own marriages and divorces; ask for alimony; report violence against them; ask for financial support from husbands; and demand child custody and financial support from husbands and ex-husbands.[46] The use of precedent was essential in these courts, where basic principles were followed in a form of common law. The picture Sonbol paints of Ottoman-era courts is one in which judges, though affiliated with one legal school, took advantage of the principles of *istishān* and *istihbāb* (preference within a specific school) as well as *talfīq* (preference between schools) to make their decisions. In any case, judges were more likely to rely on *'urf,* or custom, and these principles combined to direct judges in "what was expected and preferable depending on the sociocultural and economic context of the people he served."[47] Sonbol further points out that the homogenization of legal codes and court procedures, beginning in the modern period with the creation of the nation-state, had the effect of limiting judicial options and, hence, women's rights. A major reason for this turn toward reduced judicial options was that modern states did not apply precedents from premodern shari'ah courts when they built separate shari'ah courts—just as we see no precedent in Lawal's trial. Rather, Sonbol observes, modern states relied on committees to construct legal codes and then handed these to *qādīs*—who were educated in newly built law schools—

to exercise in the courts. "In the process," concludes Sonbol, "the logic of the court system, the philosophy behind shari'ah law, and the maneuverability and flexibility it provided to the public and *qādīs* alike were curtailed."[48]

Yadudu's work on the modern Nigerian legal system supports Sonbol's general observation that with the advent of colonization came a form of legal reductionism. Given the marked diversity of cultural legal traditions on the African continent, this process was quite extreme. "African law" developed as a catchall for the customary laws of the varied people and communities that came under a colonial power.[49] A. N. Allot, a scholar of the development of East African legal systems, argues that the coinage of "customary law" is directly tied to imperial interests; to understand their subjects better, colonial administrations often commissioned studies that were put to use in the service of imperial power: "The anthropologists were followed—or, some would say, were preceded—by legal and administrative officers in the service of the colonial office."[50] Yadudu characterizes the colonial attitude toward Islamic law as a "tolerated nuisance" and believes that this legacy of "emasculating" the Islamic legal code continues today by means of institutions that survive as a colonial legacy. Islamic law has survived as an appendage, causing the procedural rules of Islamic law to be judged, not on their own terms, but through the lens of "the English gentleman," now repackaged as "Nigerian law."

JOSEPH SCHACHT'S REPORT ON NORTHERN NIGERIA

The journey of Joseph Schacht (d. 1969) to northern Nigeria allows us to focus on these Nigerian scholars' suspicions of a colonial agenda meant to disempower Islamic law. Perhaps the most important Western scholar of Islamic law in the modern era, Schacht was sent by the British Colonial Office to northern Nigeria during February–April 1950 to "report on the position of Muhammadan law."[51] In his reflections on his travels, given during lectures in 1957 at the University of Madrid and at the Sorbonne in Paris, Schacht portrayed the Sokoto *jihad* history as warlike and uncompromising, and he described the introduction of their iteration of Islam—which, as we have seen, emphasizes Islamic law—as "propogandizing." A bifurcation is drawn between the "outward" success of the *jihad*'s instantiation of Islam in contrast to the presumably more authentic synchronism of "paganism" and "lighter" versions of Islam. On several occasions, the effect of the colonial encounter with Hausaland is spoken of only indirectly. In a discussion of the rise of native courts, for instance, Schacht writes:

> Now the pagans whose leader, incidentally, was a Christian, asked for the establishment of so-called 'native courts' all over the district, which would have transformed the tribunal of the chief cadi [alternative spelling of *qāḍī*] and his assessors into a so-called 'mixed court.' The District Officer called a meeting in order to discuss the question with the interested parties, and the cadi appeared girt with his ceremonial sword, and made a statement in which he opposed all change. "We have conquered you with the sword," he said to the pagans; that was his last word, and if it were not accepted, he would appeal to the District Officer, the Resident, the Governor, and the British Government.[52]

In this scene, both Schacht and the British authorities are portrayed as standing back and watching a power struggle between two "native" Hausaland groups. One of these groups, the "pagans," whose leader is nonetheless a Christian, is appealing to the British authorities to set up a native court just as courts had been set up for the Muslim population. The "chief cadi" is represented as responding with great rhetorical brutality to this request—even though, in the final analysis, he will, as if naturally, "appeal to the District Officer, the Resident, the Governor, and the British Government." Later in the essay, Schacht describes the state of language dominance in Hausaland, writing that "the Hausa language, which is the lingua franca of the region, used to be written in Arabic characters, but is nowadays printed and written in Latin characters only; so this traditional kind of teaching does not even produce young people literate in modern Hausa."[53] What is elided in this construction is the fact that Hausa is now written in Latin script as a result of colonial influence, which set English as the official language of the burgeoning civil service sector, especially in the southern areas of what would become Nigeria. This process left the north at a professional and economic disadvantage. The English language, taught mainly in missionary schools concomitantly with Christianity, inevitably benefited Christians in these schools, who could then go on to obtain high-paying and relatively powerful civil-servant jobs. Northerners who resisted Western education often fell behind, as Schacht himself recalls, without self-consciousness, about this process:

> There was, originally, a strong reluctance on the part of the leading Muslim families to send their children to British sponsored schools. I know, for example, of the son of a former notable and the son of his former slave. This last, having nothing better to do, went to the modern elementary school, whereas the son of the notable naturally could not go to the same school as the son of slaves. Today, thanks to his elementary education, the son of the slaves owns half his village, whereas the son of the notable is the servant of a European official.[54]

Schacht does not account for the fact that it is a particular economic reconfiguration set in motion by colonial authorities that disrupted social norms such that a slave could "own half of a village," whereas the son of a "notable" is reduced to serving a European official. This European official is again represented as passively occupying the most powerful position of all, as if naturally.

On the specific issue of Islamic law, Schacht perceives the British to have exerted a largely positive influence, with the effect of drawing Hausaland closer to doctrinaire Islamic law. Interestingly, Schacht frames this discussion by recalling what an "old cadi of a small emirate" described as "the progress which Islamic law had made, at the expense of the *siyāsa* or discretionary justice dispensed by the emir, since British influence made itself felt in the region."[55] In one example, the "Fulani" (Schacht's frequent term for the Sokoto Caliphate leaders) are described to have taken "by tyranny" much of the estate of a high official who had died.[56] In another example, when a witch doctor died, the Fulani "destroyed his house and the houses around it and took from them what they liked." [57] According to Schacht's account of what the "old cadi" told him, in 1900 these practices were ended in favor of the strict Islamic law of inheritance, "out of fear of the British." In this account, the *siyāsa* of the emir is described as a doctrine that is taken advantage of to allow for abuses at the hands of the Fulani. Schacht writes that by the 1920s, the emirs "still took the exercise of *siyāsa* by the Emir, parallel with the application of the sharī'ia by the cadi, for granted." [58] In the section that follows, Schacht makes a distinction between two categories of Muslim scholars: "the Muslim ruling class" and "others, who are not really specialists of Islamic law (of the old school)." Those in the first category aim to continue in the "direction of progress" made by Islamic law since colonial rule, with their next ambition described as follows:

> Seek[ing] the removal of the few restrictions which the British administration had to impose on the full application of Islamic law. Their immediate objective is either to be left free to apply the Mālikī doctrine of homicide to the letter, or to be relieved altogether of this matter, in which there is an obvious conflict of Islamic and British ideas of justice.... Some scholars from among the best are content with this, and they accept the abolition of slavery and the abolition of mutilation as a punishment for theft; as regards lapidation as a penalty for unchastity, they recognize themselves that the conditions for its application have not existed since the time of the Companions of the Prophet, and hardly even then, and that it had not been applied under the Fulanis before the arrival of the British.[59]

In this account, the acceptance of British influence on Islamic law is characterized as the acceptance of "progress" in Islamic law, and the evidence for this progress is the abolition of slavery and the abolition of mutilation and lapidation (stoning) as a penalty for unchastity. However, Schacht also notes that lapidation for "unchastity" *(zinā)* "had not been applied under the Fulanis before the arrival of the British." This raises the question of why, then, it was necessary to outlaw stoning in the first place. It seems clear that outlawing a legal punishment that was not in practice could risk stirring the passions of those most committed to a doctrinaire reading of the law.

Schacht's second category of Hausaland Muslims who have weighed in on the issue of British influence on Islamic law, which he describes as "not really specialists in Islamic law (of the old school)," would like for "theoretical Islamic law, as taught by the Mālikī school, recognized in its entirety as the only law of Northern Nigeria." Interestingly, this same group, according to Schacht, declared that they wanted to "follow the lead of the other Islamic countries in interpreting the rules of the sharī'a with regard to slavery and *ḥadd* punishments," recalling the contemporary desire to affiliate with a wider Islamic civilizational complex. Schacht expresses surprise at this desire for affiliation, saying that

> They did not seem very well-informed as to conditions prevailing there, because one member of an Emir's council quoted Egypt, Syria, Iraq, Saudi Arabia and Pakistan, without distinction, as possible models, whereas another declared himself shocked to hear that in Egypt and in other Islamic countries Muslim judges should judge by a law other than that of the sharī'a, and asked indignantly how they could justify this if they claimed to be Muslims. The debates of the House of Chiefs and of the House of Assembly show how jealously the members of these bodies watch over the sharī'a, and how apt they are to oppose even the most innocent administrative measures on the grounds that they interfere with pure Islamic law. It was rare indeed for me to hear a very learned cadi of the old school set out the orthodox Islamic doctrine of the restriction of the competence of cadis by the rulers who had appointed them, and to accept the restrictions on repudiation which had been enacted under this rule, as normal and legally valid in that country.[60]

In his evocation of the restrictions of the authority of the *qāḍī* in Egypt, Schacht elides a history that reveals much of what might be at stake for the second group—whose rhetoric is notably similar to that of supporters of post-1999 shari'ah. Assuming that Schacht is referring to legal reforms in Egypt in the first part of the twentieth century, it is important to note the synthesis of legal codes that ruled Egypt starting in the late Ottoman era. In other words, insofar as Egyptian judges adjudicated according to a law "other than that of shari'ah," this was the case as a result of colonial imposition. Ruud Peters notes that, even before French law was introduced in 1883, criminal law in nineteenth-century Egypt was governed by both statute and Islamic law. Although these various penal codes specifically refer several offenses to the *qāḍī*, these, as a rule, were not heard by the *qāḍī* alone but were tried first by the *qāḍī* and then by secular authorities. Notably, as far back as the nineteenth century, cases of homicide were to be tried by a regional council—first the *qāḍī* deals with the *shar'ī* (pertaining to shari'ah) aspects of the case, applying shari'ah rules on evidence; then the council tries these cases according to the al-Qānūnnāme al-Sulṭānī (Ottoman penal code).[61] Lama Abu-Odeh further notes that in the late nineteenth and early twentieth centuries in Egypt, *taqlīd* law (a style of Islamic law that "imitates" or builds upon hermeneutically closed precedent) became greatly transformed amid "intense European influence":

> First of all, as the Code came to be seen by the Europe-identified elites of Egypt as the universal, the modern, and the embodiment of advanced legal thought, Taqlid came to be seen as the local, the pre-modern, and the primitive. This was so despite the fact that the introduction of the Code in Egypt was the culmination of a long process of imperial pressure by European interests.[62]

Abu-Odeh considers the change in the *qāḍīs'* status, beginning in the last two decades of the nineteenth century, one of the most significant institutional transformations of *taqlīd* law. As the Egyptian state centralized regulatory powers, it created a surplus of laws atop the *taqlīd* until the *taqlīd* laws themselves became exceptions. New statutes were passed that forced *qāḍī* courts to pass European laws of procedure "as they adjudicated cases included under their shrunken jurisdiction." The final culmination of this annexation of the *qāḍī* institution was the reinforcement of the "very European, modern, and historically un-Islamic idea that the privileged and sole source of the law is the regulatory power of the state and not that of the private *ijtihād* of the jurists, as was the case under the *Taqlid* legal system."[63]

Schacht's surprise that the "old school" did not champion the doctrine of the restriction of the competence of *qādīs* by the rulers who had appointed them is yet more surprising when one considers that Schacht deployed the very same argument to justify British domination of the Islamic legal system in the north in his report on the state of Islamic law in Nigeria for the British crown. Muhammad Sani Umar has documented this, arguing that Schacht used the doctrine of *siyāsa* as the basis for colonial appropriation and containment of Islamic law. In this context, Schacht defines *siyāsa* as an unavoidable tension between Islamic practice and theory. According to Umar, Schacht, having "thus elevated *siyāsa* to the same level with Qur'anic injunctions," then posits a technical meaning of *siyāsa* as covering "the whole of administrative justice dispensed by the sovereign directly or through his political instruments of government." Having established this dualism, which, as Umar notes, Schacht attributes to "competent scholars everywhere, including in Northern Nigeria," Schacht asserts that "judicial powers rested finally with the sovereign, and Muslim judges did not possess the power to enforce Islamic law." The result, as Umar argues, was a partial breakdown in the administration of Islamic law. Umar concludes that, in Schacht's interpretation, judges are bound to make themselves subservient to rulers under the power of *siyāsa,* within the limits of shari'ah:

> The cadis are bound to follow the directives which the rulers may give them under their powers of *siyasa* within the limits assigned it by the sharī'a.... This is the Islamic basis for the enforcement by the cadis of [colonial] government ordinances and Native Authority bye-laws. The cadis are also bound by any limitation of the competence which the appointing authority may have imposed.[64]

The result is an Islamic sanction for judges enforcing the ordinances and bylaws of the colonial native authority. Thus, in the first place, these judges are bound by whatever rules of competence the native authorities might impose. The scheme therefore renders judicial competence nearly totally subservient to colonial authority. In this chapter, I have tried to excavate the history and thus the symbolic value of *ḥudūd* punishments for contemporary northern Nigerians. The theme of this strain of history is the wielding of the power of life and death to lend legitimacy to the Islamic legal system—which, in turn, lent legitimacy to the Sokoto *jihad* leaders who followed the logic of the sunnaic paradigm to amass cultural power. The British, sensing this power, moved to outlaw the stoning punishment—despite the fact that it was never practiced—and seize control over the legal and moral mechanisms of life and death. Today's shari'ah proponents attempt to regain this control.

What does this mean for the historiography of these periods and the philosophical problems raised by these histories? Most Western historians mark the beginning of the period of modernity with the Industrial Revolution in Europe in the eighteenth century, which precipitated—or, at the least, was contemporaneous with—a period of European imperial adventurism in Africa, Asia, and the Middle East. This period in the European context was preceded by a florescence of philosophy, arts, and literatures that reflected, expounded, and buttressed this period of European history. A well-known trope of this literature is the move away from theocratic states and beliefs toward Enlightenment valorizations of rationality, science, and secularism. Until very recently, Western historiographical trends have, moreover, been frequently marked by a Hegelian teleology that describes this pattern of human history as universally inevitable. Those whose histories differed—or who suffered setbacks and incursions as a result of European invasions—were often characterized as historically "behind the curve" for reasons often described as "natural" and even, starting in the nineteenth century, biological. Therefore, from the perspective of African history, I find the use of the term *modernity*—insofar as the above features characterize the term—problematic and Eurocentric. Given these dynamics, it is not surprising that much contemporary history written by Nigerian scholars in the vein of "African modernity" strikes a defensive posture vis-á-vis European historical accounts of the same period. Sulaiman's books are sophisticated examples of this trend; though he does not explicitly state that challenging Eurocentric historiographical methods is his aim, I believe that this motivation is abundantly clear in his use of the *sīra* narrative structure to describe the Sokoto Caliphate. Ahmad Muhammad Kani, another Nigerian historian of the period, accordingly begins his book like this: "This book debunks some notorious conceptions of the orientalist who contended that the *Jihad* was motivated by the tribal chauvinistic sentiments of the Sheikh."[65] Muhammad argues that most previous scholars had fundamentally misrepresented Dan Fodio and, by extension, Islam:

> That [characterization] is the exposition of the dishonest, mean and dispositional biases and prejudices of the orientalist reflected in their misrepresentations of Islam through deliberate falsehood and historical fallacies overtly and covertly manifested in their writings.[66]

One of the first pieces of evidence Muḥammad offers to rehabilitate Dan Fodio's image is what he describes as the latter's elevation of Muslim women, which is doubtlessly meant to address a criticism specific to his time:

> The single-handed battle he fought for the emancipation of Muslim women from spiritual ignorance was highlighted though his insistence that it was more dangerous to the religion to keep women at home in ignorance than to let them out to acquire knowledge with the proviso that the limitation prescribed by Islam against the intermingling of sexes was not compromised.[67]

Here, a complexity is introduced that will be explored in the following chapter, which is focused on the stoning trial of Amina Lawal.

RELATIONSHIP TO CHRISTIANS AND THE SOUTH

Do contemporary northern Nigerians consider Christians a legacy of colonial rule? I did not meet anyone in northern Nigeria who believed that the shari'ah should be extended to Christians or other non-Muslims, and most hold that the shari'ah will not and does not affect Christians. The literature written by southern Nigerian analysts who beg to differ is quite prolific and easily accessible to Western scholars. In fact, it is the reintroduction of post-1999 shari'ah that provides the rhetorical grist for the mill of terrible and deadly sectarian strife in Kaduna and Jos—though, I would argue, it is vastly reductionist to explain these conflicts using only this factor. Because this chapter is focused on painting shari'ah as a social text in northern Nigerians' own terms, I will limit this analysis to voices from northern Nigeria.

Shaykh Rabi'u Daura of the Izālā spoke to me on a mat outside his home, where a sizable audience of his followers was gathered to listen to his views, which were all expressed in flawless classical Arabic. He said:

> Shari'ah is for Muslims only, so what is the problem? Christians invented many problems, even starting a *jihad* in Kaduna. They killed and we killed, but in the end, thank God shari'ah brought an important result: services for the poor, and ending drinking, *zinā*, and homosexuality.[68]

Shaykh Daura, significantly, did not mention an end to corruption in the list of shari'ah's accomplishments. He went on to elucidate what many in northern Nigerian claimed differentiated them from the south: "In the south wives have to come out to work so both can eat, which is completely different to Muslims. Muslims take care of their wives." Here is an example—one of many—in which women as passive agents of male attention are tied to national pride. He describes Kaduna today as a split city, "like Beirut. Muslims are in the majority, but some of the Christians are good people."[69]

Shaykh Daura speaks out of a belief in the natural inevitability of shari'ah in Muslim-majority lands and, thus, does not focus much attention on the specifics of how such a return to shari'ah might negatively affect non-Muslims. Dr. Muzzammil Sani Hanga of the Kano shari'ah commission takes up this factor more thoughtfully:

> In Kano before 1999, people had lost hope completely. Life was chaotic, all eleven states were somehow steeped in crisis. People lost hope completely, there was a collapse of the social structure, armed robbery and muggings. Shari'ah is bringing order. It has brought an increased level of tolerance and the value of man and the purpose of religion.... Shari'ah has created an environment where it's actually possible to look at a Christian as a fellow citizen. It's the political interpretation that leads Christians to think this will affect them adversely.[70]

Dr. Hanga thinks it is "obvious" that people will panic about this change, and it is their right to do so. What people need to remember, according to Hanga, is that the Prophet lived with Jews but did not impose his system on them. Listening to this conversation, Christian Obo, the leader of the Yoruba community in Kano, agreed with many of Dr. Hanga's points, but he added that "much depends on who is doing the implementing."[71]

Guadebe looks at the differences between the north and south from a wider point of view. He describes the massive rise of Pentecostalism in the south as "dances for wealth and very little worship."[72] He adds that

> Southern politicians are just as corrupt [as northern ones]. There they have kidnappings—it's the same issue in another context. On top [socially] there is no religion problem, [because] they have common interests. In the south south[73] it's more difficult because of the nature of the land. Saro Wiwa was one of the activists from the south south that was hanged by Sani Abacha. These military leaders stole money for themselves. They perceive the north as more corrupt because of its military leaders. But the employees of oil companies are mostly Yorubas.[74]

Some people I spoke to in northern Nigeria believed that southerners were so dead-set against the shari'ah out of a concern that if shari'ah worked, it would drive people from Christianity to Islam. The northerners say that the Christians in the south don't live in Zamfara and, thus, don't understand that Christians there are protected. Dr. Ibrahim expands on this theme: "The south talks about the north as being backward, but the south does not have their own law. They have the customary system which is worse than the Islamic."[75]

It was interesting here that Ibrahim viewed customary law as "worse" than Islamic law. This implies that Ibrahim has some sense that Islamic law is considered, at least by some, to be "bad."

There are some points we can unquestioningly make about northern Nigeria's colonial era: Europeans who first came to the region in the nineteenth century for business reasons began to slowly amass political control; and in the early twentieth century, the British attacked militarily and began a period of official colonial rule. With Lord Lugard's Native Courts Proclamation of 1900, a bifurcation was clearly drawn between acceptable forms of punishment and Islamic ones, which happened to offend "natural justice." When we look at British penal law simultaneously imposed in northern Nigeria, it becomes clear that this appeal to "universal" repugnance toward Islamic punishments like stoning—which were never even meted out—served the British purpose of seizing power, particularly the power of life and death. Islamic law was also changed at the formal level during the colonial era. Those in support of 1999 shari'ah, the "true believers," those who identify with political Islam and Islamism, resurfaced this colonial legacy in their justifications for shari'ah—especially since shari'ah could be argued to violate the Nigerian constitution. The constitution itself was then called "colonial." I suspect that this appeal and particular construction of the colonial era was not in wide circulation when Muslim northerners held the presidency of Nigeria, as they did virtually uninterruptedly until 1999. Today, this particular form of historiography of the colonial era is folded into the sunnaic paradigm to flatten inconvenient complexity and contradiction in the singular quest to live within God's law.

CHAPTER FIVE

The Trial of Amina Lawal

Amina Lawal was arraigned in August 2002 in the lower house of Bakori, Katsina, for committing the crime of *zinā.* She was found guilty and sentenced to death by stoning in her first trial. She unsuccessfully appealed this ruling at the Upper Shari'ah Court Funtua on March 28, 2002. On August 27, 2003, before the Katsina State Judiciary, Lawal won her second appeal. Her attorneys used Islamic arguments and constitutional arguments to win her freedom, and did so against the backdrop of a massive international reaction to Lawal's case. Several actors projected their interests and concerns onto Lawal's trial, to the point that, early on, the trial all but ceased to be about Lawal as an individual. Rather, the legal and political forces animating Lawal's trial came to construct what it meant to live under Islamic law in Nigeria in the postmodern period.

In what follows, I analyze the form and substance of both the prosecution's and the defense's arguments. I also reach back into history to focus on legal education in northern Nigeria and to trace changes to the penal code implemented in the colonial period (such as precedent). These events affected Lawal's trial because these histories inspired the desire for an "Islamically authentic" legal process.

The 1999 Constitution of the Federal Republic of Nigeria also played a central role in Lawal's trial for both the prosecution and the defense. Lawal's prosecutors and defenders favored primary sources over substantive engagement with Mālikī jurisprudence, even as this direct engagement with primary sources uses explicitly Western legal forms and, in some cases, legal content. When jurisprudence is deployed, it is mainly symbolic. Moreover, trials are recorded in a form that is colonial in origin. The use of precedent in the British magistrate sense—whereby reference is made to previous cases—is abandoned in favor of developing legal proceedings in real time.

AMINA LAWAL'S TRIAL: JANUARY AND FEBRUARY 2002

Just nine days after giving birth to her daughter Wasila on August 1, 2002, Amina Lawal arrived in the dusty courtroom presided over by Judge Alhaji Nasuru Lawal Bello Dayi, took a seat, bowed her head, and held her daughter to her chest. The proceedings[1] against Amina Lawal—for violating section 124 of Katsina State Law prohibiting *zinā*[2]—commenced on January 15, 2002, in Bakori, Katsina State, northern Nigeria. The state prosecutor, who also functioned as commissioner of police of Katsina State, Corporal Idris Adamu, opened the historic trial with this statement:

> I, Police Prosecutor, Corporal Idris Adamu of the Nigeria Police Command, on behalf of the Katsina State commissioner of Police, do hereby charge Amina Lawal and Yahayya Muhammad [Kurami], both of them residing in Kurami, of committing the offense of *zinā*. Both of the accused persons were arrested on 14/1/2002 by Police Constable Rabi'u Dauda and one other policeman, both of the Nigeria Police Criminal Investigations Department, Bakori Divisional Command. The accused are being charged jointly with committing the offense of *zinā* from the time their courtship began, that is about eleven months ago, and continuing up until quite recently. As a result of their commission of this offense the 1st accused,

Amina Lawal, has given birth to a baby girl. As this is contrary to Katsina shari'ah Law, we are hereby charging them before this court.

COURT TO LAWAL: Did you hear the charge against you by the police? What do you have to say?

LAWAL: Yes. It is true. I committed the offense of *zinā* as a result of which I gave birth to a baby girl about nine days ago, on 8/1/2002.[3]

The circumstances of the arrest of Amina Lawal and her alleged lover, Yahayya Muhammad Kurami, are sketchy—today the stuff of lore. The consistent fact that emerges from the different accounts is that Lawal and Kurami's crime was tipped off by the *hisba* police, who, as I described in chapter 1, are something like a ragtag militia of exuberant youths charged with upholding the morality of the citizens of shari'ah-compliant states. In the words of Lawal's appeals attorney, Aliyu Musa Yauri, "People don't like them."[4] The *hisba* police force supplement, or even counter, the federal police, who are not trained to enforce shari'ah penal codes and, in any case, may refuse to do so if they are non-Muslim. The excesses prompted states like Kano to attempt to regulate them by creating special units in their shari'ah divisions. It is probable that some of the *hisba* volunteers, sensing the failure of the shari'ah revolution, have since joined the ranks of Boko Haram to exercise their need for authority.

Amina's testimony during her first appearance in trial—proclaimed, as it was, just nine days after giving birth—betrays a certain naïveté. She answered questions plainly and sincerely, suggesting an absence of legal coaching. In what scholar Kamari Maxine Clarke calls an "alternative moral economy," post-1999 shari'ah is understood in Nigeria as a legal system that "both parallels and challenges the Federal strategy for crafting a liberal subject governed through democratic constitutionalism."[5] I agree that the structure of democratic constitutionalism serves as both a pillar and a foil in Lawal's trial, and I further concur with Clarke that Islamic *belief* in the context of shari'ah trials is manifested through submissive actions such as Lawal's, in an instantiation of what she calls the "micropolitics of acquiescence."[6]

Yahayya Muhammad Kurami, however, did not seem to perform what Clarke calls this "particular form of dualism—that of questioning the propriety of the law while at the same time submitting to it."[7] Instead, from the very beginning of the trial, Kurami adopted what would turn out to be the successful and time-efficient strategy of categorically denying any involvement in the crime of which he is accused:

> COURT TO KURAMI: Did you hear the charge against you?
>
> KURAMI: I heard the charge. It is not true. I did not commit the offense of *zinā* with her. I know that I approached her for marriage but I never committed *zinā* with her. It was when she delivered that I was called to the palace of the village head of Kurami and I was confronted with the allegation that I committed the offense of *zinā* with her. I denied this allegation. They then brought me to the police station where they threatened me that I should accept to have committed the offense of *zinā* or else they would break my bones. So, I have not committed this offense.[8]

In response to this, Corporal Adamu told the court that Kurami's statement was not true and that he had witnesses to prove his guilt. Court was adjourned until January 30, 2002, and the corporal was ordered to bring these witnesses when court resumed.

When the trial reopened on that date, Corporal Adamu was duly asked if he had witnesses, to which he replied: "Yes. There is a witness. That is the baby delivered 25 days ago who is the product of that *zinā*. The baby has not yet been given any name."[9] Kurami was then asked, "Do you agree that she is the baby that was delivered as a result of the *zinā* that you committed?" He replied, "No. I do not agree. This is an attempt to tarnish my image."[10]

Although Corporal Adamu could not produce four sane, male Muslim witnesses to the actual act of penetration, as decreed by all major schools of Islamic law, he took advantage of a ruling found only in the Mālikī school, which holds that pregnancy is proof of adultery. Kurami's deft response to the charge, "This is an attempt to tarnish my image," clearly raises the specter of *qathf*, or false accusation, a crime in Islamic law that is itself punishable by eight lashes.[11]

The remainder of the legal proceedings pertaining to Yahayya Muhammad Kurami is brief:

COURT: Do you have any witnesses who knew that you were not committing the offense of *zinā* with Amina during the period of your courtship?

KURAMI: No, I do not have any witness.

COURT: Will you take an oath by the Holy Qur'an to the effect that you did not commit the offense of *zinā* with Amina, which resulted in the birth of this child?

KURAMI: Yes, I will take an oath.

RULING: The court has accepted Yahayya's request to take an oath by the Holy Qur'an, in its presence, to the effect that he did not commit the offense of *zinā* with Amina Lawal and that he was not responsible for her pregnancy. He also states that her allegation that he was responsible was an unwarranted defamation. [Evidently the oath-taking followed; no record of it was made.]

COURT TO ADAMU: The 2nd accused has taken an oath by the Holy Qur'an to the effect that he did not commit the offense of *zinā*. In view of this, what do you have to say?

ADAMU: I agree, since he has taken an oath by the Holy Qur'an.

RULING: Based on what has transpired above, the court having given the 2nd accused person an option to take an oath by the Holy Qur'an in obedience to Shari'ah as provided for in Tuhfa as translated by Usman Daura … [The text here becomes illegible at the bottom of the page.][12]

With the taking of this oath, Yahayya Muhammad Kurami was excused from the courtroom and acquitted of the accusation of *zinā*. The option of taking an oath was not made available to Amina Lawal, however, because of the presence of her child—proof of her crime in the Mālikī school—and because of the confession that she had previously made. In the penal code that was adopted in northern Nigeria after 1999, the section "Limits to Applying *Ḥudūd*" states the fact that there are several Prophetic *ḥadīth* that express reservations about meting out *ḥudūd* (corporal Qur'anic punishments). However, while circumstantial evidence *(lawth)* is ordinarily not allowed, there are two exceptions to this rule in Mālikī doctrine:

1. Reeking of alcohol.
2. Pregnancy—for *zinā* (unlawful sexual intercourse).[13]

The court then asked Lawal if she had understood the meaning of the charge against her. She said she had. After a forty-day period and a hot bath associated with the delivery of newborn babies, Lawal was back in court. She had been granted bail for those forty days with one "Idris" as a surety. When she returned to court on February 13, 2002, the proceedings were again short:

COURT TO LAWAL: Have you named this baby of yours?

LAWAL: I have named the baby Wasila.

FINDING OF GUILT: I, Nasuru Lawal Bello Dayi, the judge of this Shari'ah Court Bakori, have charged, and I find you, Amina Lawal Kurami, guilty of the offense of *zinā* of which the Commissioner of Police of Katsina State complained against you and Yahayya Muhammad [Kurami] to this court on 15/1/2002. The COP complained that both of you committed the offense of *zinā* in the town of Kurami for the past eleven months and as a result of this act, you gave birth to a baby girl. You confessed to the act and pleaded guilty of the offense without wasting the time of the court while the 2nd accused person, Yahayya Muhammad [Kurami], denied committing the offense. This court finds you guilty based on the charge I preferred against you and your confession to this court to the effect that you committed the offense of *zinā* and the prosecutor's physical evidence of the baby girl you delivered, by name Wasila, which you confirmed to this court was a product of *zinā*.
As a result of your confession to this court and the evidence of the prosecutor of your newborn baby, by name Wasila, your offense is contrary to Shari'ah as Allah (SWT) [*subhānahu wa-ta'ālā:* glory be to him, the exalted] stated in the Holy Qur'an in Suratul Bani Isra'il verse 32:

> And come not near to unlawful sex *[zinā]*. Verily, it is *fahishah* (immoral sin) and an evil way.

So, this court has found you guilty of this offense which is contrary to Shari'ah in your capacity as a Muslim, sane, adult and even once married as you explained to this court. As a result, this court will judge

> you according to the provisions of Shari'ah in Risala at. p. 128, where it is stated that:
>
> A *muhsinat* who commits *zinā* is to be stoned to death until she is dead.[14]

In this decision, the judge referred to Qaywarānī's (d. 386 A.H./996 C.E.) *Risālā,* a Mālikī legal compendium that has been in circulation in Hausaland since the Sokoto Caliphate. In this first trial, Lawal's defense team was not able to raise a number of conditions for the prosecution of *zinā* that would surely have aided her case. The theater of this first trial mirrors the process of judgment portrayed in the *ḥadīth,* whereby an accused person is put before the Prophet's questioning without counsel. This is, however, not seventh-century Arabia but rather a postmodern courtroom, subject in some heretofore unclear sense to the 1999 Nigerian constitution and, in any case, though they formed the basis of a sophisticated legal system that would develop in the first through fourth Islamic centuries, the *ḥadīth* are not its entire substance.

This trial was marked by its extreme brevity compared to the proceedings for murder trials in three cases from the colonial period—one in Hausa (1943), one in Arabic (1959), and one in English (1943)—that I collected from the Waziru Junaidu Archives in Sokoto, Nigeria. To the best of my knowledge, proceedings from precolonial shari'ah trials in Hausaland were not widely recorded in writing. Recording trials by written record is itself a borrowed British practice, now enshrined in section 36(7) of the 1999 Constitution of the Federal Republic of Nigeria.[15] The formatting used is moreover that of the British magistrate system. These factors characterize the "postmodern Islamic law" in evidence during Lawal's trial.

ON THE EDUCATION AND TRAINING OF JUDGES

To gain a deeper understanding of some of the dynamics described above, let us take a look at the biographical data available on Alhaji Nasuru Lawal Bello Dayi, Lawal's first judge:

> **Alhaji Nasuru Lawal Bello Dayi.** The officer was born in 1957 at Dayi, in what is now Malmfashi Local Government Area, Katsina State. He obtained Diploma in Law in 1984 from Hassan Usman Katsina Polytechnic. He joined the Judiciary as an Assistant Registrar on G.L. 06 with effect from 16th April, 1988. His cadre was changed from Registrar on G.L 07 to Area Court Judge II on G.L. 07 with effect from 1st August, 1990. He was promoted to Area Court Judge I on G.L. 08 with effect from 1st January, 1991. His salary was reviewed from G.L. 08 to G.L 09 with effect from 1st January, 1992 as Higher Area Court Judge in accordance with Federal Civil Service Commission's circular No. B. 63279/ S. 43/349. He was promoted to Senior Area Court Judge on G.L. 10 with effect from 1st January, 1997, Principal Area Court Judge I on G.L. 13 with effect from 1st January, 2000 [Alhaji Dayi appears to have been on this same level, although now a principal *shari'ah court* judge, when he tried Lawal's case]. He was appointed as an Upper Shari'a Court Judge II on G.L. 14 with effect from 5th August, 2004. He is presently an Upper Shari'a Court Judge II at Kankara Upper Shari'a Court.[16]

Like any qualified law practitioner in Nigeria—including those in shari'ah courts, the personnel of which are often the same as in magistrate courts (now, post-1999 shari'ah, having undergone retraining to serve in the new, hastily assembled shari'ah courts)—Alhaji Dayi graduated from a "secular" faculty of law, in this case at Katsina Polytechnic University. In these law schools, all students are trained in Nigerian constitutional law, with Islamic law as a secondary field. We can also see from Alhaji Dayi's biography that he has established his legal career fully within the Nigerian legal bureaucratic structure.

Some have argued that British High Commissioner of the Northern Region Lord Lugard's insistence on becoming personally involved with selecting judges for the office of the Alkalai (Hausa: judges) reduced their overall quality. Hence, with colonial influence came a pattern of appointing judges that didn't rely on internal shari'ah rules and that often favored not the candidate who was most learned or pious, but the one most agreeable to colonial authorities. The objective of these changes was to conform the traditional system to English procedures.

Nigerian legal scholar Auwalu Yadudu, however, thinks that the colonial encounter is not the only, or even the primary, cause of the reduction in the quality of judges.[17] Before the colonial encounter, he argues, it must be conceded that the overall quality of Islamic learning had been in decline—indeed, this is a reason that Muslim lands became more vulnerable to colonial attack. More specifically, Yadudu cites the abandonment of independent judicial reasoning, or *ijtihād,* which is essential to the process of *tajdīd* (renewal), as a chief factor in this decline. Attending the devaluation of independent reasoning came the loss of a lively jurisprudential discourse, a lack of innovative new commentaries, and the adoption of rulers loyal to one school of law at the expense of the practice of *talfīq,* or borrowing across legal schools. Where the colonial encounter did have a major effect, Yadudu argues, was in the decline of the training of judicial personnel, a decline that was concomitant with the desire to train judges primarily in English common law, as training in Islamic law was reduced to the periphery of legal training. The first law school to offer this type of curriculum was formed in Kano in 1934—today called the School for Arabic Studies. Yadudu argues that the increase in formality in these schools was inversely proportional to the depth that a student would have acquired informally in the context of traditional Islamic education.

Before the British came to the region with a "Euro-Christian concept of education,"[18] traditional forms of legal education were the norm in Hausaland. British educational initiatives were initially met with severe resistance, as Muslims suspected that the education system was a ruse to convert their children to Christianity. According to author Abubakre Deremi, this fear was not misplaced. However, with Western education came improved living conditions for the law students, especially much-improved health care, which "compensated their jettisoning of Islam for Christianity or a state of mind akin to agnosticism."[19] To complicate matters and further entrench suspicion, these Western schools were sponsored by government and fueled by the money of taxpayers, the majority of whom were non-Christians.[20]

To counter the rise of Western education, two new forms of Islamic education were developed in the first half of the twentieth century. The first, called "piazza schools," "modernized" Islamic education. Subjects were now learned by rote and taught in a more authoritarian manner to compete with Western education. The second new form of education explicitly mimicked its Western counterparts. These government schools, established in Islamized areas, included Arabic and Islamic education in their curriculum. This pattern of response to Western education, intended to adapt to Western colonial influence as a necessary measure to ensure the survival of Islamic education, continued not only in Nigeria but also in West Africa more generally.[21] In contemporary Nigeria, modernized schools that specialize in Arabic do not receive government funding (known locally as "Islamiyya schools"); these operate alongside government schools that teach Arabic and Islam. Some of these private Arabic schools do include some secular subjects in their curricula.[22] Once many African countries gained independence, a new and wider engagement with Islamic countries around the world became possible as embassies from Arab and Islamic countries opened their doors. These new cultural and political spaces in West Africa granted books, capital, and manpower, enabling Islamic education to improve its postcolonial lot.[23]

STRUCTURE OF ISLAMIYYA EDUCATION

From 6 to 8 A.M., Islamiyya schools open and children gather for the sole purpose of memorizing Qur'an. From 9 A.M. to 12 P.M., students study *fiqh* (Islamic law), *sunnah* (the example of the Prophet Muḥammad), and *ḥadīth* (sayings of the Prophet). From 4 P.M. to 6 P.M., the curriculum is open to miscellaneous Islamic topics. More advanced students continue a pattern of learning that has been present in the region for centuries: the study of *tafsīr* (Qur'anic exegesis). For example, students read and memorize *al-Jalālayn,* first composed by Jalāl al-Dīn al-Maḥalī in 863 A.H./1459 C.E. and then completed by his student Jalāl al-Dīn al-Suyūtī in 910 A.H./1505 C.E., who we noted was a major influence in the West African medieval period of Islamic consolidation. For Mālikī *fiqh,* in addition to the *Mukhtasar,* students study *Kitāb Ṭaḥāfuth al-Ḥukām* by al-Qādī Ayyād ibn Mūsā (d. 549 A.H./1149 C.E.), the great Almoravid judge at Granada. In this way, the Islamiyya schools keep traditional forms of Islamic learning alive, but their use in preparing students for the postmodern marketplace is negligible.

Much has been written on how the Izālā movement, considered northern Nigeria's chief organized Islamist presence, figures into Nigerian modernity.[24] An interesting question within this inquiry is the Izālā's approach to education. While traditional *'ulema* (Islamic scholarly authorities) are educated in the tracks outlined above, the Izālā's founders, Abubakar Gumi (d. 1992) and Ismaila Idris (d. 2000) were educated at the Kano School of Arabic Studies mentioned earlier.[25] Modeled after the School for Arabic Studies that emerged from the colonial Northern Provinces Law School, the British established the school to "increase Arabic fluency and legal competence of the traditional *'ulema* who until that point had been educated by traditional means. The structure of this school followed Western forms: clearly defined syllabi, graded classes, school uniforms and fixed periods of graduation following a written exam."[26] In an irony familiar to students of non-Western modernities, it was this type of Islamic learning that came to hold the most valuable cultural capital in northern Nigeria, winning mass support that has been deftly transformed into political capital.[27] However, the cultural capital in this contemporary age of Boko Haram is undergoing still another shift, with Western-educated Muslims now scrambling to emphatically demonstrate their Islamic credentials to ease suspicions that arise as a result of their Western education.[28] I believe that it follows from these dynamics that, while traces of Western legal education underlie all of Lawal's legal proceedings, geopolitical dynamics compel legal professionals to hide them by deploying an Islamic legal rhetoric that unwittingly veers significantly from classical Islamic jurisprudential form and content.

My respondents in northern Nigeria often told me that the advent of post-1999 shari'ah made many who were previously uninterested seek Islamic education in Islamiyya schools. Today, the distrust for the *'ulema* and cynicism about politicized shari'ah among some northerners is such that there is little enthusiasm for leaving interpretations of sacred texts solely to them.

AMINA LAWAL'S APPEAL TO SHARI'AH COURT FUNTUA

By the time of her appeal on March 28, 2002, Amina Lawal had the good fortune of being personally visited by Aliyu Musa Yauri, who holds a combined legal degree in Islamic law and common law.[29] Yauri traveled to Lawal's village in Katsina to offer her his legal services pro bono after a Nigerian non-governmental organization, the Women's Rights Advancement and Protection Alternative, implored him to help. Yauri told me that he was confident that he would prevail in an appeals court; he had known there would be problems in the lower court because of what he described as "extraneous circumstances,"[30] perhaps referring to the bubbling international scandal around the case. Yauri thought that the best way to approach Lawal's appeal would be procedurally—attacking the conviction using human rights arguments would not be feasible because of "the people's conviction." When I asked about arguing against the stoning punishment within Islam itself, Yauri began nervously shuffling his papers: "It is in the *ḥadīth* of the Holy Prophet. The *'ulema* are not ready to open the scope."[31]

While the *'ulema* are not ready to critically examine *ḥadīth,* according to Yauri, the people are analogously unwilling to question the criminalization of *zinā:* "It's a no go area. Before the shari'ah, people were tolerant of *zinā*—there was open prostitution. It was tolerated because there was no punishment. People became zealous when shari'ah was first implemented."[32] Yauri is willing to say, however, that he finds Imam Mālik's provision that pregnancy can be admitted as evidence in a stoning case "too stringent." Based on this, I suggest that criticism of jurisprudential heritage by questioning the implications of *'uṣūl al-fiqh* was culturally permissible, whereas *aḥadīth* that had come to take the force of law in the Islamic tradition was surely off the table for critique. Primary sources were weighed much more heavily than derivative jurisprudence.

There was no mistaking a certain confusion that overtook Yauri as he reflected on why he defended Lawal—he seemed to feel guilty about any money he had made during this process, a self-recrimination no doubt aided by angrily being called a "non-Muslim" by his pro-stoning critics. As we left his office in Abuja, several children ran up to him. He patted one little boy on the head and said to me, "You see, this is my life. In my culture, I am responsible for these children." His struggle fell between upholding shari'ah as a social text and proof-texting shari'ah with medieval texts. In the end, however, it was clear to me that in his case the social consequences of his method of defense were more important to him than fealty to a strict constructionist reading of Islamic law—hardly surprising, as he was not arguing an abstraction but rather the most famous trial Nigeria had seen in living memory. Whatever the "academics" had to say, it meant little to someone who had to live and work within this society and its mores for the rest of his and his family's life.

So why did Yauri decide to defend Amina Lawal? He told me that he was concerned that proper procedures were not followed. It was unfair to introduce the *ḥudūd* to Nigerian society at this time. Echoing a story from the *ḥadīth* often told in Nigeria, in which Caliph 'Umar ibn Al-Khaṭṭab suspended the *ḥudūd* during a time of famine, Yauri said: "It is not fair to punish someone in need. Criminal behavior should not be colored by deprivation and poverty." Speaking from 2010, with the advantage of hindsight, Yauri further reflected on the dynamic of poverty. I could feel a palpable sadness as he spoke:

> The shari'ah had died down, but people feel betrayed. The poorest of the poor are the ones who get punished. The rich steal and revel in corruption. The common man trusts the *'ulema* so much. The *'ulema* were supposed to

guide them; but the legal system has failed them. The common law courts are slow and delay justice. People were fed up with them. People have to hold on to what they have or their values will be imposed by the outside.[33]

APPEAL

These were the twelve grounds for appeal Yauri submitted to the registrar at the Upper Shari'ah Court Funtua on March 28, 2002. The judges in this appeal were Alhaji A. Abdullahi, Alhaji Umar Ibrahim, Alhaji Bello Usman, and Alhaji Mamuda Suleiman.

Notice of Appeal

Please be informed that Amina Lawal has appealed the judgment and sentencing to *rajm* [stoning] passed on her by the Shari'ah Court, Bakori on 20th March, 2002 in the case number 9/2002 between C.O.P. KTS VS. AMINA LAWAL AND YAHAYYA MUHAMMAD [KURAMI].

Grounds of Appeal

1. The judgment of the Shari'ah Court Bakori is contrary to the provisions of Islamic law and procedure.
2. The appellant will provide additional grounds of appeal as soon as she receives record of proceedings from the Shari'ah Court Bakori.
    (b) Proceedings 15th April, 2002.
    (c) Additional grounds of appeal.
        1. The Shari'ah Court Bakori erred when it convicted the appellant and sentenced her to *rajm* without interpreting and explaining to her the offense of *zinā* even when the appellant did not understand what was meant by *zinā.*
        2. The Shari'ah Court Bakori convicted and sentenced the appellant even before the court heard her defense.
        3. The Shari'ah Court Bakori sentenced the appellant to *rajm* without taking her plea and without giving the appellant the opportunity to present her defense.
        4. The judgment of the Shari'ah Court Bakori is a nullity in that the court convicted and sentenced the appellant without observing the *i'izār,* which is a mandatory requirement.

5. The judgment of the Shari'ah Court Bakori is null and void because under the Shari'ah, the police or any other authority does not have the power to arrest or prosecute Muslims for the offense of *zinā*.
6. The Shari'ah Court Bakori erred in convicting and sentencing the appellant to *rajm* when there was no evidence before the court that the appellant was a *muhsinat*.
7. The Shari'ah Court Bakori erred when it convicted and sentenced the appellant to *rajm* upon a meaningless charge.
8. The Shari'ah Court Bakori erred in convicting and sentencing the appellant to *rajm* based on the appellant's purported confession whereas the appellant never confessed before the court.
9. The Shari'ah Court Bakori erred when it convicted and sentenced the appellant based on the fact that the appellant delivered a baby without a husband whereas this does not constitute a conclusive proof of *zinā* against the appellant.[34]

The first arguments made by the defense were procedural, arguing that the Katsina State Shari'ah Courts Law (Law No. 5 of the year 2000) provides that courts shall rely in their proceedings on "(1) The Quran, (2) The *ḥadīths* of the Holy Prophet (SWT), (3) *ijma'* [consensus of the scholars], (4) *qiyās* [analogy], (5) *ijtihād* [independent juridical reasoning], and (6) *'urf* [custom]."[35] On this point Lawal's counsel further added that, while section 9 of the law provides that the grand *qāḍī* may make rules of practice for the shari'ah courts, he had not yet done so, and even if he eventually does, these must be in compliance with Islamic law. These comments appear to be an objection to a lack of classical jurisprudential method in Lawal's case, as the five sources mentioned are the classical *maqāsid al-shari'ah* (foundations of jurisprudence) set forth by al-Shāfi'ī (founder of the Shāfi'ī school of Islamic law, who standardized Sunni Islamic jurisprudence). Also regarding procedure, the defense took issue with the fact that Amina was granted bail "after judgment," stating that "we went through the Qur'an but fail to find any authority empowering a court to grant such bail after judgment. Therefore the court did not rely on any Qur'anic authority in making this order. The *Ḥadīths [sic]* of the Holy Prophet also do not provide for this power." The defense goes on to argue that they found otherwise in a *ḥadīth* recorded in *"Muwatta Malik" [sic]*, where it was only after a condemned woman found someone to look after her child that she was stoned to death.[36] "Therefore," the defense argued, "the order given by the Shari'ah Court Bakori is contrary to the provision of Islamic law." [37]

There are a few points to note regarding the above. The first is that, while the first part of the defense's argument upheld traditional methods of jurisprudence as a strategy to delegitimize the courts, the defense then immediately deployed one *ḥadīth*—without providing an edition, source, or alternative versions of this *ḥadīth*. Moreover, there is a conflation of *ḥadīth* with Islamic law that indicates a lack of substantive engagement with jurisprudence, even as the genre of jurisprudence is raised to make a strategic point. Following from this observation is a more general one that the procedure seemed to be developed as the trial proceeded; it is unclear that the defense was operating according to a protocol of procedure previously set in place.

BETTING ON SHARI'AH AS SYMBOL: ARGUING AGAINST BAIL

A special focus is warranted on the question of bail that was raised by the defense. While the concept of bail *(kafalāt)* does exist in classical Islamic law, the bail described by this court, bail as a surety, is more closely found in Nigerian criminal and constitutional law. Granting bail for capital offenses in Nigeria is rare: sections 118(1) and 34(1) of the Criminal Penal Code both provide that a magistrate court in Nigeria cannot grant bail to a person charged with the commission of an offense punishable with death. By section 118(1), the high court in the south may grant bail for capital offenses. In practice, however, bail is rarely granted, especially in northern states. Under section 341(1), the high court in the northern states appears to be completely prohibited from offering bail to a person charged with a capital offense, except where there are no reasonable grounds for the court to believe that the accused has committed the offense—section 341(3).[38] Given that the granting of bail is rare in Nigerian criminal law, and given that an Islamic explanation of bail procedure was not put forth, it is noteworthy that Lawal's counsel was willing to put their client at risk by pointing out that granting her bail post-judgment contradicted Islamic law. What this suggests is that the performance of the procedure of Islamic law was judged by Lawal's counsel to be so potentially persuasive that it would be worth making this argument—even at the risk of landing their client in jail.

The defense made a complex argument following this questioning of the bail's legality. They argued that once a court has passed judgment, it ceases to have any jurisdiction over that case, and only a higher court then has jurisdiction over the case. This is according to section 3(1) of the Shari'ah Courts Law of 2000, which provides for both shari'ah courts and upper shari'ah courts. Section 32 gives upper shari'ah courts jurisdiction to hear appeals from lower shari'ah courts. Therefore, argued the defense, any application for bail should have been entertained by the upper court, not the lower court. In that case, section 271(3) of the Criminal Procedure Code, applicable before the Shari'ah Courts Law came into effect, provides that pregnant women who are sentenced to death will have those sentences commuted to life imprisonment. It does not provide for bail.[39] In sum, the structure of the defense's argument is the following: the lower court granted Amina Lawal bail after her judgment, a precedent for which we cannot find in the Qur'an or in *ḥadīth*. In any case, the Shari'ah Courts Law of 2000 says that such a decision should have been made in a higher court during appeals. But in that case, the court would have to consider section 271(3) of the Criminal Procedure Code—not a shari'ah court—which says that a pregnant woman sentenced to death must have her sentence commuted to life imprisonment. To parse this logic further, we have

1. An Islamic argument against bail.
2. A "jurisdiction of sharī'ah courts" argument.
3. A "higher court should have jurisdiction" argument.
4. A constitutional argument that says, "If you take the case to higher court, it should revert to the laws of a pre-shari'ah court." This pre-shari'ah court will argue against bail because it is too risky when facing a sentence of life imprisonment.
5. A constitutional argument that says, "When the lower court assigned bail, it was acting illegally, and thus their decision should be null and void."

Here the lower court's grant of bail is reframed as "personal opinion," and *ijtihād* is declared appropriate only for jurists. However, the defense used *ijtihād* in their argumentation in this case. I focus on this example to highlight a new form of litigation in the shari'ah courts that unfolded with this trial, whereby (1) the form of magistrate law—in the assignment of both prosecution and defense attorneys who make subjective arguments that reflect their legal training—is at least somewhat in the Western tradition; and (2) the Nigerian constitution or criminal law is cited when it is expedient for the client. This direct engagement with primary texts like the Qur'an and *ḥadīth* using explicitly Western legal forms, and in some cases legal content, makes up some features of post-modern Islamic law. We see here that the defense used an argument that aimed to nullify the judgment of the lower court by appealing to the laws of a non-shari'ah court. In response, the prosecution did not address this gesture for authenticity from a non-shari'ah source, but rather employed the surprising strategy of arguing that the *ḥadīth* cited by the defense was not applicable in this case:

> I believe it is not contrary to the Qur'ān and *Ḥadīths*. The *ḥadīth* in *Muwatta Malik* is distinguishable from the present case. In that *ḥadīth* it was the woman who voluntarily submitted herself to the Holy Prophet with a request that he should purify her. In the case at hand the appellant was

> arraigned before the court. In the case before the Holy Prophet there was not fear that the lady would run away. In this case there is such fear. It is not certain that if she is released the appellant would report back to the court. The Bakori Shari'ah court judge relied on his *ijtihad*.[40]

The prosecutor also relied on *ijtihād* to make his case, arguing that this *ḥadīth* is not applicable to Lawal's case. Recourse to this particular understanding of the concept of *ijtihād* was built into the language of the Zamfara Penal Code, which states that enforcement of uncodified aspects of the Islamic penal code, "declared to be an offense under the Qur'an, Sunnah and *ijtihād* of the Maliki School of Islamic thought *[sic]*," is legal. Most northern Nigerian codes contain articles stipulating that

> Any act or omission which is not specifically mentioned in this Shari'ah Penal Code but is otherwise declared to be an offense under the Qur'an, Sunnah and ijtihad of the Maliki school of Islamic thought shall be an offense under this code and such acts or omissions shall be punishable.
>
> A. With imprisonment which may extend to 5 years
> B. Caning which may extend to 50 lashes
> C. Fine which may extend to 5000 Naira (= 100 kobos)[41]

Therefore the defense could argue:

> State counsel misconceived the issues involved. Islamic law does not provide for forceful execution of the punishment of *rajm*. In *Ḥadīth Ma'iz* when Ma'iz felt the pains of the stoning he ran away. People pursued him and caught him and executed the judgment on him. The Holy Prophet queried them, saying why did they not let him be? It is therefore wrong to rely on any fear that Amina might run away from justice. The State did not cite any Qur'anic authority or *ḥadīth* to support the ruling of the trial court. Islamic law unlike English law does not rely on personal opinion. Therefore this is an error. Only Islamic jurists can perform *ijtihad*.[42]

The judge ruled in favor of the defense, citing the same *ḥadīth Ma'iz* that the defense used to show that an accused person could run away from the stoning punishment. However, this is a selective use of *ḥadīth*. In another *ḥadīth* found in *Sahih Muslim*, Book 17, a woman from Ghamid who had been sentenced to death by stoning is said to have said, "It seems that you will do the same that you did with [unknown character]"—indicating that this is something she perhaps wished the Prophet would do. This would not be—the Prophet is represented as having sent her away until she weaned her baby, after which time she was stoned to death.[43]

COMPETING READINGS OF *ḤADĪTH* TO RETRACT CONFESSION

Lawal's lawyers filed to have the confession she made before the Bakori court retracted:

> Her reason for the retraction is that at the time she made the confession nobody explained the offense to her and she did not know the meaning of *zinā* which is an Arabic word. Also, she had never been to court before. It was in this confused state that she made the confession. Likewise, she is a village woman who is not familiar with courts and their proceedings.[44]

These are the sociocultural arguments, ones that may be persuasive to a court familiar with the particular culture at hand. The prosecution, for its part, argued later that although the word *zinā* is an Arabic word, it is clear from the record that Lawal understood its meaning. The following are the textual considerations:

> She relies on *Mukhtassar* vol. 2 p. 285 and *Fiqus Sunnah* p. 423 and *Fiqu ala Madhahibil Arba'a* vol. 1 as authorities for making this retraction. We also rely on *Jawahirul Ikili* and *Mugni* vol. 10 p. 188.[45]

The fact that these legal sources are given without citing the edition of the works suggests that naming the texts fulfills a more performative, rather than substantive, legal function. Indeed, *"Fiqus Sunnah"* (Arabic: *fiqh al-sunnah*) could be the title of countless texts. *"Fiqu ala Madhahibil Arba'a"* (Arabic: *fiqh al-Mathāhib al-arba'a*) is a consolidation of the codes of all four legal schools—an interesting choice for a Mālikī-dominated society. Perhaps this was the text that was in circulation at the time, having come in recently from Cairo or Beirut—where the booksellers in Kano told me they received their books.

The following argument from the defense further contributes to the idea that citation of jurisprudence is performative:

> A charge must of necessity be comprehensive. It must incorporate the date, time and place of commission of the offense; it must indicate the co-accused. For these we rely on Subulus Salam, a commentary on Bulughul Marami, vols. 3–4 p. 6. When Ma'iz went to the Prophet (SAW) and confessed that he had committed *zinā*, the Prophet said perhaps you mean you kissed her. The Prophet explained the meaning of *zinā* fully to Ma'iz. However, the charge stated against Amina Lawal on p. 5 lines 25–30 and p. 6 lines 1–25 fails to incorporate this comprehensive explanation of *zinā*. The word *zinā* is an Arabic term while the appellant is Hausa by tribe. Even though Ma'iz was an Arab, the Prophet (SAW) asked him to define *zinā*. Ma'iz gave a comprehensive definition of the word. Furthermore, the charge failed to indicate the place where offense was committed. Instead the court on p. 6 lines 1–22 stated in its charge that it was fully satisfied that the appellant had committed the offense of *zinā* as charged. "This court agrees and is satisfied that Amina has committed *zinā*."

The point of the compendiums first cited is to clarify the *ḥadīth*. But these are cited here merely as placeholders, and the interpretation of the *ḥadīth* is undertaken by the defense directly. Later, when the prosecution came back to this argument centering on *ḥadīth Ma'iz*, they undertook their own detailed engagement with the *ḥadīth*:

> We submit that Hadith Ma'iz is not a relevant authority: it is distinguishable from the facts of this case. Ma'iz reported himself to the Holy Prophet (SAW), without waiting for anybody to arrest and arraign him. Ma'iz's conduct was strange: that is why the Prophet asked him whether he was sane. The Prophet also asked him about the offense he had committed and the date and the place he committed it. That is why when the Holy Prophet (SAW) heard all this he ordered Ma'iz to be stoned to death.[46]

This level of engagement with the interpretation of primary sources such as the *ḥadīth* suggests that although the post-1999 shari'ah experiment was undertaken with the aim of re-enlivening a disrupted, divinely inspired jurisprudential tradition to improve the present, there is a sense that—in the absence of recourse to an uninterrupted jurisprudential tradition (as a material result of some combination of natural decline and the colonial disruption of this process)—exegesis and the interpretation of primary-source legal material is essentially taking place from scratch. In this sense, Amina Lawal's trial is not much about Amina Lawal; rather, the international attention garnered by the case, in addition to the internal controversy over it, rendered Lawal's trial the stage upon which existential questions about postmodern shari'ah would play out.

INFLUENCE OF THE COLONIAL PROJECT ON ISLAMIC LAW

Proponents of shari'ah argue that its speed, inexpensiveness, and ready availability to all citizens are among its benefits. Traditional courts were held in a mosque, architecturally open spaces with universal accessibility. Procedurally, the rules for the arbitration of disputes are easily understood by those who have undergone even a basic Islamic education. Yadudu argues that the traditional shari'ah system is "free" of the arcane language and "incomprehensible legal terminologies" by which contemporary legal practitioners "make their livings."[47] It was only when this system came into contact with the English common law system, Yadudu goes on to argue, that the speed and accessibility of the traditional system became increasingly endangered—a process he calls "legal warfare."

Precedent

The English common law doctrine of precedent is, for Yadudu, one of the chief weapons of this "legal warfare." In a system in which courts are hierarchized according to a common law jurisdiction, the decisions of a court will be used to govern similar decisions in the future. This process is unknown in the theoretical Islamic legal system (though *fatāwā* [plural of *fatwa*] have been consulted in courts to make decisions), which instead returns, by and large, to hermeneutic tools such as *qiyās* (analogical deductions) to deduce new rulings from legal *principles,* not cases. In the nontheoretical realm of Islamic law, there is a form of precedent known as *taqlīd,* which compels certain categories of persons to follow the rulings of earlier jurisconsults.[48] Yadudu favors the traditional court structure that was not built on a defined hierarchal order in Muslim communities or nations, today or in the past, and worries that a turn toward Western-style precedent will turn Islamic law into a "jungle made law," as he claims it did in the Indo-Pakistani subcontinent. For Yadudu, such a fate in Nigeria would be tantamount to trading the "treasure and knowledge" of traditional Islamic law for a lesser system.[49]

British judicial institutions in Nigeria were originally given quite a bit of leeway to function according to tradition. But it was not long before the bureaucracy of the British magistrate system combined to make lasting changes to the procedure of Islamic law: clerks now kept records that gave reasons for rulings, summoning of witnesses was now done by written record, and court members were eventually picked according to their qualifications and not their traditional role. According to Yadudu, "the end result was that by the close of the period of British colonial rule, the so-called native courts bore little resemblance to the traditional institutions which they gradually replaced."[50]

Ibrahim El-Zakzaki[51] makes this point even more starkly, seeing the birth of Nigeria in the context of colonial rule as the chief obstacle to mandating Islamic law. The "legal warfare," for Zakzaki, began with the 1914 colonial amalgamation of northern Nigeria with the non-Muslim colonies of southern and eastern Nigeria, which he interprets as a colonial device to dilute the north's power, which had been harnessed by identification with the larger Islamic civilization. As the townships of Kano, Zaria, Kaduna, and Jos were established, each had a *sabon gari* section (Hausa) outside of town, which traditionally housed the southern Nigerians who now came to the north for trade and commerce. It was not deemed appropriate to apply the shari'ah to these non-Muslim populations. This forced mixture with "paganism," for Zakzaki, served to buttress colonial economic interests.[52]

In contrast to Lawal's trial, the records of murder trials in the colonial period collected in the national archives in Sokoto focus heavily on the details of the case at hand. In the English transcript, very little attention is paid to legal matters in the proceedings themselves. In keeping with the norms of English magistrate law, mention is also made of previous cases. This is in contrast to Lawal's case, the bulk of which seemed to elide the person of Amina Lawal in favor of establishing the concept of legality in a postmodern shari'ah court. Aliyu Yauri indicated that part of his desire to argue Lawal's defense was precisely to participate in setting outward limits of the practice of Islamic law.

Constitutional Arguments

Another aspect of Lawal's defense's argumentation that I categorize as characteristic of "postmodern Islamic law" is the deployment of constitutional arguments where necessary to strengthen her case. The use of constitutional arguments reveals that—despite the hopes to recreate a full shari'ah legal order as understood by "idealized shari'ah"—in the practical context of Lawal's trial, northern Nigerians cannot escape their historically situated subjection to the Nigerian constitution. Nor, I believe, do they wish to do so in many cases. Recalling chapter 1, some of shari'ah's most enthusiastic proponents cited disrespect for the constitution, and religiously based reservations about following it instead of the laws of God, as grounds for their support for post-1999 shari'ah. The tension between this idealized vision and pragmatic considerations is evident in Lawal's trial. The following passage from the proceedings of Lawal's trial contains the first of several deployments of the 1999 constitution:

> We next draw the attention of the court to p. 6 lines 20–22 of the trial court record where the court passed its judgment without giving the appellant an opportunity to defend herself.... This means that the court passed two separate judgments—the first before the appellant was given the opportunity to defend herself, and the second in explaining the sentence. But it is necessary for the court to hear prosecution witnesses and to give the accused person the right to defend himself before it passes its judgment. This error committed by the court has resulted in the breach of the appellant's fundamental right to a fair hearing as granted by section 36 (1) and (6) of the 1999 Constitution. *[SWITCHES NOW TO* ḤADĪTH *ARGUMENT.]* Furthermore, the appellant's plea was not taken.... The court failed to take the appellant's plea. This is contrary to what occurred in Hadith Ma'iz where the Holy Prophet (SAW) asked Ma'iz whether he knew the meaning of *zinā*. "Did you commit this offense?" "Are you a muhsin?" The Prophet did not convict Ma'iz until he had given him all possible opportunities to defend himself. In the matter at hand, contrary to the practice adopted by the Prophet, the court passed its judgment without hearing the appellant in her defense. We rely on Al-Tashi'u al-Jina'i. We submit that it is necessary that the court should ask Amina all the questions the Holy Prophet asked Ma'iz, not withstanding Amina's alleged confession. The Bakori court judge failed to ask these questions. After the Prophet was satisfied that Ma'iz was sane, all the same he asked the above questions. Amina was not asked these questions. *[SWITCHES BACK TO CONSTITUTION.]* This error has also resulted in the breach of section 36 (5) of the 1999 Constitution. Section 36 (6) (b) of the 1999 Constitution gives the appellant the right to receive every assistance and sufficient time to prepare for her defense. She was denied this right to defend herself.[53]

Ḥadīth-based and constitutional arguments are made in the same breath at this stage of the trial. This weaving between constitutional and *ḥadīth*-based arguments did not escape the attention of the prosecution, who responded that

> This court should not be intimidated by the counsel's citation of the provisions of the Constitution. This case is based on the laws of Allah (SWT). The laws of Allah take precedence over any argument that may be proffered in this case.[54]

This is what the 1999 constitution says regarding criminal law, in section 36(12):

> Subject as otherwise provided by this Constitution, a person shall not be convicted of a criminal offense unless that offense is defined and the penalty therein is prescribed in a written law; and in this subsection, a written law refers to an Act of the National Assembly or a Law of State, any subsidiary legislation or instrument under the provisions of law. So, application of Shari'ah criminal law without codification by the National Assembly or a State House of Assembly will be unconstitutional.[55]

The counterargument that the prosecution could have made, should they have chosen to make a constitutional argument, is that shari'ah law as stated in the Qur'an, *ḥadīth,* and other sources is not a "written law" corresponding to what is meant by the former in section 36(12) of the 1999 constitution. But they chose to eschew the constitution altogether, I believe, to uphold idealized shari'ah as a persuasive strategy.

The use of the constitution here is noteworthy, given that part of the raison d'être for post-1999 shari'ah was to establish a legal system independent of the Federal Republic. It is also noteworthy because the road to establishing the shari'ah system involved, as Andrew Ubaka Iwobi puts it, "tiptoeing through a constitutional minefield." Article 10 of the 1999 Constitution of the Federal Republic of Nigeria reads: "The Government of the Federation or a state shall not adopt any religion as State religion." Both sides of the shari'ah question—which can somewhat reductively be grouped into the Muslim north vs. the Christian south—interpreted this article to their advantage. On the southern/Christian side, shari'ah violates section 10 because it infringes on the establishment of a state religion. The northern/Muslim argument is that nothing in this clause presupposes that Nigeria is a secular state. Still other northern Muslims argue that prohibiting a state religion is an unfair de facto declaration of a secular state.

However, in an interesting defense of the constitution, supporters of shari'ah do not argue, by and large, that the establishment of shari'ah is tantamount to declaring a state religion. The governors of Zamfara and Niger states, for example, took pains to stress that the establishment of shari'ah did not mean that Islam was a state religion—only that Muslims, and Muslims only, were to be subject to that law. When it is pointed out that shari'ah is derived from Islam, it is in turn pointed out that Nigerian common law is derived from Christianity. Yadudu argues, therefore, that such "legislative borrowings from a religious code" cannot be equated with the adoption of Islam as a state religion.[56]

Perhaps one's surprise at Lawal's defense strategy is lessened in view of the fact that shari'ah proponents did not argue against the articles of the 1999 constitution in the conservative opening years of shari'ah, but rather argued that the constitution's provisions gave them what they needed to establish shari'ah. Ironically, however, this strategy put shari'ah proponents in the position of having to advocate a constitution whose legitimacy is shaky. The legality of the 1999 constitution has been questioned on the grounds that it was not the product "of a wide ranging debate, or the popular will."[57] The federal government declined to intervene in the shari'ah debate, and as such there is confusion about the level of the federal government's scope in testing its constitutionality. The question of jurisdiction is also murky: can the constitution recognize the competency of these courts to adjudicate criminal matters, or does it limit their jurisdiction to matters of personal law, as has been the tradition not only in Nigeria but in many other Islamic postcolonial societies?[58]

The most dramatic test of the constitutionality of shari'ah came with the attempt by northern states to establish a federal shari'ah court of appeals in 1979, 1989, and 1999. The 1989 attempt was met with stiff resistance by many in Nigeria, particularly the intellectual elite in the south. A federal committee was formed to adjudicate the matter, with its non-Muslim members aiming to strike out any reference to a shari'ah court of appeals in clause 6, arguing that these would violate section 10, which forbids the establishment of a state religion. Some of the arguments from the Muslim side were unequivocal: to leave the shari'ah court of appeals out of the constitution would amount to "expunging Muslims from the body politic of Nigeria and would signal the dismemberment of Nigeria."[59] In the end, the anti-shari'ah faction won by a majority of five to eleven, causing chaos that led to a tabling of the issue until November 1988, at which point the federal government intervened to exclude shari'ah from the constitution and impose an alternative proposal: any state that wished to could establish its own shari'ah court of appeal, which would exercise jurisdiction only over civil cases involving Islamic law. The jurisdiction of these courts would apply only when all parties were Muslims. These provisions were included in the 1989 constitution, which, it was hoped, would precede the establishment of Nigeria's third republic. However, since the presidential election of 1993 was annulled, resulting in a coup that installed General Sani Abacha's military rule, these provisions never came into force. In 1994, General Abacha convened a National Constitutional Conference to replace the defunct 1989 constitution and revisit the issue of a federal shari'ah court of appeals. These proceedings did not please shari'ah proponents: it was decided that the Nigerian state should remain secular, with no establishment of religion, whereby no government or state could promote or hinder the practice of any religion; the government could not be a member of any international religious organization (this was no doubt a consequence of the northern attempt to join the Organization of Islamic Conferences in 1986); and, finally, the government could not patronize or promote any religious pilgrimages. This is in response to the government's subsidization of the hajj. Today, both Christians and Muslims receive subsidies for pilgrimages to Jerusalem and Saudi Arabia, respectively.

Things changed with General Abacha's sudden death in 1998. When General Abdulsalami Abubakar took power thereafter in another coup, he initiated the debate once again on the 1995 draft constitution under the direction of the Constitution Debate Coordinating Committee. The Provisional Ruling Council of the federal military government decided that the provision in the 1979 constitution prohibiting the establishment of a state religion should remain, with minor revisions, in the 1999 constitution, which came into force on May 29 of that year. This was not the end of the shari'ah controversy: four months after the ratification of the 1999 constitution, Governor Ahmed Sani Yerima of Zamfara State unilaterally declared the adoption of shari'ah in his state.

It is unclear whether the shari'ah courts, or the shari'ah courts of appeal, are empowered by the 1999 constitution to exercise jurisdiction. Section 277(1) of the 1999 constitution declares that a shari'ah court of appeals

> Shall, in addition to such other jurisdiction as may be conferred on it by the laws of the State, exercise such appellate and supervisory jurisdiction in civil proceedings involving questions of Islamic personal law which the court is competent to exercise in accordance with the provisions of subsection (2) of this section.

Section 277(2) elaborates on the shari'ah court's competency:

> a. Any question of Islamic personal law regarding a marriage concluded in accordance with that law, including a question relating to the validity or dissolution of such a marriage or a question that depends on such a marriage and relating to family relationship or the guardianship of an infant;
> b. Where all the parties to the proceedings are Muslims, any question of Islamic personal law regarding a marriage, including the validity or dissolution of that marriage or regarding family relationship, a founding or the guardianship of an infant; [. . .]

Restricting the shari'ah court's competency to issues related to marriage and family is not surprising to scholars of the transformation of Islamic law under colonial rule, as we have previously discussed. Ibraheem Sulaiman criticized this state of affairs, claiming that the 1999 constitution "reduced [the shari'ah] to the narrow confines of Personal Status"—a fact that would be recalled to argue for the legitimacy of post-1999 shari'ah.[60] Returning to Lama Abu-Odeh's study of the transformation of family law in Egypt, she argues that while "European transplants" in the legal system made possible dismissal or radical reordering of medieval Islamic jurisprudence with respect to family law, it is this same Europeanization/secularization process that places limits and sets a ceiling for progressive reforms of family law. The reason is that family law became a "sacrificial lamb" to allow for all other laws to be secularized; to allow family law to be reformed by progressively minded secular judges or protected by constitutional judges, "outer limits" have to be defined for a reticent religious audience: "It is through making patriarchal pronouncements on the outer limits that the 'reformer' gains legitimacy for his or her reforms in the eyes of watchful religious contenders."[61] Women therefore tend to bear the brunt of this most politically restricted—and, hence, ideologically stringent—manifestation of Islamic law.

MARRIAGE VS. *IḤSĀN*: THE SLEEPING FETUS DOCTRINE

The most suggestive piece of evidence pointing to Lawal's guilt is no doubt the presence of her baby daughter, Wasila. As we have mentioned, pregnancy can be admitted as evidence in the Mālikī school. It would therefore seem to be quite difficult to obviate such evidence. Lawal's defense did so by borrowing a medieval doctrine known as the "sleeping fetus doctrine," and by challenging the terminology regarding what is considered a "married" person. The defense argued:

> Besides, the law is not concerned with evidence of previous marriage. What is required is evidence of *ihsan*—i.e. that the accused is a sane, adult Muslim who had contracted a valid marriage which was validly consummated. It is possible to have a valid marriage but if it is consummated under conditions not approved by Islam the parties thereto will not possess the status of *ihsan*. Therefore there is a difference between marriage and *ihsan*. We rely on *Subulus Salam* vol. 3–4 pp. 6–7; As'hulul Madarik vol. 3 p. 189; and *Bidayatul Mujahid* vol. 2 p. 326. We also rely on Adawi vol. 2 pg. 58. It is necessary to adduce evidence on every element of *ihsan*. The failure to do that

> has occasioned a serious error. Because of this error it is necessary for this court to reverse the judgment of the trial court.
>
> The lower court relied heavily on the fact that the appellant delivered a baby when she was not married. The child was tendered in evidence, see p. 8 lines 11–14, p. 9 lines 2–28, p. 10 lines 1–29, and p. 12 lines 1–13. In the first place the law refers to pregnancy not the birth of a child. Therefore, the child tendered does not prove the offense of *zinā*. Furthermore, pregnancy itself is evidence only against a woman who is not under the authority of a husband. Therefore, before pregnancy becomes relevant, the court must investigate whether the accused had contracted a previous marriage. If she did, the court must find out when the marriage was dissolved. According to Imam Malik, if the marriage was dissolved within the last five years, then the pregnancy can be affiliated to the accused's former husband. We rely on *Fiqhu ala Madhahibil Arba'a* vol. 5 p. 459. There is a presumption that the former husband of a pregnant woman whose marriage was dissolved within five years is responsible for the pregnancy. The trial court found that Amina delivered her child in the tenth month of her divorce. Therefore we ask this court to set aside the judgment of the Bakori court.[62]

In chapter 2, we looked at the basis for the defense's first argument—that what is important is to establish the state of *iḥsān*. Ascertaining whether one has committed *zinā* is a matter of the status of one's virginity *(bikr)* or legally sanctioned sexual activity *(iḥsān)*—not necessarily, as the defense notes, a question of contracting a marriage. The salient point here is that one commits *zinā* only if they are a *muḥsin* (in a legally valid marriage or having had contracted one). This point leads to the defense's second argument: If Amina Lawal can be shown to still be in a legally contracted marriage, her child will be licit. The defense therefore argues: "According to Imam Malik, if the marriage was dissolved within the last five years, then the pregnancy can be affiliated to the accused's former husband."

How could a child born that same year be affiliated with a marriage that ended five to seven years earlier? The defense is referring to the so-called "sleeping fetus doctrine," an idea (originated in the fourteenth century, with roots in pre-Islamic Arabian medical practice) that a fetus can "sleep" in its mother's womb for five to seven years. This is a doctrine, developed in the Mālikī school, that creates uncertainty on the question of gestation, making it very difficult to use pregnancy as de facto proof of *zinā*. Mālikī jurist Shamsudden al-Dasuki notes that the dispute over the period of the gestation in the sleeping fetus doctrine (between five and seven years) constitutes a *shubha* (doubt). All schools of Islamic law hold that in the face of *shubha*, the *ḥadd* should not be applied.[63] Given that Lawal was previously married, this argument could cast a *shubha* on her guilt. Stoning on the basis of a dubious pregnancy is further frowned upon in the Islamic tradition, as attested to by a companionate *ḥadīth* in which a woman who was scheduled to give birth in six months was brought before Caliph Uthmān, who ordered her to be stoned. The tradition says that 'Alī (Islam's fourth caliph and son-in-law of the Prophet) protested that she should not be given the penalty, since in verse 46:15 God says, "Mothers shall suckle their infants for two complete years, if one desires to complete the suckling." Uthmān was convinced by this argument and sent after her, but she had already been stoned.[64] Given that the entire point of the post-1999 shari'ah experiment was to re-enliven an idealized notion of a pristine, divinely inspired past, the question of DNA testing did not arise.

The prosecution's response to the use of the sleeping fetus doctrine was the following:

> Counsel submitted that the appellant's pregnancy is irrelevant. I believe this is wrong. It is contrary to human nature for a woman to conceive without a man. Counsel said it is possible that the pregnancy is for the appellant's former husband. This is a mere allegation, because it is not the former husband who named the baby. Even if he didn't take the child into his custody he is supposed to be responsible for its upkeep and other things.[65]

The prosecution betrays little knowledge of the delineating jurisprudential concept of *shubha*. It is indeed the case that the establishment of doubt about the father of Lawal's child would have made it impossible to convict her with a *ḥadd* punishment. According to this logic, although it is true that this possibility brought up by the defense is mere speculation, so is the prosecution's argument that the baby was conceived illegitimately. The prosecution's claim is particularly strange in view of the fact that the court dismissed Yahayya Muhammad Kurami as the father of Wasila, raising questions as to who the prosecution presumes Wasila's father to be. Part of the point, however, is that the emphasis of the trial is not, as one might expect (and as colonial court records show to have been the case), an attempt to fill in the holes of the case, but rather the emphasis is to establish and then act in accordance with "the shari'ah."

The Upper Shari'ah Court Funtua upheld Amina Lawal's conviction. With regard to the *muḥsin* argument discussed above, the judge said:

> On ground number 6, they argued that the trial court erred in sentencing the appellant to *rajm* when there was no evidence the appellant was a *muhsinat.* This is not correct, because appellant's counsel did not bring any evidence to prove that the appellant was not a *muhsinat.* Therefore this is a mere opinion of counsel.

As we have mentioned, however, it is not necessary for evidence to be proffered on this matter; it is enough to raise doubts as to the child's paternity on the basis of the sleeping fetus doctrine, which raises a *shubha,* rendering it illegal to mete out a *ḥadd* punishment according to Islamic law. Therefore this interpretation of "evidence" seems borrowed from a magistrate-law conception of the term.

FINAL APPEAL

Lawal's second appeal, this time to the Shari'ah Court of Appeal of Katsina State, took place on August 21, 2002, and was then delayed until August 28, 2002. The final appeal, *Amina Lawal v. the State,* took place on August 27, 2003. On that date the defense team consisted of counsel Aliyu Musa Yawuri, Hauwa Ibahim, and Mariam Imhanobe, together with Yunus Ustaz Usman, who represented the Nigerian Bar Association. The counsel representing the state was Nurul Huda Muhammed Darma. State counsel Darma objected to the presence of the Usman from the Nigerian Bar Association, saying that he did not represent any of the parties of the appeal and, therefore, should be denied audience. Usman replied:

> Amina Lawal had not instructed any counsel to represent her in this appeal. We come into this appeal bearing in mind its religious importance and its importance for Nigerian law. The Bar Association has the right to send a counsel to any important case so that the counsel will assist the court. The State Counsel is a member of this association and he knows this is the practice.

By the time Lawal's final appeal began in August 2003, it had metamorphosed from a local dispute to a case that housed great "religious importance" and "importance for Nigerian Law." By 2003, the case had attracted a major reaction from the West, which we will examine in the following, concluding, chapter. For now, suffice it to say that Amnesty International generated over 1.3 million letters calling for Lawal to be released;[66] Western governments offered her asylum;[67] the European Parliament adopted a resolution in support of Amina Lawal and opposed to the death penalty on March 13, 2003;[68] the U.S. House of Representatives drafted legislation threatening Nigeria with sanctions (that was not brought to a vote) should Lawal be stoned; and American television personality Oprah Winfrey enthusiastically took up the case.[69] I believe this shift in significance cannot be disaggregated from the Western reaction to Lawal's case, in which stoning, shari'ah law, and universal human rights became international phenomena. The increased international attention to Lawal's trial gradually crowded out the person of Amina Lawal, such that her case became a cypher for projections of anxiety about "Nigerian Law," "religion," and, in the case of the Western gaze, "the universal values of human rights." The Bar Association had not attended any of the previous trials for Amina Lawal, and her defense team also increased in number.

The judgment of the majority suggests that they agreed with the plurality of the appellant's grounds for appeal, arguing that the prosecution misused *ḥadīth.* Moreover, they agreed with the logic of the sleeping fetus doctrine in so far as the doctrine raised doubts about Lawal's guilt. In the final judgment, the judges raised questions about why Police Corporal Rabiu Dauda and another police officer arrested Amina Lawal in the first place, when they themselves claimed that she had been committing *zinā* for the previous eleven months. Could they have seen the actual commission of the offense, or were they told about it by others? The court also employed *talfīq* (juridical preference between schools), arguing that

> Where a woman confesses to *zinā* four times and she mentions the name of her co-adulterer, and the co-adulterer denies the charge, Imam Abu Hanifa said the two shall not be punished. Imam Malik said the woman who confesses may be punished but the co-adulterer will not be punished.
>
> Amina Lawal's plea to withdraw her confession was granted, with the majority ruling. From what is reported concerning confession to the offense of *zinā* and the like from the rights of Allah if such a confession is retracted it shall be accepted. Because the retraction amounts to seeking forgiveness for the person who makes the retraction and therefore the prescribed punishment shall not be inflicted.[70]

Judge Ibrahim Maiangwa concluded by saying, "It is the view of this court that the judgment of the Upper Shari'ah Court Funtua was very wrong and the appeal of Amina Lawal is hereby discharged and acquitted."[71]

As she was leaving the courtroom with Wasila, Amina Lawal told CNN: "I am happy. God is great and he has made this possible. All I want to do is go home, get married, and live a normal life."[72]

CHAPTER SIX

Gender and the Western Reaction to the Case

The following comment was made anonymously on a blog after its author watched a news report on the unfolding stoning trial of Amina Lawal:

> Before seeing this program, I only knew about the wonderful story of Jesus coming upon a woman about to be stoned to death because she too was caught in adultery. What a wonderful ending for her—Jesus writing down the sins of the men who were ready to hurl a rock at her, as they slowly one by one, dropped them and disappeared. Yes, she was saved by a loving Jesus. Sadly there was no Savior for this poor woman who was buried in the earth—with only her head visible. *I don't remember if I saw the actual stoning or even if it was taped.* But it didn't have to be. She died a horrible, horrible death for a "crime" which is almost universally committed and probably by the very people who stoned her to death.[1] (Emphasis mine)

As we know, Amina Lawal was not stoned to death. But this was immaterial to the above commentator's reconstruction of what must have happened to her, indicating how profoundly different actors projected their own concerns onto Lawal's case. This commentator reads Lawal's case and the provocative image of stoning onto an understanding of Western civilization as a counterpoint to the Muslim world's barbarity.

This blogger is an untraceable voice in cyberspace, but projections onto Lawal's trial took on global dimensions. In a 2003 French television interview between Swiss-Egyptian intellectual Tariq Ramadan and then interior minister (later president) of France Nicolas Sarkozy, the civilizational claims at stake were starkly drawn. Lawal's stoning punishment was inserted into wider tensions about Islam in Europe as a stand-in for the barbarity and inadmissibility of Islamic law—and, by extension, of Islam and Muslims themselves—in Western societies. In response to this charge, Ramadan called for a "moratorium" on stoning. The subsequent exchange on Ramadan's call for a moratorium proceeded as follows:

SARKOZY: A moratorium ... Mr. Ramadan, are you serious?

RAMADAN: Wait, let me finish ...

SARKOZY: A moratorium, that is to say, we should, for a while, hold back from stoning women?

RAMADAN: No, no, wait ... What does a moratorium mean? A moratorium would mean that we absolutely end the application of all of those penalties, in order to have a true debate. And my position is that if we arrive at a consensus among Muslims, it will necessarily end. But you cannot, you know, when you are in a community ... Today on television, I can please the French people who are watching by saying, "Me, my own position." But my own position doesn't count. What matters is to bring about an evolution in Muslim mentalities, Mr. Sarkozy. It's necessary that you understand ...

SARKOZY: But, Mr. Ramadan ...

RAMADAN: Let me finish.

SARKOZY: Just one point. I understand you, but Muslims are human beings who live in 2003 in France, since we are speaking about the French community, and you have just said something particularly incredible, which is that the stoning of women, yes, the stoning is a bit shocking, but we should simply declare a moratorium, and then we are going to think about it in order to decide if it is good ... But that's monstrous—to stone a woman because she is an adulterer! It's necessary to condemn it!

RAMADAN: Mr. Sarkozy, listen well to what I am saying. What I say, my own position, is that the law is not applicable—that's clear. But today, I speak to Muslims around the world and I take part, even in the United States, in the Muslim world ... You should have a pedagogical posture that makes people discuss things. You can decide all by yourself to be a progressive in the communities. That's too easy. Today my position is, that is to say, "We should stop."

SARKOZY: Mr. Ramadan, if it is regressive not to want to stone women, I avow that I am a regressive.[2]

Note that Ramadan says, "My own position is that the law is not applicable." He had to use the word *law* because fidelity to the law is most important. As I've argued throughout this book, stoning, in the 1999 shari'ah moment, is symbolic of a serious, divinely ordained legal system—the only one that can organize Nigeria's current chaos. Understanding this symbolism makes Ramadan's argument more comprehensible. For many in a postmodern Islamic audience, what is advocated is not stoning per se, but the *legality* of stoning and thus the legitimacy of Islamic law as a synecdoche for the Islamic tradition. Hence Ramadan's challenge: "You should have a pedagogical posture that makes people discuss things." On the other hand, as long as stoning is on "the books" at any point (and as long as the legal system continues to be considered divine), it can be meted out. This problem is not addressed by Ramadan's careful maneuvering around Western and certain Muslim opinions, and perhaps it doesn't satisfy either.

This conundrum strikes me as being at the heart of the challenge of Islamic reform today: even if Muslims could agree on change, there is no organizing body that could enforce that change. And as this book has shown, in many postcolonial/postmodern societies challenged by extreme social disorder, there is little appetite for dispensing with an "authentic" Islamic tradition, especially one that can confer the "legitimizing severity" of stoning—as is evidenced by the rise of Boko Haram in Nigeria.

Sarkozy, for his part, does not have to placate diverse audiences and interests in France (or, at least, he does not choose to). The severity of the stoning issue gives him that rare political gift: a totally safe issue with respect to which demagogic rhetoric would be received as describing such an evident truism—stoning should be opposed—that it ceases to be detectable as demagoguery. Sarkozy was in the politically enviable position of being able to simply assert that stoning is the most barbarous of crimes, about which any discussion is obviously unnecessary. This outrage over an issue that was so obvious on its face was quickly picked up by an international commentariat that is frequently critical of Islam and Muslims. For example, Paul Berman, in his 2010 book *The Flight of the Intellectuals,* describes the exchange between Ramadan and Sarkozy as Ramadan's "missed opportunity" to speak with absolute clarity about violence against women:

> Ramadan couldn't do it. Here was his Qutbian[3] moment, the moment of frisson. The seventh century had suddenly appeared, poking out from beneath the modern rhetoric of feminism and rights. A moment of barbarism. A thrill. The whole panorama of Muslim women suddenly deployed across the television screens of France—the panorama of violence that is condoned, sanctified, and even mandated by the highest authorities. And here was Sarkozy, recoiling in horror: the bourgeoisie, shocked at last.[4]

Berman's invocation of Sayyid Qutb (d. 1966) is not accidental. Qutb was a Muslim Brotherhood intellectual and activist who is thought to have provided the intellectual heft for the splintering and radicalization of the movement through such binary-producing texts as *Milestones* (1964), wherein the world is divided between "the good" *Dar al-Islam* (the abode of Islam), and "the misguided" *Dar al-Harb* (the abode of war). Berman's point is to tie Ramadan's careful or obfuscating treatment of this issue—depending on your perspective—to international terrorism. This theater is aided, it must be noted, by the fact that Ramadan did not bear down on one side or another of this issue. Wider French opinion was also duly outraged. Responding to this exchange on French television, Éric Zemmour wrote in *Le Figaro:* "And suddenly Islamism has become likable ... [There is] a climate, an *air du temps,* a fashion."[5] Returning to this exchange eight years later in his 2011 presidential campaign, Sarkozy made full political use of the triumphant exchange, praising Jean-François Copé, the head of the UMP party *(Union pour un Mouvement Populaire),* for telling Ramadan—in yet another exchange on French television—that he had "no right" to give moral lessons about Islamophobia in Europe when "he had never fully condemned the stoning of women."[6] When Ramadan replied that he was attempting to spark a debate in the Islamic world, Copé predictably scoffed, "Is there a debate to be had about stoning?"[7]

This book attempts to show that there is a debate to be had about stoning, but it is not the fruitless debate demanded by Sarkozy, Berman, and Copé. Instead, the debate is much more difficult and entrenched. Can Islamic law be reformed in a postcolonial/postmodern climate in which many Muslim-majority societies understand the medieval jurisprudential tradition as conferring stability to chaotic situations, historically grounded sovereignty to weak states, and moral order to cultures fraying under economic pressure? If intellectuals like Ramadan were to move beyond the politically unsatisfying "moratorium" and declare stoning invalid, on what credible basis could she or he make that case to Muslims suffering under the aforementioned conditions? Do contemporary Muslims have the political will and the anti-corporal-punishment, and even feminist, commitments to conduct this reform? If not, how can that groundwork be established, and what would be the role of Western intellectuals, intellectual traditions, and politicians in that process? Taking a very different side of this debate, Professor Murray Last, a leading scholar of the Sokoto Caliphate, shared his reflections on Lawal's case with me in London one evening: "Stoning is not about Nigeria, but about the fantasy world of the West."[8] Stoning is considered uniquely barbarous in the modern Western consciousness, and it has now come to be associated exclusively with the Muslim world. Indeed, the stoning punishment has been found to be in violation of several human rights conventions to which Nigeria is a signatory, creating a plane of potential illegality that northern Nigerian shari'ah proponents read as the "legal warfare" I discussed in chapter 4. Shari'ah is in potential violation of the International Covenant on Civil and Political Rights (1966), the Convention for the Elimination of All Forms of Discrimination against Women (1979), the Convention against Torture and Other Cruel, Inhuman or Degrading Treatment or Punishment (1984), and the Convention on the Rights of the Child (1989).[9] The punishment can be described as torture and as cruel or degrading; children's rights may be violated and religious freedom circumscribed; and the principle that all are equal before the law can be threatened. Many of these violations of the Islamic penal code are specific to gender: the Zamfara Penal Code section 76 permits physical correction of a wife by her husband and stipulates that because of implied consent, a man is not capable of raping his wife.[10] Section 68 of Niger's penal code holds that the testimony of men is worth more than that of women in proving *zinā*.[11] Islamic penal law also brings potential violations of the right to freedom of religion, as Muslims cannot change their religion—or commit apostasy *(riḍa)*—on pain of death. *Riḍa* also entails the loss of civil rights, such as the right to be married (marriage of an apostate is dissolved immediately) and the right to own property. This international order has the optical and practical effect of placing Nigerians at odds with international human rights standards for following what they understand to be Islamic law.

Western human rights organizations' initial response to Lawal's sentencing was unequivocal condemnation, and these organizations were, in many instances, unaware of both the basic context of Lawal's case and the measures being taken by local actors to quash Lawal's conviction. Bill Graham, Canada's foreign affairs minister, remarked that "we totally reject that shari'ah law should act in a way that is contrary to international norms."[12] Amnesty International beseeched Nigerian authorities to abolish all torture and cruel, inhuman, or degrading punishments, and to observe the legally binding international human rights conventions to which Nigeria is a signatory.[13] Interestingly, Amnesty International further urged Nigeria to bring its laws in line with the 1999 Nigerian constitution, meaning that the organization was unaware of the robust debate in the north that urged precisely this position. U.S. President Bill Clinton personally pleaded for Lawal's life to be spared during a speech on democratization to an audience that included Nigerian President Olusegun Obasanjo as well as several other West African leaders. Clinton said, "I hope and pray that the legal system will find a way to pardon a young woman convicted to death for bearing a child out of wedlock." [14] President Clinton likewise did not seem to be aware that President Obasanjo, a Christian from the south, likely opposed shari'ah more than he. For all practical purposes, it was not within Obasanjo's power to stop this case.

Lawal's acquittal is often attributed to Western outrage. I believe, however, that the Western reaction did not play a direct role (and was sometimes counterproductive) in influencing popular sentiment—and I see no direct evidence that the Western reaction had an effect at the level of the judiciary and prosecution. This is an opinion that changed dramatically for me upon concluding this research. I had assumed, like many others, that Lawal was ultimately released because of Western pressure. But the reality was more complex. Regarding Amnesty International's letter-writing campaign, for example, Governor Ahmed Sani Yerima's response was typical, here recounted by Andrew Ubaka Iwobi:

> Also pertinent are comments by Governor Sani of Zamfara State, who recently stated that he had received at least 8,000 letters from human rights and nongovernmental organizations pointing out that the world is now a global community which has gone beyond the age of amputation, flogging and so on. He dismissed such letters with the observation that their writers did not appear to appreciate that such punishments had been ordained by the Qur'an.[15]

This is not to say that Western pressure had no effect. It did. I believe that Western intervention exerted influence through non-governmental organizations (NGOs)—and this influence was paradoxical. Nigerian NGOs like the Women's Rights Advancement and Protection Alternative (WRAPA), recipients of Western aid, were instrumental in getting Lawal excellent legal counsel—here the effect of Western intervention is clear, and it helped Lawal win her case. The defense, however, was savvy enough to assess the public climate as extremely hostile to arguments that drew on the language of "universal human rights"—for this, after all, would challenge "idealized shari'ah"—and were thus able to react effectively, calibrating their arguments in Islamic (and, to a lesser extent, constitutional) rhetoric. Western funding was helpful here, but Nigerian intellectual labor was essential to Lawal's acquittal.

DEFIANT NORTHERN NIGERIAN REACTIONS TO THE CRITICISM

> Modern Muslims know nothing about Islam. And that's why they're modern.
>
> Dr. Guando, Professor of Islamic Studies, University of Sokoto

The northern Nigerian reaction to the Western outcry recalls a history of Western attempts to discipline, control, and subvert an Islamic order considered "native" and thereby "authentic."[16] Northern Nigerian opposition to the various international human rights statutes that shari'ah risks violating becomes more comprehensible when viewed through this wider historical lens, as I have discussed throughout this book. However, while the stated reasons for northern Nigerian opposition to Western intervention sometimes evoke this history of legal warfare, opposition takes different forms—one of which is to defiantly assert an immutable, divinely mandated order that is frozen in time. As one informant in Nigeria put it:

> Most of the Western world believes that they have a moral obligation to stop Amina Lawal's stoning to death sentence. It is, nevertheless, far more complex. The worldviews of the two societies are different. The West has discarded God as the pivot of its philosophy and chose Man. All prohibitions of God, therefore, were legalized except for those that disturb man's pleasure. Hence sex by consenting adults is not a crime in Western societies but in Muslim societies all these are illegal because the Muslims still uphold Devine *[sic]* prohibitions.[17]

Muslim societies are framed as "still uphold[ing] divine prohibitions," as if the differences in the worldviews of the two societies are ahistorical and essentially entrenched. However, as I have mentioned, stoning and punishments for illegal sexual activity in the Islamic tradition have been exceedingly rare throughout history—while Western societies have also taken legal steps to control female sexuality throughout their history. Claiming that Islamic and Western societies stand in interminable opposition is instead a contemporary northern Nigerian attempt to reclaim an Islamic order in the face of opposition from the West by emphasizing some essential civilizational difference. In response to a historical challenge, ahistoricism is a refuge.

It thus appears as if many northern Nigerian commentators have paradoxically internalized a particular Western discourse that pits their society against "modernity." As Iwobi writes:

> Even though the Nigerian Government has shown no inclination to withdraw from treaties prohibiting cruel and inhuman punishments which it has duly ratified, the operation of these treaties within the Nigerian context has been vigorously contested by Muslim advocates of the Shari'ah reforms. The prevailing atittude in Muslim circles is vividly exemplified by a recent publication of the Supreme Council for Shari'ah in Nigeria (SCSN) which portrayed Nigeria's ratification of various United Nations instruments concerned with human rights a spat of a "United Nations covert campaign against Islam." [18]

Many northern Nigerians commented that the Western reaction played into the hands of the most conservative elements. As Hamidu Bobboyi put it, "No one took the Western reaction seriously, they simply rallied to the conservative shari'ah base. They said: 'We must be doing something right for these non-Muslims to be reacting this way.'" [19] With the Western oppostion came the hardening of conservative northern Nigerian views, summarized here, for example, by the Honorable Justice Abdulkadir Orire, retired grand *qāḍī* of Kwara State, during a seminiar on shari'ah organized by Jamaat Nasril al-Islam in Kaduna in 2000:

> There is no doubt that Shari'ah had created a lot of bad blood between Muslims and those who are not Muslims, not only in this country but anywhere whenever Muslims decided to live a life of Islam. Shari'ah to non Muslims is like red-rag in the face of a circus bull. To them, the mentioning of Shari'ah is tantamount to declaring the country an Islamic state where in their belief all people of other faiths will be forced to accept Islam or be killed. As a result of this, they maligned the law, ridiculed it and called it names such as barbaric, rigid, harsh, archaic and unsuitable for our modern age.[20]

This diagnosis understands the West's demonization of shari'ah as having caused pejorative labels of Islamic law. The response has hardened theories of an essential difference between the West and Islam among Nigerian proponents of shari'ah.

THE QUESTION OF GENDER

In the course of interviewing a group of intellectual Islamist voices in northern Nigeria, I was eventually handed a book called *Shari'ah: Ruling by Laws Other Than What Allah Revealed; Conditions and Rulings,* by Dr. Abdur-Rahmaan ibn Salih al-Mahmood, that illustrates the degree to which promotion of an unyielding, legal order is taken as essential to Muslim *faith.* This book argues against a private notion of faith, claiming in stark terms that anything short of *acting* on behalf of "Islam" is *kufr* (unbelief), thereby "putting one beyond the pale of Islam":

> As the Islamic ruling on ruling by something other than that which Allah has revealed is not clear in the minds of the majority of Muslims, most Muslims do not realize the seriousness of this deviation and its nature, because the views of the *Murji'ah* are so widespread among the masses. These views say that Islam or faith is simply the matter of what is in the heart, and if a person believes in his heart then nothing can put him beyond the pale of Islam, no matter what he does. This is contrary to the view of the *salaf* and the scholars who followed in their footsteps, who affirmed that there are certain actions which may constitute major *kufr* and thus put a person beyond the pale of Islam. One of these actions, the focus of this

> book, is the promulgation of laws and legislative systems other than shari'ah, making them binding upon the people and forcing them to refer to these man-made laws for judgment.[21]

The Murji'ah—the wayward Muslims in this formulation—were a group who opposed the Khārijite movement in the early centuries of Islam, holding that judgment of a Muslim's piety should be left to God in the afterlife, and, as such, an assessment could not be made by mere men. It is this private notion of religion, resonant with a Protestant Western notion of religion, that al-Mahmood objects to. If Islam is not active, then it cannot help solve Nigeria's pressing problems. If one peasant woman is caught in the fray, according to this thinking, it does not invalidate the overall structure.

The promulgation of these laws and other such histories seemed to inform Dr. Sadiq's reaction when I asked him his opinion about the lack of punishment for Lawal's alleged lover, which he then attributed to "rules and regulations." Desires of individual women are subsumed under the more "important" imperative of collective political interest—be it expansion of empire, state, or, in this case, shari'ah order.[22] I believe that this theme—sublimating women's individual desires to the imperatives of a larger political order—is recurrent, both intellectually and especially legally, in Islamic history. Dr. Sadiq waves this concern away, saying:

> For the women, unfortunately or not there is evidence with a pregnancy. The man cannot be prosecuted because there's only the evidence of the woman [pregnancy]. In Islamic history, notice the Prophet won't even listen to the woman [who said she was guilty of adultery and asked to be punished], he says she is crazy and should go home.[23]

That the Prophet told a confessing adulterous woman to "go home" is meant to suggest that because of the natural disadvantage suffered by women in the Islamic legal system, in this instance because of the evidentiary nature of their pregnancy (a rule allowed in the Mālikī school), the Prophet repeatedly attempted to give the woman a means of escape.

Dr. Sadiq also added, as if to soften the immutability of "rules and regulations": "Very few *'ulema* are capable of understanding the shari'ah in the twenty-first century. Uthmān Dan Fodio has a saying: the best *'ālim* (learned person) is the *'ālim* of the present community. Not of the past."[24] Dr. Sadiq's comment, and his invocation of Uthmān Dan Fodio's authority in keeping with the sunnaic paradigm, seems to convey ambivalence about meting out the stoning punishment, but not enough to engender sympathy for the person of Amina Lawal.

Dr. Guando of the University of Sokoto was sanguine as he reflected on the same ambivalence in Lawal's case, conveying both fatalism about the rules and regulations of her legal case and an awareness—or perhaps rationalization—that she could have escaped had she wanted to:

> Even within the context of Islam, she could have denied it. People are also eager to see her stoned. Overall, the love of Muslims for the Prophet's sunnah is more than their love of Amina Lawal. They thought the lawyers and the judges themselves did their best as Muslims. Setting her free is what the shari'ah was after.[25]

Here, the almost pro forma need to assert that Muslims love the Prophet more than Amina Lawal is juxtaposed with several caveats about the ease with which Lawal could have escaped, ending with the assertion that in the end, "the shari'ah" is trying to set her free. To insist on a literal reading of the law while at the same time foregrounding a loophole therein can be read as another instance of northern Nigerian ambivalence toward the stoning punishment.

What these controversies suggest is that individual rights are not an operative concept in this shari'ah scheme, and one woman's fate will be sacrificed for larger social continuity without much public protest. This sacrificial narrative is one that invokes longer histories of the sacrifice of women—recalling scholarship on witch sacrifice—to preserve the body politic.

By focusing on the rhetoric of "saving" Muslim women in the current U.S./allied war on terrorism, Leila Ahmed traces the contemporary manifestation of a theme that was poignantly coined by Gayatri Spivak: "white men saving brown women from brown men."[26] In this complex terrain wherein the politics of outrage about the oppression of Muslim women often conceals imperial and other agendas, scholars and activists for Muslim women's rights who are aware of these dynamics take up a difficult and delicate topic. I present now the strategies and ethical admonishments of two scholars with both scholarly and practical experience engaging this problematic issue. Asifa Quraishi, in her 2011 essay, "What If Sharia Weren't the Enemy? Rethinking International Women's Rights Advocacy on Islamic Law," draws upon her experience as a legal scholar and advocate in her critique of human rights organizations' treatment of Islamic law, arguing that Western-based advocacy on behalf of women should omit reference to Islamic law altogether. Quraishi observes that feminist advocacy that positions itself in opposition to shari'ah contributes to a false dichotomy between being "pro-Islam" and "pro-women," a bifurcation that is unnecessary and counterproductive. Quraishi suggests an alternative strategy for transnational feminist work:

> My proposal requires a significant paradigm shift. Specifically, I ask internationally-active women's rights advocates, especially those in or from the West, to eliminate any reference to Islamic law (positive or negative) from their advocacy and international pressure campaigns. I make this request both as a feminist and as a Muslim. In my observation, the presumed conflict between women's rights and *sharia* may have ultimately brought more harm than good to the women ... that women's rights advocates seek to help. I believe that a simple but serious change in the way these advocates address Islamic law would go a long way toward breaking this destructive pattern.[27]

Drawing on her scholarship about an infamous northern Nigerian case in which the proposed flogging of a young girl was hastened—not stopped—by Western involvement in the case, which was often couched in zero-sum oppositional rhetoric against Islamic law, Quraishi concludes that Western arguments that engage shari'ah are counterproductive and hinder future human rights efforts.

Quraishi's position follows logically from the fact that NGO strategies hindered the case that Quraishi references. Therefore, while the call for NGOs to stop referencing Islamic law makes sense, I believe that such a suggestion must be accompanied by Muslim scholars making a commitment to engage Islamic law in critical ways. In the absence of that commitment, it is difficult to ask NGOs to cease and desist this work that must be done by someone.

In her 2006 essay "Taking Islamic Law Seriously: INGOs and the Battle for Muslim Hearts and Minds," Naz K. Modirzadeh takes a medial position in relation to Quraishi's, arguing that the failure of international NGOs (INGOs) to engage shari'ah leaves open the dangerous possibility that interpretation will be left to those deemed most authentic. This would be determined simply by identifying who claims a Muslim identity, making it difficult to ascertain actual expertise. Modirzadeh therefore argues for a strategy whereby NGOs expand their mandate to "deepen their expertise, develop new research techniques, or enter fields that were previously considered ill-suited to human rights work."[28] Modirzadeh's suggestions for NGOs include hiring shari'ah experts, developing a permanent presence in the Middle East (the geographic focus of her article), and devoting large portions of reports to discussing the rules and debates that animate a particular Islamic legal struggle; finally, the NGOs should craft recommendations based largely on Islamic approaches to legal reform. These methods could aid in the development of

> Bold and creative thinking on Islamic law tying together various parts of the world, from Cairo to New York, and from Brussels to Baghdad. INGOs could also marshal their significant resources (intellectual, financial, and political) to create alliances and networks among activists, Islamic legal scholars, judges, and lawyers working in different ways on similar issues.[29]

Modirzadeh's approach would generate a cadre of legal scholars that directly aid in policy formation. It is worth wondering how the dynamic relationship between NGOs and Islamic legal scholars would influence those scholars; perhaps their participation would enliven a more contemporary form of Islamic jurisprudence. Modirzadeh's suggestion would seem to open an avenue for the difficult and elusive task of Islamic legal reform that I touched on earlier.

NIGERIAN VOICES

One evening in Nigeria, I was sitting on a couch in the dimly lit, stylish living room of a woman I had come to know.[30] She began to ask me about myself. I cut to the chase and told her that I was not married, which I correctly suspected was the purpose of her polite probing. She seemed relieved at the confession, attributing this status to my "open-minded Westernism." She continued, "You know, I didn't want to tell you this earlier in the car but... well, we have this 'problem' here in Nigeria," and she began to recount in extreme detail the story of a woman from a certain northern state who had sexually propositioned her. She described her feelings toward this woman—exhilaration and confusion—her words came out in a flood; she spoke of other instances in which she had heard of lesbian activity, and how much of an interest she took in this "problem," and it soon became clear to me that she knew all of the lesbian enclaves in the north and maybe one or two in the south.

She spoke floridly of the sensuality of scents, and then, lit by a lone light, showed me her very extensive collection of perfumes. These scents, she told me, bring sexual feelings out in her when she smells them on a woman, and that scares her. Sometimes she travels with prominent women of the town, and they share the same bed and she smells them. "I am vulnerable to this," she said. "I just try to keep myself safe. One slip-up, and there could be a disaster." Not a moral disaster, I sensed, but a social one—or perhaps it was I who made this distinction so easily.

She described a woman she had met in a neighboring state who had clearly captivated her. This woman was driving a jeep and smoking a cigarette—outside! Not hiding in the bathroom. She told me that a friend of hers had called her one day and said, "Have you had an orgasm?" She replied, "I have had sex more times than I can count. But orgasm? Please! Ask the next person!" Through her laughter at recalling this conversation, she estimated that 80 percent of Hausa women have not had orgasms; they have sex simply to please their husbands. "It's all about men," she said, shaking her head. "You don't even trust the man you're lying with. They might leave you tomorrow. Justice is a word that is not even known in our dictionary. Love is not an issue in Nigeria. It is all about what you have—your position in society." For example, HIV affects the wife because it is thought that only she should be tested. If she is positive, he "sends her packing."

Aliyu Yauri, Lawal's lawyer, agrees that, in practice, shari'ah tends to disproportionately regulate and target women, describing this as the "mentality and tradition in the north. Even without shari'ah, the society pays a high level of attention to women. There is a culture of regulating women and 'putting eyes on them.'"[31] Shaykh Malam Sanusi Khalil of the Izālā movement agrees, perhaps a bit surprisingly, with this sentiment, saying simply, "It is part of ignorance that women are singled out."[32] These men seem to recognize the disproportionate focus on women, but they attribute it to a misapplication of shari'ah that is rooted in "northern culture" rather than in shari'ah itself.

The story recounted above illustrates the complexity and diversity of the society that shari'ah was meant to order. It is a culture that has internalized fears about difference, particularly on the part of women. It can be argued that the desire to render elites and common people on the same level has created the unintended consequence of endangering expressions of all difference, while elites continue to flout these conventions.

TWO VISIONS OF SHARI'AH AND GENDER: IBRAHEEM SULAIMAN AND BILKISU YUSUF

Ibraheem Sulaiman, one of northern Nigeria's most important historians, writes that "Shari'ah is often described as the core and kernel of Islam, being the practical manifestation of the faith, both being two faces of the same coin. Any threat to Shari'ah is also a threat to Islam, therefore, an existential threat to Muslims."[33] Sulaiman makes an argument for the superiority of the Muslim worldview, saying of northern Muslims: "They rightfully expect that the strategic decision to commit Muslims to higher standards of morality, character and justice should manifest itself not only in behaviour of society but also in politics and governance."[34] He then contrasts Muslims and some others in Nigeria's "shared environment" in order to stake the claim for shari'ah's legitimacy:

> Nigeria is a shared environment. This fact alone accounts for some of the problems being encountered in the application of the Shari'ah. Here live side by side and with equal claim to fundamental rights and privileges those who worship the One Supreme Being and those who worship trees, snakes and lizards, as well as those who earnestly desire a moral and upright atmosphere to live in and those who regard higher values as a burden. Those who derive their inspiration from the "white man" live under the same roof with those who derive their law and way of life from the Lord of Creation. The moral gulf between the contending forces can be so wide and irreconcilable as the gulf, if you can imagine, between those who eat only wholesome food over which the sublime name of God is mentioned and those who would eat anything that comes their way, even, as unimaginable as it would sound, the flesh of primates of all kinds, from the lowest to the highest.... In a country ruled by surrogates it was only natural that the centre caved in.[35]

For Sulaiman, to assert that Nigeria is a secular state is to "question the very existence of Muslims, as individuals and as a community."[36] Having staked this defiant claim for the legitimacy of shari'ah, Sulaiman describes how shari'ah gives hope and is an alternative vision for those suffering in Nigeria:

> Those who have lost hope of the prospect of ever escaping from the suffocating tyranny of the prevailing economic system which had all along been unjustly protected by law and state to the detriment of the people now know that the Islamic alternative is available with little or no legal

> impediments. In short, with the opportunity offered by the ethical, humane and moral alternatives in the judicial, economic, social and governmental spheres, Nigeria does not have to endure an inexorable decline, decay and degradation. The Shari'ah therefore offers a prospect for rebirth; even in the most bleak of circumstances.[37]

Sulaiman asserts the "natural right" of shari'ah in Nigeria both out of a clear conviction of its legitimacy and because of a sense, shared by many in northern Nigeria, that only this system can offer hope against an economic and social situation that is largely thought to be hopeless. Islamic law offers a way to cut into the disorder and injustice "with little or no legal impediments." He says simply: "The dramatic failure in the prevailing economic systems and the exposure of gross materialism, greed and godlessness that power it are driving people toward the alternative presented by the shari'ah." [38]

What does this alternative look like, particularly with regard to gender? The ideal worldview is framed against the background of a world that is divided between those who possess technological capacity and wealth and those who do not:

> Today's reality also indicates that whoever produces better tools in quality and quantity will have all the advantages in their favour. That is why our world is divided by technology in two. One half, technology-driven, is rich, powerful, resourceful, the other half technology-starved, poor, weak, hungry. Knowledge encompasses every field that is needed for a human being to excel in character and capability, to understand the world entrusted to him by Allah and take full advantage of its resources, its possibilities, its limitations. No one field of knowledge is superior to the other, or more or less holy, all must be required with equal zeal and passion.[39]

An understanding of the world emerges here that takes into account hard realities about the need for economic advancement through the embrace of modern systems of technologization. This vision of Islam as manifested through shari'ah is not one that only looks back in an attempt to reclaim a past heritage and lifestyle, but one that draws inspiration and strength from that past to gear up Muslims to create a better future. Passionate engagement in all tasks is also valued—Islam is the vehicle through which people become enlivened through work, helping their societies in the process. To this end, Sulaiman says clearly:

> Therefore, it is imperative for Muslims to deploy all the resources needed to educate their children. Every male child should receive education as far as his ability and aptitude can carry him without any hindrance or inhibitions whatsoever. He is the child of the Muslim Ummah or of the state as the case may be, and so it does not matter whether the parents are rich or poor. The same applies to the female child. She too must receive education to whatever level her ability and aptitude can take her, without any hindrance and inhibition whatsoever, and in whatever branch of knowledge she feels she can excel. What makes a human being is not the physique as such, but the knowledge by virtue of which he can live. Even if education should take up to half of our resources for many years to come, we must oblige.[40]

This articulation of a gender-fair Islamism, at least with regard to education, is formed in view of a particular, "realist" assessment of economic and social imperatives that demand the full participation of well-educated Muslim boys and girls. We can see that Sulaiman makes the case for female education rather more forcefully, no doubt in view of societal attitudes that contradict his vision. The justification for this worldview is grounded in a particular understanding of the Islamic tradition and its texts, one that calls on Muslims to fight against injustice and excel at all costs.

To actualize this vision, Sulaiman encourages his readers to look beyond the idea of the nation-state and its boundaries, toward a new regional vision where, "to the north of this heart of Africa," one sees "a cluster of Muslim nations with which they share common history and faith." He extends this cultural and geographical observation to say that "you can consider them all as one people, sharing a common vision of life and common destiny."[41] To the west of the map of Africa we find a "vast ocean of Muslims, from Benin Republic all across to Senegal"; still farther to the north are Sudan, Libya, Morocco, and Algeria; "and beyond them you are in the Muslim East." Sulaiman ends this reflection with the thought that "viewed globally this is a 'New World.'"[42] To advance toward the future, finally,

> The Muslim states must begin a process of self-integration by which they pool resources together, work out a common strategy for development and growth, and move together in a form of commonwealth. They are of course a part of Nigeria, indeed the nucleus of this great nation. It is the duty of Muslims to make Nigeria work, viable, stronger.[43]

Sulaiman seems to advocate two seemingly contradictory, yet perhaps interrelated, ideas: questioning Nigeria's and surrounding states' status as "nation-states," while at the same time working toward these states' betterment, with an eye toward realpolitik concerns regarding the logic of the world economy. The way to accomplish this goal is to educate every young Muslim boy and girl at equal levels, so that they can meet their potential and fight for the values of an Islamic society in what could be seen as a "new world." In Sulaiman's vision, gender equality within an Islamic framework is a strategy for the survival of Africa in the contemporary world, and Islam and Islamic law are the mechanisms through which northern Nigeria can be redeemed.

The late northern Nigerian journalist and women's rights activist Bilkisu Yusuf's[44] conception of contemporary Islam in northern Nigeria also looks outward, but with a focus on her deep engagement with women's issues, about which she makes global connections: "The history of Nigerian women's struggle to improve their situation is similar to that of their counterparts in other areas of the world."[45] From Yusuf's perspective, Western education, rather than being a threatening imposition from outside, is today necessary for Nigerian women's empowerment. That Christian missionaries first brought Western education to the non-Muslim south has for Yusuf, at this moment, resulted in a disadvantage for Muslim women. Islam's history in the north had a different effect: "The north, however, was influenced by Arab North Africa. Islam was introduced through the trans-Saharan trade, along with an educational system quite distinct from that of the West. Because Islam pervades every aspect of life, it has had a greater effect on its adherents in northern Nigeria than any other single factor."[46] This effect includes limiting "spacial freedom"and therefore education and political engagement. She cites Speaker of the House of Representatives of the Second Republic Benjamin Cha'aha, who spoke of why women were excluded as committee chairpersons: "If women were picked to head any of the thirty-four committees, men would refuse to serve under them.... Such committees would die natural deaths."[47]

Yusuf attributes this poor level of education and political representation to women's vulnerability to "superstition." Interestingly, Yusuf links this state of deprivation to the days of the Sokoto Caliphate, where, Dan Fodio's highly learned daughter notwithstanding, "minimal literacy skills and religious tenets were taught to women—just enough to allow them to say their obligatory prayers." Since that time, Yusuf argues that men have "deliberately interpreted laws to deprive women of their legal rights." However, while evoking this history in a surprising way—perhaps to signal the deep pervasiveness of the cultural problem—she argues (necessarily, I believe) that these conditions have no relevance or justification in Islam and are, in fact, in opposition to Islamic principles and injunctions.[48] Here we see a subtle indictment of the negative consequences for women resulting from gendered space delineation in the dominant Islamic tradition in the north, followed by a rhetorical statement that distances the tradition as a whole from these restrictions. The same move that exposes and then elides misogynistic histories is deployed for the Sokoto Caliphate; while Yusuf criticizes the lack of emphasis on female literacy in the caliphate, she provides the following quote from *jihad* leader Uthmān Dan Fodio to challenge that version of the history of the Sokoto Caliphate:

> Oh Muslim women, do not listen to the words of the misguided ones who seek to lead you astray by ordering you to obey your husband instead of telling you to obey Allah and his messenger. They tell you a woman's happiness lies in obeying her husband. This is no more than a camouflage to

> make you satisfy their needs. They impose on you duties which neither Allah nor his messenger impose on you. They make you cook, wash clothes, and do other things which they desire while they fail to teach you what Allah and his apostle have prescribed for you. Neither Allah nor his apostle charges you with such duties.[49]

Yusuf dates this statement from Uthmān Dan Fodio to "1981," indicating that the quotation is derived from a secondary source that perhaps paraphrased and idiomized the language. Yet the insistence on coupling critiques of the Islamic tradition with alternate Islamic visions suggests, at the very least, that grounding one's critiques in Islamic terms is fundamental to the success of any attempt at social change.

Adult education is one of the many programs Yusuf has participated in to improve women's position in northern Nigerian society. Describing free evening classes in Kano City that include courses in literacy, child care, income-generation projects, and Islamic religious knowledge, Yusuf laments that "perhaps the most difficult" is the stipulation that "women may attend these classes only with the permission of their husbands: the agency does not want to be responsible for conflict between partners."[50] This hurdle makes attendance of evening classes possible for women, even though they are frequently exhausted from a day of domestic labor. To undergird this activism, Yusuf cites the example of Maalam Aminu Kano, founder of the Northern Elements Progressive Union, who urged northern women, according to Yusuf, to "'escape the state of total subjugation' in which Hausa-Fulani women found themselves and to react against centuries-old concepts of respect, deference, modesty and their 'proper place.'"[51] Here again, an appeal is necessary to a respected male authority to argue for wives to be allowed to leave their homes alone for non-family-related activities.

In another appeal to male authority, Yusuf recalls a conference held by WIN (Women in Nigeria) in 1982, where a "pious Muslim male" argued that "No nation can be said to be developed or civilized if its menfolk relegate its womenfolk to the background.... Such nations must be condemned as primitive."[52] One of the most serious manifestations of this relegation of women to the "background" for Yusuf is around the issue of early pregnancy, childbirth, and divorce:

> Pregnancy at too young an age may result in death during childbirth; it may also cause internal rupture of the bladder and rectum (vesico vaginal fistula; *Newswatch,* April 17, 1989, pp. 36–37). In the latter case, the condition is often worsened through treatment by some midwives, whose unsuccessful surgery leaves a young girl with permanent internal damage. Thus she becomes "undesirable" to her husband, who promptly divorces her, leaving her suited only for a life of prostitution.[53]

Yusuf is one of northern Nigeria's most prominent activists against early pregnancy and the damage it can cause to the developing sexual organs of young girls (see chapter 4). For this activism, for which she is sometimes awarded money from Western NGOs, she is often the target of suspicion and criticism by northern Islamists, as I noted in chapter 1.

As a broader strategy for addressing these concerns, Yusuf advocates a reinterpretation and perhaps re-imagination of what the Islamic tradition in the north has to say about women's role in an Islamic society. Reflecting on the WIN conference, Yusuf writes, "Participants stressed that no solution to these problems was possible without radical social change and the complete elimination of all forms of human exploitation."[54]

A NOTE ON "CRITICAL THINKING"

As president of WRAPA, the organization that commissioned Amina Lawal's legal counsel, Saudatu Mahdi is familiar with accusations of Islamic "inauthenticity." WRAPA, which was founded by former president Abdulsalami Abubakar's wife, is one of the most prominent organizations in northern Nigeria advocating the rights of women. By Mahdi's account, conservatives' willingness to work with her organization has steadily increased since 1999, and today her group works with Islamist voices as "stakeholders" in the shari'ah debate, as she put it using NGO terminology.

Both Mahdi and Aliyu Yauri take refuge in their belief that the Qur'an itself makes a distinction between *"al-zānia wa al-zānī"* (the adulteress and the adulterer) and a "fornicator," the latter being a married person. Mahdi told me she believes that this distinction is made out of Arabs' prioritization of lineage *(nasb),* which leads them to hate the idea of "mixing semen." There is quite a bit of evidence to support Mahdi's claim, but the point, for our purposes, is her willingness to reach outside the Islamic tradition to think critically about its injunctions, a conceptual leap I found rare in northern Nigeria. Mahdi further mused, "If Islam had come to Africa, what would it have been like?" Another interesting question that destabilizes orthodoxy. She and I contemplated this question for a few moments. When I commented that she seemed unusually willing to ask these types of hypothetical questions of the Islamic tradition, Mahdi replied, "People are afraid of scholarship because if you read, you are bound to ask questions. Then their power is threatened. A few people have cornered religion and used it for power. Nigerians don't like to rock the boat."[55] In other words, the stifling of critical thought is linked to political domination by elites, a theme I often heard during my research. And perhaps the most dangerous questions to address through critical thought are those about gender roles and the place of women in society—the destabilizing fissure in the shari'ah project, as I suggested earlier. Dr. Bobboyi took a sardonic historical perspective on the matter: "If you had a question in the 1970s, you were either a Marxist or an Islamist."[56]

Despite the general pall on publicly expressed critical thought concerning questions of religion, I found a willingness to critique the *'ulema* in somewhat surprising places. For example, though he also remarked that the use of Lawal's pregnancy as proof of *zinā* was "fortunately or unfortunately" the unchangeable result of Islamic law's rules and regulations, Dr. Sadiq was nonetheless critical of the *'ulema* for, interestingly, their lack of Western education. "They don't know the structure of government, the political situation, current affairs. They can't speak English, and therefore you really won't know anything."[57]

Here we have evidence that knowledge of the structure of governance currently in place in the Nigerian nation-state is deemed of obvious importance to at least one champion of post-1999 shari'ah. But Dr. Sadiq's statement also touches on the notion that Western education is connected to critical thinking.

Dr. Asmau, a professor of public policy at Kaduna Polytechnic University who has been thoroughly educated in the Western tradition, fully acknowledges that "Western education came with colonial rule and Christianity, and these go hand in hand." At the same time, she says, "colonialism brought Western education, which is different from Christianity. Western education trains you for employment and wages: here in Nigeria, you have to pay for everything."[58] Therefore, Western education is very important to basic survival in Nigeria. But beyond this, Dr. Asmau believes that both Western and Islamic education involve critical thinking. Reflecting on the importance of Western education, Dr. Asmau said, "We must acknowledge that we live in the twenty-first century, which is a global village, a knowledge-ized world."[59]

It is unsurprising that elites who have benefited from Western education are more sympathetic to its aims and convinced of its epistemological neutrality. This attitude toward Western education is forcibly challenged, however, by groups like Boko Haram, which is wreaking havoc in northern Nigeria with a series of terrorist attacks under their simple banner that all books (except the Qur'an)—and "books," here, are a symbol for "Western education"—are a sin, *harām*. These youths connect Western education with the West, which they connect with the elites, whom they see as the corrupt harbingers of their poverty. A noteworthy midpoint between these positions is the Izālā movement, which manifests one form of modernity in its use and promotion of Western education to further its neo-traditionalist social and theological aims.

There are other ways that Western education is seen as threatening. Dr. Aliyu Ibrahim and I discussed his problems with the Convention on the Rights of the Child. He is against the general concept of United

Nations human rights charters, and seems to reserve special ire for the "child rights act," insofar as it affects women: "Women don't need this—shari'ah has made all their provisions. Our culture is different from the culture on which this was based."[60] Western "sexuality" education was seen as particularly threatening, with many northern men expressing anger and disbelief that their wives would be asked personal questions about their sex lives by Western researchers—strangers. Northern states, according to Dr. Ibrahim, are opposed to sexuality education, yet some groups attempt to impose it, "while in London, children can be excepted from it."[61] In this example we see opposition to a form of education based on the fact that it emerges from another culture, out of a fear that this education will divide or change society in new ways that, it must be noted, may not "benefit" the men who are opposed to this change. On the other hand, there is the frequently made observation that education must be tailored to local needs; otherwise the situation is a simple transposition of Western values—and "people are opposed to Western values."[62]

Dr. Abba Yusuf, assistant secretary of the Kano Emirate Council, also encourages a notion of progress that does not necessarily assume Western education: "Even without Western education you can have a well-enlightened, well-spirited citizenry." How?

> If I'm properly guided I can be more patriotic and disciplined. In the jihad days, people were well-enlightened to the civic responsibilities. There was less corruption, more morality. Moral decadence holds back morality. There is a notion that morality has to come first. We must look back to before colonial times. People were more content, judicious. There was a political system in place and there was law and order. People were contributing effectively to society. There is not actually development here (with Western development efforts): people have to develop from within. The easiest way to develop from within is through the most authentic structures. Why isn't democracy accepted globally? The normal man on the street knows the answer, even if the secretary general of the United Nations does not: you can't import a system from China and say people in Australia or in the Middle East should accept it wholesale.[63]

Dr. Yusuf"s is a sophisticated articulation of how "shari'ah" has always been and can only be expressed politically, and of the importance of "authentic" structures, a major theme of this study. Again, I believe that the category of gender is the major fault line in this constructed "authenticity," because of its exposure of other fault lines in the Islamic tradition. Concerns about women and gender expose the limitations of a static understanding of shari'ah; gender is a living regulator that refocuses energy on ascertaining the "universal message" of Islam while, at the same time, exposing the various traditions' historicity.

• • •

Driving through the streets of Kano one night, I talked about critical thinking with a friend of mine—a Western researcher with extensive experience teaching in Nigeria. He insisted that critical thinking must be developed from the ground up, that there is no innate propensity to think critically. I found this idea shocking. He described a British philosopher's notion—he couldn't recall the name—that there is a relational amount of "furniture" in the mind depending on how much you read, how many languages you speak. The greater the number, the more furniture you will be able to use in order to assemble multiple factors as you think through one topic. My friend argued that most Nigerians—his experience was largely at the university—just do not have the mental architecture to, for example, question the divinity of Islamic law itself. I recalled what Dr. Guando said about different "Western" and "Islamic" "logics," the latter premising all subsequent thought on a literal reading of primary Islamic texts.

While I agree that the education-based critical thinking my friend refers to has become an internalized threat in the view of the people it would most help, I find myself in slight disagreement with him about the genesis of critical thought. Whereas he understands critical thought as something that must be taught, and that it is only through this education that a society can change, my own reading of the situation in northern Nigeria is that difficult societal conditions have a way of rendering critical thinking an actual threat—and, therefore, critical thinking is suppressed and discouraged. But in my experience in northern Nigeria, I found people to be more than capable of critical thought; there was simply no social reward for expressing it. Critical thinking, it seemed clear to me, could further disrupt an already weak order. The notion that critical thought is safer to express in stable societies is dispiriting. Boko Haram's campaign to wipe out "foreign" architectures of the mind is disheartening evidence of how threatening critical thought is to the forces of conformity, and how difficult it is to actualize critical thought in societies with a weak social order. In such a context, as in northern Nigeria, those with the most simple and seemingly unified message are winning the day, especially when they tether these constricting impulses to "Islam" and its legal instrument, political shari'ah, represented as the ideal.

CONCLUSION

Northern Nigerians went out into the streets in 1999 demanding the laws of God where the laws of man had failed. Exhausted by endemic corruption and poverty, regular, struggling citizens put their faith behind politicians who promised them a new era of justice energized by the ideal of shari'ah. Many northern Nigerians already carried this shari'ah in their hearts, as a reservoir of strength to summon in times of stress and strife.

This very difficult situation in which northern Nigerians found themselves was a result of their colonial legacy, contemporary geopolitical corruption—particularly of the global financial system—and inter-Nigerian corruption. It was time for a radical change, and idealized shari'ah—launched through the conceptual power of the sunnaic paradigm—was the only force powerful enough to do the job. The sunnaic paradigm is made up of three layers of history, looking backward in time: the present tense and its concerns, which looks to the second layer, the nineteenth-century Sokoto *Jihad,* for inspiration, both of which look to the third layer, the classical period of Islam, specifically the Prophetic period of Muhammad and the Islamic law that would be formed 150 years after his death.

This sunnaic paradigm was formed to animate a new sense of idealized shariʿah as a solution to northern Nigeria's problems. This powerful conceptual force is characterized by three factors: it offers a fast, "silver bullet" solution to northern Nigerians' problems; it appeals simply to the laws of God to hold all "men" equally accountable before a force unquestionably higher than all mortals, no matter how rich and powerful they may be; and it offers a simplified version of history to reduce confusion and give people direction. This is the shariʿah, bolstered historiographically and intellectually by the sunnaic paradigm, that people from across northern Nigeria's ideological spectrum supported in massive numbers.

Once enacted into law, this idealized shariʿah almost immediately turned into "political shariʿah." Questions arose, such as who are shariʿah judges to be? What is their training? Which courts have authority? How do we negotiate the federal state structure? Amina Lawal's trial for committing the crime of *zinā*, her sentence to death by stoning, and her various appeals became the first time shariʿah was put on trial in Nigeria—and the first time that stoning was put on trial internationally. Lawal's trial, though made possible through state laws that sanctified reductionist versions of the Mālikī school of law, a tradition that has been around since the Sokoto Caliphate, instead displayed the razor-focused ideals of the sunnaic paradigm by referring to primary texts like the Qur'an and *ḥadīth* far more often than it referred to Mālikī jurisprudence. The trial also made use of the Nigerian constitution, creating a mixture of influences—including the retention of a form of British magistrate law—that I call exemplary of "postmodern" Islamic law.

Continuing the contingency and ambiguity, Lawal was released in an Islamic court, but before eyes tuned in worldwide and with the help of lawyers who, while using Islamic arguments instead of human rights arguments, did benefit from Western soft power in the form of financial support from the NGOs that hired them. The very strong Western reaction to the case—riddled with blind spots as many parts of the West readied themselves to send troops to attack Iraq, an operation that would result in hundreds of thousands of deaths—increased Nigerian suspicions of Western reactions and caused the conservative "true believers" who championed the 1999 shari'ah revolution to double down on their convictions. Women often pay the price for these stringent readings of Islam and Islamic law, but their voice is hampered by myriad internal factors and intense external politics—whether it be Western hegemonic powers who may use Nigerian women's complaints to justify interventions in Nigeria, or Western feminist scholars who caution about expressing Muslim women's voices in scholarship without robust contextualization. If those Muslim women express opposition to shari'ah itself, we scarcely have the tools to represent their voice in Western scholarship or discourse more widely without risking undesirable co-optation.

The danger of the sunnaic paradigm lies in the same factor that lends it strength and appeal: its simplicity. That same simplicity can be abused by actors like Boko Haram, whose raison d'être is reductionism, a stripping away of all ambiguity and difference. On the surface, the answer to fanaticism would seem to be the encouragement of more critical thinking, difference, heterogeneity, and complexity. Yet I was surprised by my own thoughts at times, walking the long streets of Kano. At times I thought I understood why critical thinking and difference would be threatening to a society facing such massive internal and external problems, one that instinctually understands that it must, somehow, stay bound together to resist what seem like ever-thickening forces aiming to fragment it.

Has "Islam" redeemed the north? As Boko Haram wreaks havoc on the region and regular citizens depend on the Nigerian military to maintain order, Nigerians have suspended their existential critique of the Nigerian state. Boko Haram's rise and sworn allegiance to ISIS in

2015 signals the final failure of the post-1999 shari‘ah experiment. With much sadness, I suspect that the resilient everyday people of Hausaland have had to reach back into idealized shari‘ah and a more private, safely protected, idealized Islam to find the faith to weather this latest storm. Meanwhile, increasingly militant forces of conformity that have lost legitimacy among common people continue to instrumentalize shari‘ah for their own nihilistic ends.

NOTES

INTRODUCTION

1. While shari'ah is idealized, God's law, so perfect it is fundamentally unknowable in its totality to humans, *fiqh* are the man-made traditions of law that attempt to uncover God's divine law. It is noteworthy and not coincidental that these concepts are conflated in northern Nigeria.

2. Copied from original manuscript of the declaration, Kaduna National Archives, Kaduna, Nigeria.

CHAPTER ONE. A REVOLUTION FOR SHARI'AH

1. Ruud Peters, *Islamic Criminal Law in Nigeria* (Ibadan, Nigeria: Spectrum Books, 2003).

2. "Native Courts Proclamation" administered by Lord Frederick Lugard, British High Commissioner for the Protectorate of Northern Nigeria, 1900. In Kaduna National Archives.

3. See 1999 Transparency International Corruption Perceptions Index: www.transparency.org/research/cpi/cpi_1999/0/.

4. "In general, not only did the economic stabilization measures and reforms prove inadequate in dealing with the seemingly intractable problems of the economy, some of them, were to a large extent, counter-productive, thus defeating the attempts to use them successfully in restoring normalcy to economic activities. After more than a decade of SAP [structural adjustment programs], structural imbalances still persist and abound. The reforms have

not been far-reaching with low economic growth and more people becoming poor." ("Structural Adjustment Programme in Nigeria: Causes, Processes and Outcomes," National Centre for Economic Management & Administration, Ibadan, Nigeria; no date—sometime after 2003)

5. Murray Last, "Notes on the Implementation of Sharī'ah in Northern Nigeria," *FAIS Journal of Humanities* (2002): 1–17.

6. *Zinā* is best translated as "illegal sexual activity," though it is often translated as "adultery." This translation is flawed in that "adultery" in English connotes extramarital sex, whereas *zinā* includes both premarital and extramarital sex. Whether homosexual male and female sex is considered *zinā* is subject to debate in the tradition (see, e.g., Fakhr al-Dīn al-Rāzī's [d. 606 A.H.] discussion in Mu'jam al-Ghayb; for a good contemporary discussion, see Khaled El-Rouayheb, 2005).

7. Aliyu Musa Yauri, Esq., "Issues in Defending Safiyyatu Husseini and Amina Lawal," in *Sharī'ah Penal and Family Laws in Nigeria and in the Muslim World: Rights Based Approach,* ed. Jibrin Ibrahim (Zaria, Nigeria: Aḥmadu Bello University Press, 2004).

8. Section epigraph: Dr. Haruna Wakili, interview with the author, April 2010, Kano, Nigeria.

9. Aliyu Musa Yauri, Esq., interview with the author, February 2010, Abuja, Nigeria.

10. Hauwa Ibrahim, Esq., interview with the author, November 2009, Cambridge, Massachusetts, USA.

11. From an untitled essay given to me by Ibraheem Sulaiman.

12. Adamu Adamu (*Daily Star* columnist), interview with the author, April 2010, Zaria, Nigeria.

13. Ibraheem Sulaiman, interview with the author, April 2010, Zaria, Nigeria.

14. Adamu Adamu, interview with the author, April 2010, Zaria, Nigeria.

15. Dr. Usmanu Bugage, interview with the author, April 2010, Zaria and Kaduna, Nigeria.

16. Just outside Jos, on the border of Bauchi State.

17. Branches of Islamic law, understood as the human manifestation of the shari'ah. The Mālikī school is the dominant branch of *fiqh* in Nigeria.

18. See Saadi A. Simawe, "Rushdie's 'The Satanic Verses' and Heretical Literature in Islam," *The Iowa Review* 20 (winter 1990): 185–198.

19. Dr. Aliyu Tilde, interview with the author, March 2010, Bauchi, Nigeria.

20. "'Urwa related from 'A'isha that Usama spoke to the Prophet, may Allah bless him and grant him peace, on behalf of a woman and he said, 'Those before you were destroyed because they used to carry out the *hadd* punishment on the weak and did not carry it out on the noble. By the One who has my soul in His hand, if Fatima were to do that, I would cut off her hand.'" (Sahīh al-Bukhāri, *Book of Ḥudūd,* chapter 89, no. 6405; trans. Aisha Bewley)

21. The spareness with which I recount this story reflects the way it was told to me by Dr. Abdulkareem Sadiq. The story is that Alī is said to have lost his shield in battle, and a Jew took it. When Alī asked him for it back, the Jew refused to return it. Alī took him to court, insisting that he not be called by the honorific "Emīr al-Mu'manīn," since all are equal before the law. Due to a lack of evidence, the Jew was allowed to keep the shield, and then he converted because he was so moved by the justness of this decision. It is noteworthy that all of the fleshed-out details of this story were not necessary for Dr. Sadiq to make his point, indicating that there is a sense in which stories of the classical period of Islam enjoy a credibility based on their form in addition to their substance.

22. An oft-complained-about pattern in Nigerian politics happens when governors are voted out of their posts by the opposition. The deposed or ex-governor then immediately becomes a member of the Senate, which grants them immunity from the often inevitable investigation the new governor launches of the corruption of the old regime.

23. Dr. Abdulkareem Sadiq, interview with the author, March 2010, Zaria, Nigeria.

24. Ibid.

25. Dr. Muzzammil Sani Hanga (Kano shari'ah commission), interview with the author, May 2010, Kano, Nigeria.

26. Dr. Aliyu Ibrahim, interview with the author, April 2010, Zaria, Nigeria.

27. Dr. Asmau, interview with the author, March 2010, Kaduna, Nigeria.

28. Dr. Guando is again referencing the problem of granting former governors immunity against investigation in the Senate.

29. Dr. Guando, interview with the author, May 2010, Sokoto, Nigeria.

30. Dr. Aliyu Ibrahim, interview with the author, March 2010, Zaria, Nigeria.

31. Adamu Adamu, interview with the author, March 2010, Zaria, Nigeria.

32. Section epigraph: Jude O. Ezeanokwasa, "Obasanjo's Sharī'ah Incoherence," *Nigeria World,* September 7, 2007.

33. Islamic call to prayer.

34. Interview with Dr. Mustapha Muhammadu Guadebe, a senior lecturer of history at the Ahmadu Bello University, Zaria, March 2010, Kaduna, Nigeria.

35. Dr. Auwalu Yadudu, Professor of Law, Bayero University, interview with the author, May 2010, Kano, Nigeria.

36. Ibid.

37. Dr. Muzzammil Sani Hanga, interview with the author, April 2010.

38. Sam Olukoya, "Eyewitness: Nigeria's Sharia amputees." *BBC News World Edition,* December 19, 2002.

39. Ibid.

40. Dr. Muzzammil Sani Hanga, interview with the author, April 2010.

41. "Fundamentals of Islamic law."

42. Shaykh Malam Sanusi Khalil, interview with the author, March 2010, Kaduna, Nigeria.

43. See S. Abul al'la Maudidi, *Islamic Law and Its Introduction* (Lahore, Pakistan: Islamic Publications, 1955), 13–14.

44. In keeping with the methodology of this chapter, these short descriptions reflect the perception of these groups on the ground in northern Nigeria, as reflected in my ethnographic data. The reader is referred to scholarly supplementary material in the notes.

45. Khadija Asaiko, interview with the author, February–March 2010, Jos, Nigeria.

46. Shaykh Malam Sanusi Khalil, interview with the author, March 2010, Kaduna, Nigeria.

47. See Elizabeth Archibong, "Yerima's Bride Is the Daughter of His Egyptian Driver," *Next,* October 7, 2011.

48. Secretary general of the Women's Rights Protection and Advancement Alternative.

49. Dr. Abdulkareem Sadiq, interview with the author, March 2010, Zaria, Nigeria.

50. "The Destruction of Innovation and the Reinstitution of the Sunnah" (my translation).

51. See Ramzi Ben Amara, "The Izālā Movement in Nigeria: Its Split, Relationship to Sufis and Perception of Sharī'ah Re-implementation" (PhD dissertation, Universität Bayreuth, Germany, 2011), 88.

52. "Amen."

53. Literally "remembrance of God": a practice closely associated with Sufi movements that involves repeating certain prayers from Qur'an, *ḥadīth,* and other Islamic sources in a meditative, ritualized gathering of worshippers.

54. "Exegesis." Gūmi's writing of his own *tafsīr* is reminiscent of Sayyid Qutb (1906–66 C.E.), one of the most famous figures to be associated with the Muslim Brotherhood in Egypt, who likewise wrote his own *tafsīr* of the Qur'an with a distinctly modernist bent.

55. The first major Sufi order in Nigeria; sharing its prominence with the Tijāniyya, it was founded in the twelfth century in Baghdād and came to Hausaland through al-Maghīlī's travel's south from al-Maghreb (modern Morocco, Mauritania, Algeria, and Tunisia).

56. My translation.

57. "Submission, faith, and beauty."

58. Aliyu Ibrahim, interview with the author, April 2010, Zaria, Nigeria.

59. *Zakāt* is the yearly tax required of Muslims for the care of the needy that was established at the time of the Prophet.

60. Proselytizing Islam.

61. Dr. A.N. Umar, interview with the author, May 2010, Sokoto, Nigeria.

62. Dr. Muzzammil Sani Hanga, interview with the author, May 2010, Kano, Nigeria.

63. This principle of jurisprudence that Dr. Hanga upheld was not honored, however, in the cases of Saffiyatu Hussaini, a woman who had been sentenced to death by stoning for committing *zinā* in 2000, and Amina Lawal, whose convictions for adultery were on the basis of hearsay and circumstantial evidence, respectively. I argue that these deviations from the spirit of Islamic jurisprudence are characteristic of "postmodern shari'ah" (see chapter 4), whereby proactive punishments are foregrounded as a shortcut to re-enliven an image of a pure, shari'ah-ruled society that is perceived to have been lost through the disruptions of colonialism and what many describe as neocolonial economic policies and geopolitical circumstances.

64. See Gilbert da Costa, "'Nigeria's Taliban': How Big a Threat?," *Time,* July 30, 2009. www.time.com/time/world/article/0,8599,1913796,00.html.

65. Aminu Gamawa in personal correspondence with the author.

66. Jamila Nasr, dean of the law faculty at the University of Jos, interview with the author, March 2010, Jos, Nigeria.

67. Aliyu Ibrahim, interview with the author, March 2010, Zaria, Nigeria.

68. Bilkisu Yusuf (journalist), interview with the author, April 2010, Kano, Nigeria.

69. Dr. Mustapha Muhammadu Guadebe, interview with the author, February 2010, Kaduna, Nigeria.

70. Dr. Asmau, interview with the author, March 2010, Kaduna, Nigeria.

71. Dr. Hamidu Bobboyi, interview with the author, February 2010, Abuja, Nigeria.

72. Moḥammad Bashir Sambo, *Shari'ah and Justice* (Zaria: Sankore Educational Publishers, 2003).

73. Saudatu Mahdi, interview with the author, February 2010, Abuja, Nigeria.

74. Dr. Muzzammil Sani Hanga, interview with the author, May 2010, Kano, Nigeria.

CHAPTER TWO. HAUSALAND'S ISLAMIC MODERNITY

1. Chapter epigraph: Dr. Muzzammil Sani Hanga, chairman of the Kano shari'ah commission, talking about post-1999 shari'ah efforts (interview with the author, April 2010).

2. "Jibrīl went on his second pilgrimage at a time when the Waḥḥābīs were at the height of their first empire in Arabia.... Jibrīl could hardly have been in the holy lands and failed to notice this Waḥḥābī progress based on nothing other than the claim and will to reform Islam." Ismail A. B. Balogun, *The Life and Works of Uthman Dan Fodio* (Lagos, Nigeria: Islamic Publications Bureau, 1975), 31.

3. C. N. Ubah, *Islam in African History* (Kaduna, Nigeria: Baraka Press, 2001), 93.

4. Pade Badru, *The Spread of Islam in West Africa: Colonization, Globalization and the Emergence of Fundamentalism* (Lewiston, NY: Edwin Mellen Press, 2006), 87.

5. Ubah, *Islam in African History*, 105–107.

6. Razaq Deremi Abubakre, "The Academic and Non-academic Study of Islam in Sub-Saharan Africa: Nigeria as a Case Study," in *The Study of Religions in Africa: Past, Present and Prospects*, ed. Jan Platvoet, James Cox, and Jacob Olupona (Cambridge, UK: Roots and Branches; Stockholm: Almqvist & Wiksell, 1996).

7. Ibid., 256.

8. Ibid., 257.

9. Ubah, *Islam in African History*, 98.

10. Nehemia Levtzion, "The Eighteenth-Century Background to the Islamic Revolutions in West Africa," in *Eighteenth-Century Renewal and Reform in Islam*, ed. John Obert Voll (Syracuse, NY: Syracuse University Press, 1987).

11. Ibid., 21.

12. Ibid., 165.

13. Ibid.

14. Ibid., 168.

15. Badru, *The Spread of Islam in West Africa*, 101.

16. Arab-dominated in the sense of an Arabic-language-dominated epistemic tradition.

17. Ibn Farḥūn (d. 799 A.H./1396 C.E.), *al-Dibāj al-madhāhib fī marifat ayān ulama al-madhhab* (Cairo: Dar al-Turath lil-Tab wa-al-Nashr, 1975).

18. Muḥammad b. Uthmān b. Fūdī Bello, *Infāq al-Maysūr fī tarīkh Bilād al-Takrūr* (Rabat [al-Rabāṭ]: Ma'had al-Dirāsāt al-Ifrīqīyah, 1996).

19. Mervyn Hiskett, *The Sword of Truth: The Life and Times of the Shehu Usuman dan Fodio* (Evanston, IL: Northwestern University Press, 1994). The Arabic style conforms to Hiskett's observation of being short and to the point, simple and more legalistic—the point seems to be for pedagogical and clarifying purposes. Hiskett also contends that *Hawsawas* are likely to refer more to these manuals than to the original texts.

20. Uthmān Dan Fodio, *Kitāb 'uṣūl al-dīn wa kitāb 'ulūm al-mu'amala* (Norwich, UK: Diwan Press, 1978).

21. *"khayr(un) Umūr(i) al-dīn(i) mā kāna sunnah(tan), wa sharr(un) al-umur(i) al-muhadithāt(u) al-bidā'a'."*

22. Uthmān Dan Fodio, *Ihya' al-Sunnah wa Ikhmād al-Bid'ah* (Cairo: 'Abd Allāh al-Sayyār, al-Maktabah al-Ifrīqīyah, year unknown).

23. Ibid., 35.

24. *"surat al hasar: 7: wa mā ātākum al-rasūl fa khathūhū wa mā nahākum 'anhū fa antahū; ḥadīth: 'alaykum bi-sunnahti wa sunnaht al-khulafā' min ba'dī, 'aḍu 'alayhā b-il nuājith wa b'il ijmā'a lā na'qāduhu 'ala thalika."*

25. Ghazālī: *"wa haq al-'awām an yashtaghalū bi 'abādatahum wa bi m'ashātuhum wa yatrakū al-'ilm lilulama'."* Dan Fodio: *"marāduhu an yatrakū lahum al-'ilm fī bāb al-takalum lā fī bāb al-ta'alum." Ihya' al-Sunnah*, 7.

26. Sabo Bako, "The Development of Political Thought and Public Administration in Africa: The Sokoto Caliphate Example," paper prepared for the

Conference on the Celebration of Two Hundred Years After the Caliphate (organized by Arewa House, Kaduna), Abuja, June 14–16, 2004, 5–6.

27. Mohammad Bello, "Political Leaders of the Jihād Leaders" (master's thesis, Ahmadu Bello University, 1975), 41–42.

28. It should be noted that the term *emirate* was introduced by the British. Caliphate leaders were known locally by the Islamic term *Amīr al-Mu'manīn* (Commander of the Faithful).

29. Ibid., 12. My translation.

30. Unpublished manuscript, Arewa House Archives, Kaduna, Nigeria.

31. Amir al-Mu'minin Muḥammad Bello B. Uthmān b. Foduye, *The Dignity of Labor: Being the Text and Translation of Tanbīh al-sāhib 'ala ahkām al-mākasib,* ed. and trans. Omar Bello (unpublished manuscript, Arewa House Archives, Kaduna, Nigeria).

32. Ibid., 6. Called by the author an *arewa* (Hausa: "north," scholar).

33. Ibid.

34. Ibid. See also Murray Last, *The Sokoto Caliphate* (London: Longman, 1967).

35. R.A. Adeleye, *Power and Diplomacy in Northern Nigeria, 1804–1906* (London: Longman, 1971), 17.

36. Ibid., 17–18.

37. Ibid., 7.

38. Ibid., 16–17.

39. Bako, "The Development of Political Thought and Public Administration in Africa," 4.

40. Smith (1971, p. 70) cited in Bako, "The Development of Political Thought and Public Administration in Africa," 8.

41. Ibraheem Sulaiman, unpublished manuscript, 9.

42. Ibraheem Sulaiman, unpublished essay, 3.

43. Ibid., 4.

44. Ibid., 100.

45. 'Abdallahi ibn Muḥammad, *Ḍiyā' al-ḥukkām / ta'līf 'Abdallahi ibn Fūdīyū* (Zaria [Zāriyā], Nigeria: Maktab Nūlā, 1956).

46. Uthmān Dan Fodio, *Bayān wujūb al-hijra 'ala 'l-'ibad / Uthmān ibn Fūdī,* ed. and trans. F.H. El Masri (Khartoum: Khartoum University Press; New York: Oxford University Press, 1978).

47. Adeleye, *Power and Diplomacy in Northern Nigeria,* 47.

48. Hamidu Bobboyi, interview with the author, March 2010, Kaduna, Nigeria.

49. *"innama halaka man kāna qablakum 'innahum kānu yaqūmun al-ḥaḍ 'ala al-waḍi'a wa yatrukūn al-sharī'ah īf, wa allathi nafsī bi-yaddahū law an Fāṭima fa'alat thālik l'iqaṭa'at yaduhā." Ihya' al-Sunnah,* 243.

50. Interestingly, Dan Fodio's reference to those who erroneously prefer to "pay money" mirrors a *ḥadīth* in which the father of an adulterous son attempts to do the same until he is stopped by "learned scholars." Dan Fodio speaks of this desire to replace stoning with payment as if it happened in Hausaland; I have uncovered no evidence to confirm this presumed claim. This is the *ḥadīth* indirectly referenced:

> Narrated Abu Huraira and Zaid bin Khalid Al-Juhani: A bedouin came and said, "O Allah's Apostle! Judge between us according to Allah's Laws." His opponent got up and said, "He is right. Judge between us according to Allah's Laws." The bedouin said, "My son was a laborer working for this man, and he committed illegal sexual intercourse with his wife. The people told me that my son should be stoned to death; so, in lieu of that, I paid a ransom of one hundred sheep and a slave girl to save my son. Then I asked the learned scholars who said, "Your son has to be lashed one-hundred lashes and has to be exiled for one year." The Prophet said, "No doubt I will judge between you according to Allah's Laws. The slave-girl and the sheep are to go back to you, and your son will get a hundred lashes and one year exile." He then addressed somebody, "O Unais! go to the wife of this (man) and stone her to death." So, Unais went and stoned her to death. (*Ṣahih Bukhārī*, 3:49:860)

51. *"rafaḍa kathīr minhā ka had al-zinā rajman wa jaldan, iktifā' b'il māl raghba fīhū, wa huwa bid'ah muḥaramah ijmā'an." Ihya' al-Sunnah,* 245.

52. Muḥammad b. Uthmān b. Fūdī Bello, *al-Ghayth al-wabl fī sirāt al-imām al-'adl,* ed. and trans. Omar Bello in "The Political Thought of Muḥammad Bello (1781–1837)" (PhD dissertation, Ahmadu Bello University, 1975).

53. Ibid.

54. *"itha saraqa fīhim al-sharīf tarakuhū, wa itha saraqa fīhim al-ḍa'īf aqāmū 'alayhu al-ḥadd." Sahih Muslim,* Book 11, report 186.

55. Ibid.

56. Abba Yusuf, interview with the author, May 2010, Kano, Nigeria.

57. Dr. Bashir Galadanci, interview with the author, April 2010, Kano, Nigeria.

58. Dr. Abdulkareem Sadiq, interview with the author, March 2010, Zaria, Nigeria.

59. Shaykh Malam Sanusi Khalil, interview with the author, March 2010, Kaduna, Nigeria.

60. Shaykh Rabi'u Daura, interview with the author, March 2010, Kaduna, Nigeria.

CHAPTER THREE. ORIGINS OF THE STONING PUNISHMENT

1. Aliyu Musa Yauri, Esq., interview with the author, February 2010, Abuja, Nigeria.

2. Saudatu Mahdi, interview with the author, February 2010, Abuja, Nigeria.

3. Mu'āwiyah ibn 'Abī Ṣufyān (d. 60 A.H./680 C.E. First caliph of the Umayyad Caliphate (r. 40 A.H./661 C.E. to 60 A.H./680 C.E.).

4. This history is further explored in chapter 4.

5. *Naskh* is a form of abrogation that allows for the abrogation of verses that were never recorded as having been recited, while retaining the legal value of those verses *(naskh al-tilāwa duna al-ḥukm).*

6. Pavel Pavlovich, "The Stoning of a Pregnant Adulteress from Juhayna: The Early Evolution of a Muslim Tradition," *Islamic Law and Society* 17 (2010): 1–62.

7. Harald Motzki, "The *Muṣannaf* of 'Abd al-Razzāq al-Ṣan'ānī as a Source of Authentic *Aḥadīth* of the First Century A.H.," *Journal of Near Eastern Studies* 50 (1991): 1–21. The *isnād cum matn* method can be seen as a compromise method that Motzki (a contemporary Dutch Islamicist) developed in response to Schacht. Motzki studied 'Abd al-Razzāq's *Muṣannaf* (see Motzki, *The Origins of Islamic Jurisprudence: Meccan Fiqh before the Classical Schools,* Leiden, The Netherlands: Brill, 2002), which is one of the earliest surviving *ḥadīth* collections that had not previously been given much scholarly attention. Motzki concludes that most of the *isnāds* from 'Abd al-Razzāq to his main informants are authentic. These informants include ibn Jurayj (d. 150 A.H./767 C.E.), Ma'mar b. Rāshid (d. 153 A.H./770 C.E.), and Sufyān al-Thawrī (d. 161 A.H./778 C.E.).

8. Ibid., 15.

9. Patricia Crone, *Roman, Provincial and Islamic Law: The Origins of the Islamic Patronate* (Cambridge, UK: Cambridge University Press, 1987), 3.

10. Walter Young, "Stoning and Hand-Amputation: The Pre-Islamic Origins of the Hadd Penalties for *Zinā* and Sariqa" (master's thesis, Institute of Islamic Studies, McGill University, 2005).

11. Martha T. Roth, *Law Collections from Mesopotamia and Asia Minor* (Atlanta, GA: Scholars Press, 1995), 17–20 (quoted in Young, "Stoning and Hand-Amputation," 123).

12. Rev. C. H. W. Johns, *Babylonian and Assyrian Laws, Contracts, and Letters* (Union, NJ: Lawbook Exchange, 1999), 53–34; Chilperic Edwards, *The Hammurabi Code and the Sinaitic Legislation with a Complete Translation of the Great Babylo-*

nian Inscription Discovered at Susa (London: Kennikat Press, 1971), 46–47; Russ VerSteeg, *Early Mesopotamian Law* (Durham, NC: Carolina Academic Press, 2000), 119 (quoted in Walter Young, "Stoning and Hand-Amputation," 123).

13. J.M. Powis Smith, *The Origin and History of Hebrew Law* (Chicago, IL: University of Chicago Press, 1931) (quoted in Young, "Stoning and Hand-Amputation," 123).

14. T.G. Pinches, "Crimes and Punishments (Assyro-Babylonian)," in *Encyclopædia of Religion and Ethics,* vol. 4, 259; Martha T. Roth, "'She Will Die by the Iron Dagger': Adultery and Neo-Babylonian Marriage," *Journal of the Economic and Social History of the Orient* 31 (1988): 201; Rev. C.H.W. Johns, *Babylonian and Assyrian Laws, Contracts, and Letters* (quoted in Young, "Stoning and Hand-Amputation," 124).

15. W.H. Bennett, "Crimes and Punishments (Hebrew)," in *Encyclopædia of Religion and Ethics,* vol. 4, 280–283 (quoted in Young, "Stoning and Hand-Amputation," 149).

16. Poucher, J. "Crimes and Punishments," in *A Dictionary of the Bible,* ed. J. Hastings (Edinburgh: T&T Clark, 1898), 520–527 (quoted in Young, "Stoning and Hand-Amputation," 152).

17. *The Jewish Study Bible: Tanakh Translation,* ed. Adele Berlin and Marc Zvi Brettler (Oxford: Oxford University Press, 2004), 417.

18. Ibid., 217–218.

19. Young, "Stoning and Hand-Amputation," 164.

20. Noel J. Coulson, *A History of Islamic Law* (Edinburgh: Edinburgh University Press, 1964).

21. "The mnemonic device of reducing more complicated legal concepts to easily-memorized rhythmic or rhyming phrases is more than merely a teaching device, but a means by which the legal traditions of orally-focused societies can no doubt attain astounding longevity." (Young, "Stoning and Hand-Amputation," 82)

22. It is important to note that this was a society in which fathers wanted as many children as possible.

23. Uri Rubin, "'Al-Walad li'l-Firash': On the Islamic Campaign against 'Zinā,'" *Studia Islamica* 78 (1993), 5–26. The utterance can be found, for example, in the traditions of Abu Hurayra, Bukhari, VII, 191 (85:18) (as cited by Rubin).

24. Ibid., 6. In this era, slave girls often worked as prostitutes—and if they gave birth, various men could claim to be the father, in a practice known as *di'wa.* The Qur'an tried to outlaw this practice.

25. Patricia Crone, *Roman, Provincial and Islamic Law.*

26. Rubin, "Al-Walad li'l-Firash'," 7.

27. Ibid.

28. The following classical and medieval scholars are representative of a wide swath of the tradition—all mandate stoning as the punishment for married adulterers: Mālik ibn Anas (d. 178 A.H./794 C.E.); al-Shāfi'ī (d. 204 A.H./ 819 C.E.); al-Buhkāri (d. 256 A.H./869 C.E.); al-Ṭabarī (d. 310 A.H./922 C.E.); Sarākhsī Ḥanafī (d. 483 A.H./1090 C.E.); Al-Tūsi (Shī'ī, d. 459 or 460 A.H./1066 or 1067 C.E.); al-Ghazāli (Shāfi'ī, d. 505 A.H./1111 C.E.); Al-Ṭabarāni (Shī'ī, d. 548 A.H./ 1153 C.E.); al-Rāzī (d. 606 A.H./1209 C.E.); Al-Qurtubī (Mālikī, d. 674 A.H./1275 C.E.); ibn Kathīr (Shāfi'ī, d. 774 A.H./1372 C.E.). I have found surprisingly few exceptions to this ruling across the tradition. One interesting exception is that of the Khawārij, who argue that they do not accept *ahād* (single-transmission) *ḥadīth* and that, in any case, the Qur'an calls for unmarried adulterers' punishment to be "half" that of married adulterers, which would make stoning illogical in that the punishment—death—cannot be cut in half: *"qawlahu f'alayhuna nisf mā 'ala al-muḥasanāt fa law wajaba nisf al-rajam 'ala al-raqīq lākin al-rajam lā nasaf lahu."* See Fakhr al-Dīn al-Rāzi (d. 606 A.H./1209 C.E.), *Mafātīh al-Ghayb.*

29. Aḥmad Taymūr Bāshā, *Al-Mathāhib al-fiqhīyah al-arba'ah* (Cairo [al-Cāhira]: Maktabat al-Thaqāfah al-Dīnīyah, 2001).

30. Crone, *Roman, Provincial and Islamic Law.*

31. Ibid., 2.

32. Ibid.

33. Ibid., 99.

34. Young, "Stoning and Hand-Amputation," 52.

35. Crone, *Roman, Provincial and Islamic Law,* footnote 18, p. 112.

36. Ignaz Goldziher, *Muhammedanische Studien (Muslim Studies),* vol. II, ed. S.M. Stern, trans. C.R. Barber and S.M. Stern. London: Allen and Unwin, 1971, 76; Crone, *Roman, Provincial and Islamic Law,* footnote 65, p. 115.

37. Wael Hallaq, *The Origins and Evolution of Islamic Law* (Cambridge, UK: Cambridge University Press, 2005), 26.

38. Theodor Nöldeke and Friedrich Schwally, *Geschichte des Qorâns* (Göttingen, Germany: Dieterichschen Buchhandlung, 1860), 248–252.

39. Patricia Crone, "Two Legal Problems Bearing on the Early History of the Qur'ān," *Jerusalem Studies in Arabic and Islam* 18 (1994): 11.

40. Translation by Aḥmed Ali, *Al-Qur'an: A Contemporary Translation* (Princeton, NJ: Princeton University Press, 1993). Arabic: *wa allatī ya'tayna al-fāhisha min nisā'akum fi-s-tashhadu 'alayhunna arba'atun minkum fa-in shahadu fa-imsikunhunna fī bayātī hatta yatawafahinna al-mawtu aw yij'al Allahu lahunna sabīlan.*

41. Ibid. Arabic: *wal-ladhāni ya'tiyānihā minkum fa ādhūhumā fain tābā wa aṣlaḥā fa a'ariḍū 'anhumā in-nal-lāha kāna taw-wābar raḥiymā.*

42. A full discussion of *naskh* (abrogation) and *mansūkh* (the abrogated) is given later in this chapter.

43. Ali, *Al-Qurān: A Contemporary Translation.* Arabic: *az-zāniyatu waz-zāni fajlidā kul-la wāḥidim minhumā miata jaldah wa lā ta'khudhkum bihimaa ra'fatun fā ydiynil-lāhi in kuntum tu'minūna bil-lāhi wal yawmil ākhir* walyash-had 'Adhaabahumā Tāifatum minal mu'miniyn.*

44. Ibid. Arabic: *az-zāni lā yankiḥu il-lā zāniyatan aw mushrikataw waz-zāniyatu lā yankiḥuhā il-lā zānin aw mushrik* wa ḥur-rima dhālika 'al al mu'miniyn.*

45. Ibid. Arabic: *wal-ladhiyna yarmūnal muḥṣanaati thum-ma lam ya'tū bi arba'ati shuhadā fajlidūhum thamāniyna jaldataw wa lā taqbalū lahum shahādatan abadā* wa ulāika humul faasiqūn.*

46. Ibid. Arabic: *Wa-al-lathīna yarmūna azwājahum wa-lam yakūn lahum shuhadā' illa anfusuhum fa-shahadatuahadihim arba'u shahada billahiinnahu la min as-sādiqīn.*

47. Ibid. Arabic: *wal khāmisatu an-na la'anatal-lāhi 'Alayhi in kāna minal kādhibiyn.*

48. Ibid. Arabic: *wa yadrau 'anhal 'adhāba an tash-hada arba'a shahādātim bil-lāhi in-nahū la minal kādhibiyn.*

49. Ibid. Arabic: *wal khāmisata an-na gaḍabal-lāhi 'alayhā in kāna minaṣ ṣādiqiyn.*

50. Young, "Stoning and Hand-Amputation," 152.

51. Ibid.

52. In the course of my research for this project, I witnessed an Azhar-trained scholar and a scholar trained in Qom, Iran, turn to *Lisān al-'Arab* to commence their investigation of several religious topics.

53. Sayings of the Prophet Muḥammad transmitted through an oral tradition called *isnād,* later compiled into catalogs called *musanid* (singular: *musnad*), until the *ḥadīth* were finally sorted and canonized by the fourth century. See Jonathan A. C. Brown, *The Canonization of al-Bukhārī and Muslim: The Formation and Function of the Sunnī Ḥadīth Canon* (Leiden, The Netherlands: Brill, 2007).

54. These include both *ḥadīth qawlī* (that which the Prophet said) and *ḥadīth fa'lī* (that which the Prophet did). The usual translation for *zinā* is "adultery," a misnomer, as in English "adultery" refers exclusively to extramarital sex, whereas the Islamic legal definition includes premarital sex. With this caveat in mind, I will use the word "adultery" to connote the Islamic legal sense.

55. Particularly in the collections of Bukhari (d. 246 A.H./860 C.E.) and Muslim (d. 261 A.H./874 C.E.), the two most revered compilations of *ḥadīth,* called *al-Ṣahihayn.*

56. Mālik ibn Anas (d. 150 A.H.), *Al-Muwaṭṭa,* trans. Aisha Abdurrahman Bewley (London: Kegan Paul International, 1989), Muwatta 344 (41.1.1).

57. Muḥammad ibn Isḥāq (d. 150 A.H./768 C.E.), *Sīrat ibn Isḥāq, al-musammāh bi-, Kitāb al-Mubtada' wa-al-mab'ath wa-al-maghāzī / (ta'līf Muḥammad ibn Isḥāq ibn Yasār ; taḥqīq wa-ta'līq Muḥammad Ḥamīd Allāh; taqdīm Muḥammad al-Fāsī)* (Rabat [al-Rabāṭ]: Ma'had al-Dirāsāt wa-al-Abḥāth lil-Ta'rīb, 1976).

58. 'Abd al-Malik ibn Hishām (d. 218 A.H./834 C.E.), *Mukhtaṣar Sīrat ibn Hishām (al-Sīrah al-Nabawīyah) / i'dād Muḥammad 'Afīf al-Zu'bī; rāja'ahu wa-ashrafa 'ala taṣḥīḥih'Abd al-Ḥamīd al-Aḥdab* (Beirut [Bayrūt]: Dār al-Nafā'is; Ḥims, Syria [Sūriyā]: Mu'assasat Zu'bī, 1977).

59. Mālik ibn Anas, *Al-Muwaṭṭa,* trans. Aisha Abdurrahman Bewley (New York: Kegan Paul International, 1989), 345.

60. Ibid., 41.

61. Ibid., 346 (41.10). G. H. A. Junyboll supposes that this *ḥadīth* was meant to be part of Sura 33. See Junyboll, *Studies on the Origins and Uses of Islamic Hadith* (London: Ashgate Variorum, 1996).

62. 'Umar's *ḥadīth* commanding stoning: "'Abdullah b. 'Abbās reported that 'Umar b. Khattāb sat on the pulpit of Allah's messenger (may peace be upon him) and said: Verily Allah sent Muammad (may peace be upon him) with truth and He sent down the Book upon him, and the verse of stoning was included in what was sent down to him. We recited it, retained it in our memory and understood it. Allah's Messenger (may peace be upon him) awarded the punishment of stoning to death [to the married adulterer and adulteress] and, after him, we also awarded the punishment of stoning. I am afraid that, with the lapse of time, the people [may forget it] and may say: We do not find the punishment of stoning in the Book of Allah, and thus go astray by abandoning this duty prescribed by Allah. Stoning is a duty laid down in Allah's Book for married men and women who commit adultery when proof is established, or if there is pregnancy, or a confession." *Sahih Muslim,* Book 17, report 4194.

63. Avraham Hakim, "Context: 'Umar b. Al-Khaṭṭāb,"in *The Blackwell Companion to the Qur'an,* ed. Andrew Rippen (Oxford: Oxford University Press, 2009).

64. Hallaq, *Origins and Evolution,* 32.

65. Christopher Melchert, "Traditionist-Jurisprudents and the Framing of Islamic Law," *Islamic Law and Society* 8 (2001): 383–406. Melchert characterizes

Schacht's understanding of the rise of Prophetic *ḥadīth* this way: "To explain the rise of Prophetic *ḥadīth* alone, Joseph Schact pointed to one area of controversy, mainly between adherents of the different regional schools of the eighth century. Thus jurisprudents of Kufa, for example, would cite *ḥadīth* from the Prophet to trump the *ḥadīth* from the Companions cited by their Medinese opponents. Shaybani's preference for *ḥadīth* from Companions to *ḥadīth* from followers is roughly in line with opinion among traditionist-jurisprudents of the early ninth century."

66. Scott Lucas, "'Perhaps You Only Kissed Her?': A Contrapuntal Reading of the Penalties for Illicit Sex in the Sunni Hadith Literature," *Journal of Religious Ethics* 39 (2011): 399–415.

67. Ibid., 409.

68. Ibid., 410.

69. Ibid.

70. See Lucas's discussion. Ibid., 407–408.

71. Ibid., 408.

72. Ibid.

73. The early legal and exegetical Islamic tradition generally prefers, for theological and epistemological reasons, not to employ the term "contradiction" *(naqd)* to describe the difference between the Qur'anic and *ḥadīth* punishments for *zinā*. It is beyond our scope to engage this problem, so I use language that hedges this claim.

74. Jilāl al-dīn 'Abd al-Rahmān al-Suyūti, *Itqān fi 'ulūm al-Qur'an (al-juz' al-thālith)* (Cairo: al-Turath, 1985), 61.

75. John Burton, *The Sources of Islamic Law: Islamic Theories of Abrogation* (Edinburgh: Edinburgh University Press, 1990), 123.

76. Ibid., 52 (quoting Qurtubī).

77. Ibid., 7–8.

78. "Malik admitted this principle, but Shafi'i denied it, although the *fuqaha'* all admit, in the instance of the penalty for adulterer, that the flogging element of Q 24:2 has been allowed to lapse in the case of those offenders who are condemned to death by stoning. There is no explanation for the abandonment of the flogging element other than that the penalty all now acknowledge is based on the Sunnah, i.e. the practice of the Prophet." (Ibid., 65–66, quoting Qurtubī, report 52)

79. Ibid., 4, 7.

80. See Moḥammad Hashim Kamali, *Principles of Islamic Jurisprudence* (Cambridge, UK: Islamic Texts Society, 2003), especially chapter 7. For

Kamali, abrogation *(naskh)* depended upon the possibility of ascertaining a chronological order between two *ḥadīths*—in other words, Kamali argues that wherever possible, abrogation is deployed to privilege the verse that was later revealed.

81. Andrew Rippin, "The Function of *asbab al-nuzūl* in Qur'anic Exegesis," *Bulletin of the School of Oriental and African Studies* 51 (1988): 362.

82. Burton, *The Sources of Islamic Law,* 467.

83. See Robert G. Hoyland, *Arabia and the Arabs: From the Bronze Age to the Coming of Islam* (New York: Routledge, 2001).

84. Wael Hallaq, *A History of Islamic Legal Theories* (Cambridge, UK: Cambridge University Press, 1997).

85. Coulson, *A History of Islamic Law,* 240.

86. Joseph Schacht, *The Origins of Muhammadan Jurisprudence* (Oxford: Clarendon Press, 1959), 17–18.

87. Hallaq, *Origins and Evolution,* 209.

88. Jonathan E. Brockopp, "Theorizing Charismatic Authority in Early Islamic Law," *Comparative Islamic Studies* 1, no. 2 (2005).

CHAPTER FOUR. COLONIALISM: THEN AND NOW

1. "The Future of the Global Muslim Population: Projections for 2010–2030," Pew Research Center, Forum on Religion and Public Life, January 2011. www.pewforum.org/2011/01/27/the-future-of-the-global-muslim-population/.

2. Shaykh Khalidu, interview with the author, February 2010, Jos, Nigeria.

3. Shaykh Sanusi Gumbi, interview with the author, March 2010, Kaduna, Nigeria. This chapter's epigraph is from the same interview.

4. Dr. Mustapha Muhammadu Guadebe, interview with the author, April 2010, Kaduna, Nigeria. "*Juju*" can be roughly translated as "evil spirits."

5. From an essay published in a Nigerian newspaper, given to me by its author, Auwalu Yadudu. No citation information available.

6. There are no official records documenting those awaiting trials for stoning cases who are held indefinitely in northern Nigeria's shari'ah courts. Therefore, the estimates of individuals held under such circumstances vary considerably. Based on anecdotal conversations in Nigeria, I conclude that there are at least a dozen such cases. Attorney Hauwa Ibrahim, however, believes there are "hundreds." Ibrahim has compiled a report called "Visit to Bauchi Prison" that documents nine such cases in Bauchi State alone. This report is unpublished, to the best of my knowledge, but she made it available

to me through private correspondence while she was a visiting lecturer at Harvard University. I mention it here with her permission.

7. Ibraheem Sulaiman, interview with the author, March 2010, Zaria, Nigeria.

8. Aḥmed Garba, interview with the author, March 2010, Jos, Nigeria. Garba was also referring to a conference he attended in Jos (cosponsored by the Volkswagen Foundation in Germany and the University of Jos) in which a raucous debate broke out between Nigerian and Western intellectuals. See Ibrahim Ado-Kurawa's reflections on that debate: "Review of the International Conference on Comparative Perspective on Shar'ia in Nigeria." http://web.archive.org/web/20040525024413/http:/www.gamji.com/NEWS3239.htm.

9. Ibraheem Sulaiman, interview with the author, March 2010, Zaria, Nigeria.

10. Mustafa Ismail, interview with the author, April 2010, Kano, Nigeria.

11. Aliyu Musa Yauri, Esq., interview with the author, February 2010, Abuja, Nigeria.

12. Ibid.

13. Ibid.

14. Ibid.

15. Ibraheem Sulaiman encouraged me to use the term "re-enlivening" instead of "implementing."

16. Zaki Badawi is a renowned Egyptian Islamic scholar who founded the Muslim College of London.

17. Dr. Guando, interview with the author, May 2010, Sokoto, Nigeria.

18. Aḥmed Garba, interview with the author, February 2010, Jos, Nigeria.

19. Ibraheem Sulaiman, interview with the author, March 2010, Zaria, Nigeria. Polygamy is widely practiced in northern Nigeria and, as such, constitutes a major cultural difference with most of the Arab world. The issue of polygamy will be explored in more detail in chapter 3.

20. Uthmān Dan Fodio, *Bayān wujūb al-hijra 'ala 'l-'ibad / Uthmān ibn Fūdī,* ed. and trans. F.H. El Masri (Khartoum: Khartoum University Press; New York: Oxford University Press, 1978).

21. Usmanu Bugage, in conversation with the author, March 2010, Zaria, Nigeria.

22. Aliyu Ibrahim, interview with the author, March 2010, Zaria, Nigeria.

23. Ibid.

24. Christian Obo, interview with the author, May 2010, Kano, Nigeria.

25. Muzzammil Sani Hanga, interview with the author, May 2010, Kano, Nigeria.

26. Bilkisu Yusuf was tragically killed in a stampede in Saudi Arabia in 2015. The speculated cause of the stampede was an official Saudi government convoy crowding the pilgrims.

27. Bilkisu Yusuf, interview with the author, April 2010, Kano, Nigeria.

28. Ibid.

29. This organization and its location will be kept anonymous, out of concern for the safety of the actors involved. Interview with the author, March 2010, Jos, Nigeria.

30. Aliyu Ibrahim, interview with the author, April 2010, Zaria, Nigeria.

31. R.A. Adeleye, *Power and Diplomacy in Northern Nigeria, 1804–1906* (London: Longman, 1971), 117.

32. Ibid., 128.

33. Ibid., 129.

34. Ibid., 130.

35. Ibid., 213.

36. Ibid., 287.

37. Okechukwu Okeke, *Hausa-Fulani Hegemony: The Dominance of the Muslim North in Contemporary Nigerian Politics* (Engu, Nigeria: Acena, 1992), 162.

38. Copied from original manuscript of the declaration, Kaduna National Archives, Kaduna, Nigeria.

39. Edwin Arney Speed (Editor), *Laws of the Protectorate of Northern Nigeria. With an appendix containing the orders of the Sovereign council relating to the Protectorate, the royal instruction to the governors and various acts of the government* (London: Stevens and Sons, 1910; first edition, in the Kaduna National Archives, Kaduna, Nigeria).

40. Ibid.

41. Andrew Ubaka Iwobi, "Tiptoeing through a Constitutional Minefield: The Great Sharia Controversy in Nigeria," *Journal of African Law* 48 (2004): 111–164.

42. Auwalu Hamsxu Yadudu, "Colonialism and the Transformation of the Substance and Form of Islamic Law in the Northern States of Nigeria," *Journal of Law and Religion* 9, no. 1 (1991): 29.

43. Zamfara State of Nigeria, *Sharia Penal Code Law, 2000* (Zaria: Gaskiya Corporation Limited, with Consent and Authority of Zamfara State Government, 2000).

44. Ruud Peters, *Islamic Criminal Law in Nigeria* (Ibadan, Nigeria: Spectrum Books, 2003).

45. Amira El-Azhary Sonbol, "The Genesis of Family Law: How Sharī'ah, Custom and Colonial Laws Influenced the Development of Personal Status Codes," in *Wanted: Justice and Equality in the Muslim Family,* ed. Anwar and Sisters in Islam (2009).

46. Ibid., 183.

47. Ibid.

48. Ibid., 184.

49. Yadudu, "Colonialism and the Transformation," 18.

50. Ibid.

51. Joseph Schacht, "Islam in Northern Nigeria," *Studia Islamica* 8 (1957): 123–146.

52. Ibid., 127.

53. Ibid., 130.

54. Ibid., 133.

55. Ibid., 137.

56. Ibid.

57. Ibid.

58. Ibid., 138.

59. Ibid.

60. Ibid., 139.

61. Ruud Peters, "Islamic and Secular Criminal Law in Nineteenth Century Egypt: The Role and Function of the Qāḍī," *Islamic Law and Society* 4 (1997): 70–90.

62. Lama Abu-Odeh, "Modernizing Muslim Family Law: The Case of Egypt," *Journal for Transitional Law* 37 (2004): 1086.

63. Ibid., 1027–1029.

64. Muhammad Sani Umar, *Islam and Colonialism: Intellectual Responses of Muslims of Northern Nigeria to British Colonial Rule* (Leiden, The Netherlands: Brill, 2006), 198–199.

65. Aḥmad Muḥammad Kani, *The Intellectual Origin of Sokoto Jihad* (Ibadan, Nigeria: Iman Publications, 1984), iv.

66. Ibid.

67. Kani, *The Intellectual Origin of Sokoto Jihad,* v.

68. Shaykh Rabi'u Daura, interview with the author, March 2010, Kaduna, Nigeria. (My translation.)

69. Ibid.

70. Muzzammil Sani Hanga, interview with the author, May 2010, Kano, Nigeria.

71. Christian Obo, interview with the author, May 2010, Kano, Nigeria.

72. Dr. Mustapha Muhammadu Guadebe, interview with the author, March 2010, Kaduna, Nigeria.

73. "South south" refers to River State and Niger Delta State, where there have been terrible problems due to oil reserves and the abuses of the Shell Oil Company.

74. Dr. Mustapha Muhammadu Guadebe, interview with the author, March 2010, Kaduna, Nigeria.

75. Aliyu Ibrahim, interview with the author, April 2010, Zaria, Nigeria.

CHAPTER FIVE. THE TRIAL OF AMINA LAWAL

1. The proceedings of this trial were translated from the Hausa by Sama'ila A. Mohammed.

2. Kano Penal Code as pertains to the crime of *zinā:* "*Zinā* defined: Whoever, being a man or a woman fully responsible, has sexual intercourse through the genital of a person over whom he has no sexual rights and in circumstances in which no doubt exists as to illegality of the act, is guilty of the offence of *zinā*. Punishment for *zinā:* Whoever commits the offence of *zinā* shall be punished: (a) with caning of one hundred lashes if unmarried, and shall also be liable to imprisonment for a term of one year; or (b) if married, with stoning to death *(rajm)*. Explanation: Mere penetration is sufficient to constitute the sexual intercourse necessary to the offence of *zinā*. The section in Kano further stipulates that males, additional to the Zamfara penal code, face 1 year imprisonment, if unmarried." Ruud Peters, *Islamic Criminal Law in Nigeria* (Ibadan, Nigeria: Spectrum Books, 2003), 62–63.

3. Philip Ostien (Editor), *Sharī'ah Implementation in Northern Nigeria 1999–2006: A Sourcebook, vol. 5: Two Famous Cases* (translated from Hausa original) (Ibadan, Nigeria: Spectrum Books, 2007), 52.

4. Aliyu Musa Yauri, Esq., interview with the author, February 2010, Abuja, Nigeria.

5. Kamari Maxine Clarke, "'The Hand Will Go to Hell': Islamic Law and the Crafting of the Spiritual Self," unpublished manuscript, 2005, cited with permission from the author.

6. Ibid.

7. Ibid.

8. Ibid.

9. Ibid.

10. Ibid.

11. *Sūrat al-Nūr,* 4: "And those who accuse chaste women [with adultery] but do not bring four witnesses, then scourge them [with] eighty stripes and do not [afterward] accept their testimony forever, and these are they that are evil-doers."

12. Clarke, "The Hand Will Go to Hell."

13. Peters, *Islamic Criminal Law in Nigeria,* 8.

14. Ostien, *Sharī'ah Implementation in Northern Nigeria,* 55.

15. 1999 Constitution of the Federal Republic of Nigeria 36(7): "When any person is tried for any criminal offence, the court or tribunal shall keep a record of the proceedings and the accused person or any person authorized by him in that behalf shall be entitled to obtain copies of the judgment in the case within seven days of the conclusion of the case."

16. Ostien, *Sharī'ah Implementation in Northern Nigeria,* 126, including supra note 114.

17. Auwalu Hamsxu Yadudu, "Colonialism and the Transformation of the Substance and Form of Islamic Law in the Northern States of Nigeria," *Journal of Law and Religion* 9 (1991): 17–47.

18. Razaq Deremi Abubakre, "The Academic and Non-academic Study of Islam in Sub-Saharan Africa: Nigeria as a Case Study," in *The Study of Religions in Africa: Past, Present and Prospects,* ed. Jan Platvoet, James Cox, and Jacob Olupona (Cambridge, UK: Roots and Branches; Stockholm: Almqvist & Wiksell, 1996), 257.

19. Ibid.

20. Ibid., 258.

21. Ibid.

22. Ibid., 260.

23. Ibid., 259.

24. See Muhammad Sani Umar, *Islam and Colonialism: Intellectual Responses of Muslims of Northern Nigeria to British Colonial Rule* (Leiden, The Netherlands: Brill, 2006).

25. Muhammad Sani Umar, "Education and Islamic Trends in Northern Nigeria: 1970–1990s," *Africa Today* 48 (summer 2001).

26. Ibid., 134.

27. Ibid., 140.

28. Ibid., 144.

29. The proceedings of this trial were translated from the Hausa by Aliyu M. Yauri.

30. Aliyu Musa Yauri, Esq., interview with the author, February 2010, Abuja, Nigeria.

31. Ibid.

32. Ibid.

33. Ibid.

34. Ostien, *Sharī'ah Implementation in Northern Nigeria,* 59–61.

35. Ibid., 62.

36. The full text of the *ḥadīth* in question, mentioned in chapter 2, is described this way in the proceedings: "[I]t is reported that a woman came to the Holy Prophet and confessed to having committed *zinā*. The Prophet told her to go away until she had delivered. After she delivered she went back to the Prophet. He asked her to go back again until she had weaned her child. After she weaned the child she went back to the Prophet once again. The Prophet told her to go back once more until she got somebody to look after the child. It was only after she got somebody to take care of the child that she was stoned to death." Ibid.

37. Ostien, *Sharī'ah Implementation in Northern Nigeria,* 62.

38. Ijeoma Okoronkwo, "The Accused Persons Right to Bail in Nigeria," in *The Lawyer's Chronicle: The Magazine for the African Lawyer,* 1992.

39. Ostien, *Sharī'ah Implementation in Northern Nigeria,* 62–63.

40. Ibid., 63.

41. Peters, *Islamic Criminal Law in Nigeria,* 177.

42. Ostien, *Sharī'ah Implementation in Northern Nigeria,* 63.

43. *Sahih Muslim,* Book 17: Punishments Prescribed by Islam (chapter: He who confesses his guilt of adultery): "Sulaiman b. Buraida reported on the authority of his father that Ma'iz b. Malik came to Allah's Apostle (may peace be upon him) and said to him: Messenger of Allah, purify me, whereupon he said: Woe be upon you, go back, ask forgiveness of Allah and turn to Him in repentance. He [the narrator] said that he went back not far, then came and said: Allah's Messenger, purify me. Whereupon Allah's Messenger (may peace be upon him) said: Woe be upon you, go back and ask forgiveness of Allah and turn to Him in repentance. He [the narrator] said that he went back not far, when he came and said: Allah's Messenger, purify me. Allah's Apostle (may peace be upon him) said as he had said before. When it was the fourth time, Allah's Messenger (may peace be upon him) said: From what am I to purify you? He said: From adultery. Allah's Messenger (may peace be upon him) asked if he had been mad. He was informed that he was not mad. He said: Has he drunk wine? A person stood up

and smelt his breath but noticed no smell of wine. Thereupon Allah's Messenger (may peace be upon him) said: Have you committed adultery? He said: Yes. He made pronouncement about him and he was stoned to death. The people had been [divided] into two groups about him [Ma'iz]. One of them said: He has been undone for his sins had encompassed him, whereas another said: There is no repentance more excellent than the repentance of Ma'iz, for he came to Allah's Apostle (may peace be upon him) and placing his hand in his [in the Holy Prophet's] hand said: Kill me with stones. [This controversy about Ma'iz] remained for two or three days. Then came Allah's Messenger (may peace be upon him) to them [his Companions] as they were sitting. He greeted them with salutation and then sat down and said: Ask forgiveness for Ma'iz b. Malik. They said: May Allah forgive Ma'iz b. Malik. Thereupon Allah's Messenger (may peace be upon him) said: He [Ma'iz] has made such a repentance that if that were to be divided among a people, it would have been enough for all of them. He [the narrator] said: Then a woman of Ghamid, a branch of Azd, came to him and said: Messenger of Allah, purify me, whereupon he said: Woe be upon you; go back and beg forgiveness from Allah and turn to Him in repentance. She said: I find that you intend to send me back as you sent back Ma'iz. b. Malik. He [the Holy Prophet] said: What has happened to you? She said that she had become pregnant as a result of fornication. He [the Holy Prophet] said: Is it you [who has done that]? She said: Yes. He [the Holy Prophet] said to her: [You will not be punished] until you deliver what is there in your womb. One of the Ansar became responsible for her until she was delivered [of the child]. He [that Ansari] came to Allah's Apostle [may peace be upon him] and said the woman of Ghamid has given birth to a child. He [the Holy Prophet] said: In that case we shall not stone her and so leave her infant with none to suckle him. One of the Ansar got up and said: Allah's Apostle, let the responsibility of his suckling be upon me. She was then stoned to death."

44. Ostien, *Sharī'ah Implementation in Northern Nigeria*, 67.

45. Ibid.

46. Ibid.,71.

47. Yadudu, *Colonialism and the Transformation*, 41.

48. Ibid., 43.

49. Ibid.

50. Ibid., 27.

51. Shiite cleric and head of the Islamic Movement in Nigeria. Six of El-Zakzaki's sons were killed by the Nigerian military between 2014 and 2015. See

IHRC (United Kingdom), "Zaria Quds Massacre: The Role of the Military," October2014.www.ihrc.org.uk/publications/reports/11219-nigeria-report-the-zaria-massacres-and-the-role-of-the-military.

52. Ibid.

53. Ostien, *Sharī'ah Implementation in Northern Nigeria,* 67–68.

54. Ibid., 68.

55. 1999 Constitution of the Federal Republic of Nigeria & Fundamental Rights (Enforcement Procedure) Rules.

56. Andrew Ubaka Iwobi, "Tiptoeing through a Constitutional Minefield: The Great Sharia Controversy In Nigeria," *Journal of African Law* 48 (2004): 111–164.

57. Ibid., 122–123.

58. Ibid., 123.

59. Ibid., 117–118.

60. Ibid., 135–136.

61. Lama Abu-Odeh, "Modernizing Muslim Family Law: The Case of Egypt," *Journal for Transitional Law* 37 (2004): 1047.

62. Ostien, *Sharī'ah Implementation in Northern Nigeria,* 68–69.

63. For more on *shubha* as a legal maxim, see Intisar A. Rabb, "Islamic Legal Maxims as Substantive Canons of Construction: *Ḥudūd*-Avoidance in Cases of Doubt," *Islamic Law and Society* 17 (2010): 63–125.

64. John Burton, *The Sources of Islamic Law: Islamic Theories of Abrogation* (Edinburgh: Edinburgh University Press, 1990), 128.

65. Ostien, *Sharī'ah Implementation in Northern Nigeria,* 72.

66. Kimberley J. Wilson, "Stoning Sentence Creates a Nigerian Nightmare," *New Visions Commentary,* November 2002. www.nationalcenter.org/P21NVWilsonNigeria1102.html.

67. See, for example, Tony Smith, "Brazil: Asylum Offered to Condemned Nigerian," *The New York Times,* September 13, 2003.

68. Adopted by the European Parliament in Strasbourg, March 13, 2003. See www.europarl.europa.eu/sides/getDoc.do?type=TA&reference=P5-TA-2003–0105&language=EN.

69. Winfrey worked in collaboration with Amnesty International.

70. Ostien, *Sharī'ah Implementation in Northern Nigeria,* 106.

71. Jeff Coinage, "Woman Sentenced to Stoning Freed," *CNN World,* September 26, 2003.

72. Ibid.

CHAPTER SIX. GENDER AND THE WESTERN REACTION TO THE CASE

1. Source unknown; sent to me in private correspondence with a researcher in Nigeria.

2. Blog post, "The Belmont Club," May 31, 2007. http://fallbackbelmont.blogspot.de/2007/05/whos-afraid-of-tariq-ramadan.html.

3. Sayyid Qutb (d. 1966) was a leading member of the Muslim Brotherhood movement in Egypt in the 1950s and 1960s, often thought of as the figure responsible for radicalizing the movement.

4. Paul Berman, *The Flight of the Intellectuals* (Brooklyn, NY: Melville House, 2010).

5. Emma-Kate Symons, "Besieged on Left and Right, Sarkozy Clutches at a Dangerous Popularism," *The Australian,* February 26, 2011.

6. Ibid.

7. Ibid.

8. Professor Murray Last, interview with the author, February 2010, London, United Kingdom.

9. Ruud Peters, "The Reintroduction of Islamic Criminal Law in Northern Nigeria: A Study Conducted on Behalf of the European Commission" (Lagos, September 2001), 37. http://rezaei.typepad.com/hassan_rezaei/files/islamic-criminal-law-nigeria_en.pdf.

10. Ibid., 19.

11. Ibid.

12. "Sharia Law and Western Reaction," blog post, *Kano Online,* December 30, 2002 [no longer online as of this writing].

13. Amnesty International, "Amina Lawal": www.amnesty-1312.de/Main/AminaLawal.

14. "Sharia Law and Western Reaction."

15. Andrew Ubaka Iwobi, "Tiptoeing through a Constitutional Minefield: The Great Sharia Controversy in Nigeria," *Journal of African Law* 48, no. 2 (2004), 141.

16. Section epigraph: Dr. Guando, interview with the author, May 2010, Sokoto, Nigeria.

17. Ahmadu (pseudonym), interview with the author, April 2010, Jos, Nigeria.

18. Iwobi, "Tiptoeing through a Constitutional Minefield," 140.

19. Dr. Hamidu Bobboyi, interview with the author, April 2010, Kaduna, Nigeria.

20. Hon. Justice Abdulkadir Orire (Editor), *Proceedings from Seminar on Sharī'ah,* February 10–12, 2000.

21. Abdur-Rahmaan ibn Salih al-Mahmood, *Man-made Laws vs. Shari'ah: Ruling by Laws Other Than What Allah Revealed* [Conditions and Rulings], trans. Nasiruddin al-Khattab (Riyadh: International Islamic Publishing House, 2003).

22. The female body as a site in which the honor and unity of the state is inscribed is a major theme in women's studies. I see evidence for this theme in representations of the Prophet Muḥammad making light of 'Umar ibn Khaṭṭāb's hostility toward women, as reflected in several *aḥadīth.* I explore this dynamic in a separate article.

23. Dr. Abdulkareem Sadiq, interview with the author, April 2010, Zaria, Nigeria.

24. Ibid.

25. Dr. Guando, interview with the author, May 2010, Sokoto, Nigeria.

26. Gayatri Chakravorty Spivak, "Can the Subaltern Speak?," in *Marxism and the Interpretation of Culture,* ed. Cary Nelson and Lawerence Grossberg (Urbana: University of Illinois Press, 1988), 296. Quoted in Leila Ahmed, *A Quiet Revolution: The Veil's Resurgence, from the Middle East to America* (New Haven, CT: Yale University Press, 2011), 24.

27. Asifa Quraishi, "What If Sharia Weren't the Enemy?: Rethinking International Women's Rights Advocacy on Islamic Law," *Columbia Journal of Gender & Law* 22 (2011): 173.

28. Naz K. Modirzadeh, "Taking Islamic Law Seriously: INGOs and the Battle for Muslim Hearts and Minds," *Harvard Human Rights Journal* (2006): 233.

29. Ibid.

30. Details are kept sketchy in the interests of my interviewee.

31. Aliyu Musa Yauri, Esq., interview with the author, February 2010, Abuja, Nigeria.

32. Malam Sanusi Khalil, interview with the author, March 2010, Kaduna, Nigeria.

33. Ibraheem Sulaiman, "Sharī'ah Application in Nigeria: Continuity and Sustainability," paper presented at the Fourth Conference of Sharī'ah and Implementing States, Kano, Nigeria, December 2009, 2.

34. Ibid., 5.

35. Ibid., 6.

36. Ibid., 2.

37. Ibid., 4.

38. Ibid., 7.

39. Ibid., 10.

40. Ibid., 11.

41. Ibid., 14.

42. Ibid.

43. Ibid., 15–16.

44. Bilkisu Yusuf was killed in a stampede in Saudi Arabia during the hajj in 2015.

45. Bilkisu Yusuf, "Hausa-Fulani Women: The State of the Struggle," in *Hausa Women in the 20th Century*, ed. Catherine Cotes and Beverley Mack (Madison: University of Wisconsin Press, 1991), 87.

46. Ibid., 90.

47. *Sunday Guardian*, July 31, 1983, 5 (cited by Yusuf, 91).

48. Yusuf, "Hausa-Fulani Women," 92.

49. Ibid.

50. Ibid., 93.

51. Ibid., 94.

52. Ibid., 96.

53. Ibid., 97.

54. Ibid.

55. Saudatu Mahdi, interview with the author, February 2010, Abuja, Nigeria.

56. Dr. Hamidu Bobboyi, interview with the author, February 2010, Abuja, Nigeria.

57. Dr. Abdulkareem Sadiq, interview with the author, March 2010, Zaria, Nigeria.

58. Dr. Asmau, interview with the author, March 2010, Kaduna, Nigeria.

59. Ibid.

60. Dr. Aliyu Ibrahim, interview with the author, March 2010, Zaria, Nigeria.

61. Ibid.

62. Ibid.

63. Dr. Abba Yusuf, interview with the author, May 2010, Kano, Nigeria.

REFERENCES

1999 Constitution of the Federal Republic of Nigeria & Fundamental Rights (Enforcement Procedure) Rules. [Edition information unknown.]

1999 Transparency International Corruption Perceptions Index. www.transparency.org/research/cpi/cpi_1999/0/.

Abbott, Nabia. "Women and the State in Early Islam." *Journal of Near Eastern Studies* 1 (1942): 106–126.

'Abdallahi ibn Muḥammad, *Ḍiyā' al-ḥukkām / ta'līf 'Abdallahi ibn Fūdīyū*. Zaria, Nigeria: Maktab Nūlā, 1956.

Abubakre, Razaq Deremi. "The Academic and Non-academic Study of Islam in Sub-Saharan Africa: Nigeria as a Case Study." In *The Study of Religions in Africa: Past, Present and Prospects*. Edited by Jan Platvoet, James Cox, and Jacob Olupona. Cambridge, UK: Roots and Branches; Stockholm: Almqvist & Wiksell, 1996.

Abu-Lughod, Lila. "Do Muslim Women Really Need Saving? Anthropological Reflections on Cultural Relativism and Its Others." *American Anthropologist* 104 (2002): 783–790.

Abun-Nasr, Jamil M. "The Recognition of Islamic Law in Nigeria as Customary Law: Its Justifications and Consequences." In *Law, Society, and National Identity in Africa*. Edited by Jamil M. Abun-Nasr, Ulrich Spellenberg, and Ulrike Wanitzek. Hamburg, Germany: Helmut Busque, 1990, 31–45.

Abu-Odeh, Lama. "Modernizing Muslim Family Law: The Case of Egypt." *Journal for Transitional Law* 37 (2004): 1043–1146.

Adeleye, R.A. *Power and Diplomacy in Northern Nigeria, 1804–1906.* London: Longman, 1971.

Agbede, I. O. "Application of Islamic Law in Nigeria: A Reflection." *Nigerian Law Journal* 5 (1971): 119–128.

Ahmed, Leila. *A Quiet Revolution: The Veil's Resurgence, from the Middle East to America.* New Haven, CT: Yale University Press, 2011.

———. *Women and Gender in Islam: Historical Roots of a Modern Debate.* New Haven, CT: Yale University Press, 1992.

Ali, Aḥmed. *Al-Qur'an: A Contemporary Translation.* Princeton, NJ: Princeton University Press, 1993.

Ali, Kecia. *Imam Shafi'i: Scholar and Saint.* Oxford: Oneworld, 2011.

———. "Progressive Muslims and Islamic Jurisprudence: The Necessity for Critical Engagement with Marriage and Divorce Law." In *Progressive Muslims: On Justice, Gender, and Pluralism.* Edited by Omid Safi. Oxford: Oneworld, 2003.

———. *Sexual Ethics in Islam: Feminist Reflections on Qur'an, Ḥadīth, and Jurisprudence.* Oxford: Oneworld, 2006.

Amadi, Sam. "Religion and Secular Constitution: Human Rights and the Challenge of Sharia." Paper written for the Carr Center for Human Rights Policy, Harvard University, 2003.

Amnesty International. "Amina Lawal" (no date). www.amnesty-1312.de/Main/AminaLawal.

Anonymous. "Saving Amina Lawal: Human Rights Symbolism and the Dangers of Colonialism." *Harvard Law Review,* May 2004.

Archibong, Elizabeth. "Yerima's Bride Is the Daughter of His Egyptian Driver." *Next,* October 7, 2011.

Asad, Talal. "The Idea of an Anthropology of Islam." Occasional Paper Series, Center for Contemporary Arab Studies, Georgetown University, 1996.

Badru, Pade. *The Spread of Islam in West Africa: Colonization, Globalization and the Emergence of Fundamentalism.* Lewiston, NY: Edwin Mellen Press, 2006.

Bako, Sabo. "The Development of Political Thought and Public Administration in Africa: The Sokoto Caliphate Example." Paper prepared for the Conference on the Celebration of Two Hundred Years After the Caliphate (organized by Arewa House, Kaduna), Abuja, June 14–16, 2004.

Balogun, Ismail A.B. *The Life and Works of Uthman Dan Fodio.* Lagos, Nigeria: Islamic Publications Bureau, 1975.

Barry, Brian. *Culture and Equality: An Egalitarian Critique of Multiculturalism.* Cambridge, MA: Harvard University Press, 2001.

Bāshā, Aḥmad Taymūr. *Al-Mathāhib al-fiqhīyah al-arba'ah.* Cairo: Maktabat al-Thaqāfah al-Dīnīyah, 2001.

Bello, Mohammad. *Infāq al-Maysūr fī tarīkh Bilād al-Takrūr.* Rabat, Morocco: Ma'had al-Dirāsāt al-Ifrīqīyah, 1996.

———. "Political Leaders of the Jihād Leaders." Master's thesis, Ahmadu Bello University, Kano, Nigeria, 1975.

Bello, Omar. "The Political Thought of Muḥammad Bello (1781–1837)." PhD dissertation, Ahmadu Bello University, 1975.

Ben Amara, Ramzi. "The Izāla Movement in Nigeria: Its Split, Relationship to Sūfīs and Perception of Sharī'ah Re-Implementation." PhD dissertation, Universität Bayreuth, Germany, 2011.

Bennett, W. H. "Crimes and Punishments (Hebrew)." In *Encyclopædia of Religion and Ethics,* vol. 4. Edinburgh: T&T Clark, 1927, 280–283.

Benny, Philip B. *The Criminal Code of the Jews: According to the Talmud, Massecheth Synhedrin.* Clark, NJ: Lawbook Exchange, 2005.

Berlin, Adele, and Marc Zvi Brettler (Editors). *The Jewish Study Bible: Tanakh Translation.* Oxford: Oxford University Press, 2004.

Berman, Paul. *The Flight of the Intellectuals.* Brooklyn, NY: Melville House, 2010.

Brenner, Louis. "Muslim Thought in Eighteenth-Century West Africa: The Case of Shaykh Uthman b. Fudi." In *Eighteenth-Century Renewal and Reform in Islam.* Edited by Nehemia Levtzion and John O. Voll. Syracuse, NY: Syracuse University Press, 1987.

Brockopp, Jonathan E. "Competing Theories of Authority in Early Mālikī Texts." In *Studies in Islamic Legal Theory.* Edited by B. Weiss. Leiden, The Netherlands: Brill, 2002.

———. "Theorizing Charismatic Authority in Early Islamic Law." *Comparative Islamic Studies* 1, no. 2 (2005).

Brown, Daniel. "The Triumph of Scripturalism: The Doctrine of Naskh and Its Modern Critics." In *The Shaping of an American Islamic Discourse: A Memorial to Fazlur Rahman.* Edited by Earle H. Waugh and Frederick M. Deny. Atlanta, GA: Scholars Press, 1998.

Brown, Johnathan A. C. *The Canonization of al-Bukhārī and Muslim: The Formation and Function of the Sunnī Ḥadīth Canon.* Leiden, The Netherlands: Brill, 2007.

Bukhāri, Sahīh al-. Chapter 89, no. 6405. *Book of Ḥudūd.* Translated by Aisha Bewley. http://bewley.virtualave.net/.

Burton, John. *The Sources of Islamic Law: Islamic Theories of Abrogation.* Edinburgh: Edinburgh University Press, 1990.

Clarke, Kamari Maxine. "'The Hand Will Go to Hell': Islamic Law and the Crafting of the Spiritual Self." Unpublished manuscript, 2005, cited with permission from the author.

Coinage, Jeff. "Woman Sentenced to Stoning Freed." *CNN World,* September 26, 2003.

Coulson, Noel J. *A History of Islamic Law.* Edinburgh: Edinburgh University Press, 1964.

Crone, Patricia. *Roman, Provincial and Islamic Law: The Origins of the Islamic Patronate.* Cambridge, UK: Cambridge University Press, 1987.

———. "Two Legal Problems Bearing on the Early History of the Qur'ān." *Jerusalem Studies in Arabic and Islam* 18 (1994).

da Costa, Gilbert. "'Nigeria's Taliban': How Big a Threat?" *Time,* July 30, 2009. www.time.com/time/world/article/0,8599,1913796,00.html.

Dan Fodio, Uthmān. *Bayān wujūb al-hijra 'ala 'l-'ibad / Uthmān ibn Fūdī.* Edited and translated by F. H. El Masri. Khartoum: Khartoum University Press; New York: Oxford University Press, 1978.

———. *The Dignity of Labor: Being the Text and Translation of Tanbīh al-sāhib 'ala ahkām al-mākasib.* Edited and translated by Omar Bello. Unpublished manuscript, Arewa House Archives, Kaduna, Nigeria.

———. *Ihya' al-Sunnah wa Ikhmād al-Bid'ah.* Cairo: 'Abd Allāh al-Sayyār, al-Maktabah al-Ifrīqīyah, year unknown.

———. *Kitāb 'uṣūl al-dīn wa kitāb 'ulūm al-mu'amala.* Norwich, UK: Diwan Press, 1978.

Das, Veena. "Social Suffering." Special Issue of *Daedalus.* Edited by Arthur Kleinman and Margaret Lock. Berkeley: University of California Press; Dehli: Oxford University Press, 1998.

———. *Violence and Subjectivity.* Berkeley: University of California Press, 2000.

Diakho, Abou Ilyas Mouhammed. *La lapidation, précepte abrogé du droit musulman.* Beirut: Al-Bouraq, 2005.

Donnelly, Jack. *Universal Human Rights in Theory and Practice.* Ithaca, NY: Cornell University Press, 2003.

Edwards, Chilperic. *The Hammurabi Code and the Sinaitic Legislation with a Complete Translation of the Great Babylonian Inscription Discovered at Susa.* London: Kennikat Press, 1971.

El-Rouayheb, Khaled. *Before Homosexuality in the Arab–Islamic World: 1500–1800.* Chicago, IL: University of Chicago Press, 2005.

Espositio, John (with Natana J. DeLong-Bas). *Women in Muslim Family Law.* Syracuse, NY: Syracuse University Press, 2001.

European Parliament in Strasbourg. "Texts Adopted. Nigeria: Case of Amina Lawal." March 13, 2003. www.europarl.europa.eu/sides/getDoc.do?type = TA&reference = P5-TA-2003–0105&language = EN.

Ezeanokwasa, Jude O. "Obasanjo's Sharī'ah Incoherence." *Nigeria World,* September 7, 2007.

Fluehr-Lobban, Carolyn. "How Anthropology Should Respond to an Ethical Crisis: Cultural Relativism and Universal Human Rights." *Anthro Notes: Museum of Natural History Publication for Educators* 20 (winter 1998).

Goldziher, Ignaz. *Muhammedanische Studien (Muslim Studies),* vol. II. Edited by S. M. Stern. Translated by C. R. Barber and S. M. Stern. London: Allen and Unwin, 1971.

Hakim, Avraham. "Conflicting Images of Lawgivers: The Caliph and the Prophet: Sunnaht 'Umar and Sunnaht Muḥammad." In *The Blackwell Companion to the Qur'an.* Oxford: Blackwell, 2006.

———. "Context: 'Umar b. Al-Khaṭṭāb." In *The Blackwell Companion to the Qur'an.* Edited by Andrew Rippen. Oxford: Oxford University Press, 2009.

Hallaq, Wael. *The Formation of Islamic Law.* Aldershot, UK: Ashgate Variorum, 2004.

———. *A History of Islamic Legal Theories.* Cambridge, UK: Cambridge University Press, 1997.

———. *The Origins and Evolution of Islamic Law.* Cambridge, UK: Cambridge University Press, 2005.

Hasan, Aḥmad. *The Early Development of Islamic Jurisprudence.* Islamabad: Islamic Research Institute, 1970.

Ḥasanī, Muḥammad Badr al-Dīn. *Fayyid al Wahāb fī Muwāfaqāt Sayyidnā 'Umar ibn Al-Khattāb.* Beirut: Mu'assasat 'Izz al-Dīn, 2002.

Hassan, Riffat. "Muslim Women and Post-Patriarchal Islam." In *After Patriarchy: Feminist Transformations of the World Religions.* Edited by Paula M. Cooey et al. Maryknoll, NY: Orbis Books, 1991.

Hiskett, Mervyn. "Material Relating to the State of Learning among the Fulani before Their Jihād." *Bulletin of the School of Oriental and African Studies, University of London* 19 (1957): 550–578.

———. *The Sword of Truth: The Life and Times of the Shehu Usuman dan Fodio.* Evanston, IL: Northwestern University Press, 1994.

Hoyland, Robert G. *Arabia and the Arabs: From the Bronze Age to the Coming of Islam.* New York: Routledge, 2001.

Ibn Anas, Mālik. *Al-Muwaṭṭa.* Translated by Aisha Abdurrahman Bewley. London: Kegan Paul International, 1989.

Ibn Farḥūn, Ibrahim ibn ʻAli. *Al-Dibāj al-madhāhib fī marifat ayān ulama al-madhhab.* Cairo: Dar al-Turath lil-Tab wa-al-Nashr, 1975.

Ibn Fūdi, Uthmān. *Nūr Al Albāb.* Translated byYusuf Wali. *Kano Studies* 2, no. 1 (1980): 10–36.

Ibn Hishām, ʻAbd al-Malik. *Mukhtaṣar Sīrat ibn Hishām (al-Sīrah al-Nabawīyah) / iʻdād Muḥammad ʻAfīf al-Zuʻbī; rājaʻahu wa-ashrafa ʻala taṣḥīḥih ʻAbd al-Ḥamīd al-Aḥdab.* Beirut [Bayrūt]: Dār al-Nafā'is; Homs: Mu'assasat Zuʻbī, 1977.

Ibn Isḥāq, Muḥammad. *Sīrat ibn Isḥāq, al-musammāh bi-, Kitāb al-Mubtada' wa-al-mabʻath wa-al-maghāzī / (ta'līf Muḥammad ibn Isḥāq ibn Yasār ; taḥqīq wa-taʻlīq Muḥammad Ḥamīd Allāh; taqdīm Muḥammad al-Fāsī).* Rabat: Maʻhad al-Dirāsāt wa-al-Abḥāth lil-Taʻrīb, 1976.

Ignatieff, Michael. *American Exceptionalism and Human Rights.* Princeton, NJ: Princeton University Press, 2005.

———. *Human Rights as Politics.* Princeton, NJ: Princeton University Press, 2001.

Iwobi, Andrew Ubaka. "Tiptoeing through a Constitutional Minefield: The Great Sharia Controversy in Nigeria." *Journal of African Law* 48 (2004): 111–164.

Jackson, Michael. *Excursions.* Durham, NC: Duke University Press, 2007.

———. "Storytelling Events, Violence, and the Appearance of the Past." *Anthropological Quarterly* 78 (spring 2005).

Johansen, Baber. "Legal Literature and the Problem of Change: The Case of Land Rent." In *Contingency in a Sacred Law: Legal and Ethical Norms in the Muslim Fiqh.* Leiden, The Netherlands: Brill, 1999.

Johns, Rev. C. H. W. *Babylonian and Assyrian Laws, Contracts, and Letters.* Union, NJ: Lawbook Exchange, 1999.

Jumʻah, ʻAlī. *Al-Naskh ʻinda al-Uṣūlīyīn.* Cairo: Nahḍat Miṣr lil-Ṭibāʻah wa-al-Nashr wa-al-Tawzīʻ, 2005.

Junyboll, G. H. A. *Studies on the Origins and Uses of Islamic Hadith.* London: Ashgate Variorum, 1996.

Kamali, Moḥammad Hashim. *Principles of Islamic Jurisprudence.* Cambridge, UK: Islamic Texts Society, 2003.

Kani, Aḥmad Muhammad. *The Intellectual Origin of Sokoto* Jihād. Ibadan, Nigeria: Iman Publications, 1984.

Karibi-Whyte, A. G. *History and Sources of Nigerian Criminal Law.* Ibadan, Nigeria: Spectrum Books, 1993.

Khalīl ibn Isḥāq al-Jundī. *Mukhtaṣar al-Shaykh Khalīl ibn Isḥāq fī al-fiqh ʻalá Madhhab al-Imām Mālik ibn Anas al-Asbaḥī.* Paris: Maṭbaʻat al-Dawlah al-Jumhūrīyah, 1900.

Kumo, S. "The Application of Islamic Law in Northern Nigeria: Problems and Prospects." In *Islamic Law in Nigeria: Application and Teaching.* Edited by S. Khalid Rashid. Lagos: Islamic Publications Bureau, 1986.

Last, Murray. "Notes on the Implementation of Sharī'ah in Northern Nigeria." *FAIS Journal of Humanities* (2002): 1–17.

———. *The Sokoto Caliphate.* London: Longman, 1967.

Levtzion, Nehemia. "The Eighteenth-Century Background to the Islamic Revolutions in West Africa." In *Eighteenth-Century Renewal and Reform in Islam.* Edited by John Obert Voll. Syracuse, NY: Syracuse University Press, 1987.

Lucas, Scott. " 'Perhaps You Only Kissed Her?': A Contrapuntal Reading of the Penalties for Illicit Sex in the Sunni Hadith Literature." *Journal of Religious Ethics* 39 (2011): 399–415.

Mahmood, Abdur-Rahmaan ibn Salih al-. *Man-made Laws vs. Shari'ah: Ruling by Laws Other Than What Allah Revealed* [Conditions and Rulings]. Translated by Nasiruddin al-Khattab. Riyadh: International Islamic Publishing House, 2003.

Mahmood, Saba. "Agency, Performativity, and the Feminist Subject." In *Bodily Citations: Religion and Judith Butler.* Edited by Ellen T. Armour and Susan M. St. Ville. New York: Columbia University Press, 2006.

———. *Politics of Piety.* Princeton, NJ: Princeton University Press, 2005.

Maishanu, Hamza Muhammad. "Africanists' History in the Historiography of Sokoto Caliphate." Paper presented at the History Departmental Seminar Series, Usmanu Danfodio University, Sokoto, Nigeria. Manuscript collection of Harvard University Widener Library, July 18, 1989.

Makdisi, George. *Ibn 'Aqīl: Religion and Culture in Classical Islam.* Edinburgh: Edinburgh University Press, 1997.

Marsafi, Sa'd. *Shubuhāt hawla ahādīth al-rajm wa-raddih ta'līf.* Kuwait: Maktabat al-Manār al-Islāmīyah; Beirut: Mu'assasat al-Rayyān, 1994.

Marx, Anthony. *Faith in Nation: Exclusionary Origins of Nationalism.* Oxford: Oxford University Press, 2003.

Maudidi, S. Abul al'la. *Islamic Law and Its Introduction.* Lahore, Pakistan: Islamic Publications, 1955.

McAuliffe, Jane Dammen. *Encyclopaedia of the Qur'ān.* Leiden, The Netherlands: Brill, 2001–2006.

Melchert, Christopher. "Qur'anic Abrogation across the 9th Century: Shāfi'ī, Abu 'Ubayd, Muḥāsibi and ibn Qutaybah." In *Studies in Islamic Legal Theory.* Edited by B. Weiss. Leiden, The Netherlands: Brill, 2002.

———. "Traditionist-Jurisprudents and the Framing of Islamic Law." *Islamic Law and Society* 8 (2001): 383–406.

Mernissi, Fatima. "Femininity as Subversion: Reflections on the Muslim Concept of Nushuz." In *Speaking of Faith: Women, Religion, and Social Change*. Edited by Diana L. Eck. Philadelphia: New Society, 1986. [Reprinted in Mernissi, *Women's Rebellion and Islamic Memory*. London: Zed Books, 1996.]

Messick, Brinkley. *The Calligraphic State: Textual Interpretation and Domination in a Muslim Society*. Berkeley: University of California Press, 1993.

Mir-Hosseini, Ziba. *Marriage on Trial: A Study of Islamic Family Law*. Syracuse, NY: Syracuse University Press, 1993.

Modirzadeh, Naz K. "Taking Islamic Law Seriously: INGOs and the Battle for Muslim Hearts and Minds." *Harvard Human Rights Journal* (2006): 233.

Morsink, Johannes. *Drafting the Universal Declaration of Human Rights*. Philadelphia: University of Pennsylvania Press, 1999.

Motzki, Harald. "The *Muṣannaf* of 'Abd al-Razzāq al-Ṣan'ānī as a Source of Authentic *Aḥadīth* of the First Century A.H." *Journal of Near Eastern Studies* 50 (1991): 1–21.

———. *The Origins of Islamic Jurisprudence: Meccan Fiqh before the Classical Schools*. Leiden, The Netherlands: Brill, 2002.

Nadwi, Moḥammad Akram. *Al-Muhaddithat: The Women Scholars in Islam*. Oxford: Interface, 2007.

Nandy, Ahis. *The Intimate Enemy: Loss and Recovery of Self under Colonialism*. New York: Oxford University Press, 1988.

———. *Traditions, Tyranny, and Utopias: Essays in the Politics of Awareness*. New York: Oxford University Press, 1987.

"Native Courts Proclamation" administered by Lord Frederick Lugard, British High Commissioner for the Protectorate of Northern Nigeria, 1900. [In Kaduna National Archives, Kaduna, Nigeria.]

Nöldeke, Theodor and Friedrich Schwally. *Geschichte des Qorâns*. Göttingen, Germany: Dieterichschen Buchhandlung, 1860.

Oba, A. A. "Islamic Law as Customary Law: The Changing Perspective in Nigeria." *International and Comparative Law Quarterly* 51 (2002): 817–850.

Okeke, Okechukwu. *Hausa-Fulani Hegemony: The Dominance of the Muslim North in Contemporary Nigerian Politics*. Engu, Nigeria: Acena, 1992.

Okoronkwo, Ijeoma. "The Accused Persons Right to Bail in Nigeria." *The Lawyer's Chronicle: The Magazine for the African Lawyer*, 1992.

Olukoya, Sam. "Eyewitness: Nigeria's Sharia amputees." *BBC News World Edition*, December 19, 2002.

Olupona, Jacob K. "Contemporary Religious Terrain." In *Religion and Society in Nigeria: Historical and Sociological Perspectives.* Edited by Jacob K. Olupona and Toyin Falola. Ibadan, Nigeria: Spectrum Books, 1991.

Olupona, Jacob K., and Rosalind I. J. Hackett. "Civil Religion." In *Religion and Peace in Multi-Faith Nigeria.* Ile-Ife, Nigeria: Obafemi Awolowo University Press, 1992.

Olupona, Jacob K., and Sulayman S. Nyang (Editors). *Religious Plurality in Africa: Essays in Honour of John S. Mbiti.* Berlin: Mouton De Gruyter, 1993.

Orire, Hon. Justice Abdulkadir (Editor). *Proceedings from Seminar on Sharī'ah,* February 10–12, 2000.

Ostien, Philip (Editor). *Sharī'ah Implementation in Northern Nigeria 1999–2006: A Sourcebook, vol. 5: Two Famous Cases* (translated from Hausa original). Ibadan, Nigeria: Spectrum Books, 2007.

Pavlovich, Pavel. "The Stoning of a Pregnant Adulteress from Juhayna: The Early Evolution of a Muslim Tradition." *Islamic Law and Society* 17 (2010): 1–62.

Peirce, Leslie. *Morality Tales: Law and Gender in the Ottoman Court of Aintab.* Berkeley: University of California Press, 2003.

Perry, Michael J. *The Idea of Human Rights.* New York: Oxford University Press, 1998.

Peters, Ruud. "Islamic and Secular Criminal Law in Nineteenth Century Egypt: The Role and Function of the Qādī." *Islamic Law and Society* 4 (1997): 70–90.

———. *Islamic Criminal Law in Nigeria.* Ibadan, Nigeria: Spectrum Books, 2003.

———. "Judiciary: The Safiyyatu Hussaini Case." In *Dispensing Justice in Islamic Courts: Qādis and Their Judgments.* Edited by M. Khaled Masud, R. Peters, and David Powers. Leiden, The Netherlands: Brill, 2006, 219–244.

———. "The Reintroduction of Islamic Criminal Law in Northern Nigeria: A Study Conducted on Behalf of the European Commission" (Lagos, September 2001). http://rezaei.typepad.com/hassan_rezaei/files/islamic-criminal-law-nigeria_en.pdf.

Pew Research Center. "The Future of the Global Muslim Population: Projections for 2010–2030." Forum on Religion and Public Life (January 2011). www.pewforum.org/2011/01/27/the-future-of-the-global-muslim-population/.

Pinches, T. G. "Crimes and Punishments (Assyro-Babylonian)." In *Encyclopædia of Religion and Ethics,* vol. 4. Edinburgh: T&T Clark, 1927, 259.

Poucher, J. "Crimes and Punishments." In *A Dictionary of the Bible.* Edited by J. Hastings. Edinburgh: T&T Clark, 1898.

Powis Smith, J. M. *The Origin and History of Hebrew Law.* Chicago, IL: University of Chicago Press, 1931.

Qaradāwi, Yūsuf. *Islamic Awakening between Rejection and Extremism.* Washington, DC: American Trust; Herndon, VA: International Institute of Islamic Thought, 1991.

Quraishi, Asifa. "What If Sharia Weren't the Enemy? Rethinking International Women's Rights Advocacy on Islamic Law." *Columbia Journal of Gender & Law* 22 (2011): 173.

Rabb, Intisar A. "Islamic Legal Maxims as Substantive Canons of Construction: *Ḥudūd*-Avoidance in Cases of Doubt." *Islamic Law and Society* 17 (2010): 63–125.

Ramadan, Tariq. "An International Call for Moratorium on Corporal Punishment, Stoning and the Death Penalty in the Islamic World" (April, 5, 2005). www.tariqramadan.com.

Rāzī, Fakhr al-Dīn al-. *Mafātīh al-Ghayb.* Miṣr, al-Maṭba'ah al-Bahīyah al-Miṣrīyah, 1934–1962.

Reese, Scott S. (Editor). *The Transmission of Learning in Islamic Africa.* Leiden, The Netherlands: Brill, 2004.

Rippin, Andrew. "The Function of *asbab al-nuzūl* in Qur'anic Exegesis." *Bulletin of the School of Oriental and African Studies* 51 (1988): 362.

Roth, Martha T. *Law Collections from Mesopotamia and Asia Minor.* Atlanta, GA: Scholars Press, 1995.

———. "'She Will Die by the Iron Dagger': Adultery and Neo-Babylonian Marriage." *Journal of the Economic and Social History of the Orient* 31 (1988): 201.

Rubin, Uri. "Al-Walad li'l-Firash': On the Islamic Campaign against 'Zinā.' " *Studia Islamica* 78 (1993): 5–26.

Sadūsī, Qatada ibn da'āma al-. *Kitāb Al-Nāsikh wa Al-Mansūkh f'ī Kitāb Allah Ta'āla.* Beirut: Mu'asasat al-Risāla, 1985.

Sanusi, Sanusi Lamido. "Between Shari'ah and Barbarism." *Weekly Trust Newspaper* (August 3, 2003). www.nairaland.com/594835/sanusis-very-interesting-write-up.

———. "The Class Character of Religious Revival: Shar'ia and Ideology in Northern Nigeria." Paper presented at the Second Essex Graduate Conference in Political Theory, University of Essex, May 4–5, 2001.

———. "The Hudood Punishments in the Northern Nigeria: A Muslim Criticism." *ISIM News* (Institute for the Study of Islam in Modernity), Leiden, The Netherlands, 2005. www.gamji.com/sanusi/sanusi30.htm.

———. "Politics and Sharia in Northern Nigeria." In *Islam and Muslim Politics in Africa.* Edited by Benjamin F. Soares and Rene Otayek. New York: Palgrave, 2007.

———. "Power-shift and Rotation: Between Emancipation and Obfuscation." www.gamji.com/sanusi/sanusi7.htm.

Saqā, Aḥmad Muhāzi al-. *Lā Naskh f'il Qur'an.* Cairo: Dār al-Fikr Al-'Arabī, 1978.

Sarākhsī, Muḥammaḍ ibn Aḥmad. *Kitāb al-Mabṣūt.* Beirut: Dār al-Kutub al-'Ilmīyah, 2001.

Sayeed, Asma. "Shifting Fortunes: Women and Ḥadīth Transmission in Islamic History (First to Eighth Centuries)." PhD dissertation, Princeton University, 2005.

Schacht, Joseph. *An Introduction to Islamic Law.* Oxford: Clarendon Press, 1964.

———. "Islam in Northern Nigeria." *Studia Islamica* 8 (1957): 123–146.

———. *The Origins of Muhammadan Jurisprudence.* Oxford: Clarendon Press, 1950.

Scott, Joan W. (Editor). *Women's Studies on the Edge.* Durham, NC: Duke University Press, 2008.

Sen, Amartya. *Identity and Violence: The Illusion of Destiny.* New York: W.W. Norton, 2006.

Shāfi'ī, Muḥammad Ibn Idrīs al-. *Al-Umm.* al-Manṣūrah: Dār al-Wafā' lil-Ṭibā'ah wa-al-Nashr wa-al-Tawzī', 2001.

Shalbi, Abd al-Jalīl. *Al-Qānūn al-Islāmi fi Muwājahat al-Taḥadiyyāt.* Majalat al-Azhar, al-Qāhira: 1379H/1976M.

Shari'a Court of Appeal of Katsina State of Nigeria: Case No KIS/SCCA/FT/2002: Amina Lawal vs. The State." Transcript of appeals proceeding in original Hausa.

"Sharia Law and Western Reaction." Blog post, *Kano Online,* December 30, 2002 (no longer online as of this writing).

Siddiqui, Mona. "Flogging." In *Encyclopedia of the Qur'an.* Edited by J. McAuliffe. Leiden, The Netherlands: Brill, 2002, 214–215.

Simawe, Saadi A. "Rushdie's 'The Satanic Verses' and Heretical Literature in Islam." *The Iowa Review* 20 (winter 1990): 185–198.

Smith, Abdullahi. "The Early States of the Central Sudan." In *History of West Africa, vol. 1.* Edited by Jacob F. A. Ade Ajayi and Michael Crowder. London: Longman, *1971.*

Smith, M. G. "Historical and Cultural Conditions of Political Corruption among the Hausa." *Comparative Studies in Society and History* 6 (January 1964): 164–194.

Smith, Tony. "Brazil: Asylum Offered to Condemned Nigerian." *The New York Times,* September 13, 2003.

Sonbol, Amira El-Azhary. "The Genesis of Family Law: How Sharī'ah, Custom and Colonial Laws Influenced the Development of Personal Status Codes." In *Wanted: Justice and Equality in the Muslim Family.* Edited by Anwar and Sisters in Islam, 2009.

———. *Women, the Family and Divorce Laws in Islamic History.* Syracuse, NY: Syracuse University Press, 1996.

Speed, Edwin Arney (Editor). *Laws of the Protectorate of Northern Nigeria. With an appendix containing the orders of the Sovereign council relating to the Protectorate, the royal instruction to the governors and various acts of the government. London: Stevens and Sons, 1910.* [First edition, found in the Kaduna National Archives, Kaduna, Nigeria.]

Spellberg, Denise. *Politics, Gender and the Islamic Past.* New York: Columbia University Press, 1994.

Spivak, Gayatri Chakravorty. "Can the Subaltern Speak?" In *Marxism and the Interpretation of Culture.* Edited by Cary Nelson and Lawerence Grossberg. Urbana: University of Illinois Press, 1988.

Stern, Gertrude. *Marriage in Early Islam.* London: Royal Asiatic Society, 1939.

"Structural Adjustment Programme in Nigeria: Causes, Processes and Outcomes." National Centre for Economic Management & Administration, Ibadan, Nigeria (precise date unknown—after 2003). http://nairametrics.com/wp-content/uploads/2013/04/Nigeria_proposal.pdf.

Sulaiman, Ibraheem. *A Revolution in History: The Jihād of Uthman Dan Fodio.* London: Mansell, 1986.

———. "Sharī'ah Application in Nigeria: Continuity and Sustainability." Paper presented at the Fourth Conference of Sharī'ah and Implementing States, Kano, Nigeria, December 2009.

Suyūti, Jilāl al-dīn 'abd al-Rahmān al-. *Itqān fi 'ulūm al-Qur'an (al-juz' al-thālith).* Cairo: Dar al-Turath, 1985.

Symons, Emma-Kate. "Besieged on Left and Right, Sarkozy Clutches at a Dangerous Popularism." *The Australian,* February 26, 2011.

Taylor, Charles. *Multiculturalism: Examining the Politics of Recognition.* Princeton, NJ: Princeton University Press, 1994.

Tucker, Judith. *In the House of the Law: Gender and Islamic Law in Ottoman Syria and Palestine.* Berkeley: University of California Press, 1998.

Ṭūsī, Abū Ja'far Muḥammad ibn al-Ḥasan. *Fihrist kutub al-Shī'ah wa-uṣūlihim wa-asmā' al-muṣannifīn wa-aṣḥāb al-uṣūl.* Qom, Iran: Maktabat al-Muḥaqqiq al-Ṭabāṭabā'ī, 1999.

Ubah, C. N. *Islam in African History.* Kaduna, Nigeria: Baraka Press, 2001.

Umar, Muhammad Sani. "Changing Islamic Identity in Nigeria from the 1960s to the 1980s." In *Sūfīsm to Anti-Sūfīsm: Muslim Identity and Social Change.* Edited by Louis Brenner. Leiden, The Netherlands: Brill, 2006.

———. "Education and Islamic Trends in Northern Nigeria: 1970–1990s." *Africa Today* 48 (summer 2001): 127–150.

———. *Islam and Colonialism: Intellectual Responses of Muslims of Northern Nigeria to British Colonial Rule.* Leiden, The Netherlands: Brill, 2006.

'Utabī, 'Inād Najr al-'Ajrafī. *Al-zinā wa-al-khamr fī al-Yahūdīyah wa al Masīhīyah wa al Islām.* Riyadh: Dar 'Alam al-Kutub, 2002.

VerSteeg, Russ. *Early Mesopotamian Law.* Durham, NC: Carolina Academic Press, 2000.

Wahramann, Nahum. *Untersuchungen uber die Stellung der Frau im Judentum im Zeitalter der Tannaiten.* Breslau, Germany: M.&M. Marcus, 1933.

Wilson, Kimberley J. "Stoning Sentence Creates a Nigerian Nightmare." *New Visions Commentary,* November 2002. www.nationalcenter.org /P21NVWilsonNigeria1102.html.

Yadudu, Auwalu Hamsxu. "Colonialism and the Transformation of the Substance and Form of Islamic Law in the Northern States of Nigeria." *Journal of Law and Religion* 9 (1991): 17–47.

Yauri, Aliyu Musa, Esq. "Issues in Defending Safiyyatu Husseini and Amina Lawal." In *Sharī'ah Penal and Family Laws in Nigeria and in the Muslim World: Rights Based Approach.* Edited by Jibrin Ibrahim. Zaria, Nigeria: Aḥmadu Bello University Press, 2004.

Young, Walter. "Stoning and Hand-Amputation: The Pre-Islamic Origins of the Hadd Penalties for *Zinā* and Sariqa." Master's thesis, Institute of Islamic Studies at McGill University, Montreal, 2005.

Yusuf, Bilkisu. "Hausa-Fulani Women: The State of the Struggle." In *Hausa Women in the 20th Century.* Edited by Catherine Cotes and Beverley Mack. Madison: University of Wisconsin Press, 1991.

Zamfara State of Nigeria. *Sharia Penal Code Law, 2000.* Zaria: Gaskiya Corporation Limited, with Consent and Authority of Zamfara State Government, 2000.

INDEX

CPSIA information can be obtained
at www.ICGtesting.com
Printed in the USA
LVOW07s2309070118
562194LV00001B/187/P

9 780520 293786